A NEW SENSATION
TRUTH AND TEACHINGS FROM JESUS CHRIST

A NEW SENSATION
TRUTH AND TEACHINGS FROM JESUS CHRIST

A HANDBOOK TO HEALING

Jesus Christ, Laurie Stimpson,
and Elizabeth Riebe

authorHOUSE®

AuthorHouse™ LLC
1663 Liberty Drive
Bloomington, IN 47403
www.authorhouse.com
Phone: 1-800-839-8640

Published by AuthorHouse   04/21/2014

ISBN: 978-1-4918-9847-5 (sc)
ISBN: 978-1-4918-9846-8 (e)

Library of Congress Control Number: 2014905613

This book is dedicated to

YOU

CONTENTS

Chapter 1
Self-Responsibility.. 1
Everything you Need is Within You
Child Abuse
The Crucifixion
Coffee with Jesus
God Energy
Mother Earth
Teach Others
Is Death Painful?
Angels
"Heaven and Hell"
Satan loves Judgment
Preparation for the Crucifixion
Jesus is Laughing!
Mary and Joseph
The Bible
Play More!
Jesus' Phone Number

Chapter 2
Beginning to Heal 20
Sexual Preference
Love and Good Overcome Everything
The Bible
There is No reason to fear God
Was Jesus Married?
Did He have Children?
Does He have living descendents now?
Jesus' Father, Joseph
Christ Consciousness
Gratitude Comes from You
The Crucifixion
Joy
You are the Director of Your Play
Are you Always supposed to be nice?

Compassion for Yourself
There are No Mistakes
The Holocausts
It's all Planned
Connecting to Oneness
Friends and Relatives in Heaven
The Second Coming
Meeting a Spouse-The Law of Attraction
Grief
Prayer

Chapter 3
Faith 41
Universal Laws
Disease
Children with Disease
Enlightenment
Finding Faith
Compliments from Jesus
"To Thine Own Self Be True"
Self-Awareness
You are a Divine Being
Sexuality and Money
Unforgiveness Creates Disease
Healing the Emotional
The Vatican Serves a Purpose
Essay Question
Demonic Possession

Chapter 4
Understanding Free Will 60
Examples
Emotional Triggers
Effort Needed
Acceptance
Miracles
Teething
Medicine
Being a Pure Vessel

Writing in the sand
Schooling on other planets
Christ Consciousness is an Aspect of God
God
The Second Coming
Aliens
GMO'S
Belief in Lack
Mother Mary
Success in Business
Indigo Bunting
Gratitude
Murder

Chapter 5
Your Own Personal Power..**81**
Homework
Walking on Water
Stand in Your Truth
Channeling-Anyone can do it
Ask Your Heart
Step 1 of Creating your own reality
You are not alone
Start communicating-make the 1st move
Signs of communication
Jesus is teasing! LOL
Jesus talks to Adam
What is our soul's goal?
Jesus talks to Lexie
Bickering Cavemen
Erasing Cellular Memory
How One individual can have an impact
Heaven on Earth
"I AM Ready"
Jesus' Explanation of what is going on here
The Spirit of Fun
Adam & Eve
Earth's Evolution
The Darwin Theory

Dinosaurs
The Earth's Cleansing
Understanding Reincarnation
Time
John the Baptist
The Shroud of Turin
Comparing yourself to others limits you
Being Aware
Know Yourself
A Dream

Chapter 6
Compassion over Judgment...113
They Hear You
Bridging the Gap of the Religions
Understanding Truth
Killing
No Judgment
Cleaning House
ASK
Alcoholism
Abortion
Nothingness-Perception
The Impetus of the Soul
The Power of Prayer
Time Travel
Suicide
Using Time Travel to Heal
Mastery
Assisting Humanity in the Removing of the Cellular Memory
Animals
Elizabeth's Time Travel Experience

Chapter 7
Listening and Paying Attention...136
Laurie's Pain and Healing
A Description of Jesus' Physical Features
It is an Exciting Time

Becoming Aware & Mindful of your emotions
Stop and Feel the Energy
Is this Mine or does it belong to someone else?
Energy
Write a Letter
Love and Hate
Archangel Michael's Protection
Your Body
It's the Vibrations—not so much the words
Injustices
Trust that Everything is in Divine Order
Observing the Progress
Angels
Fairies, Gnomes, Unicorns, etc
Don't be so Serious
Let Go of ALL Judgment
Parenting
Schizophrenia
Walk-ins
Bigger Picture
Sadness
Fertility
Your Ticket to Freedom
A Bible Suggestion

Chapter 8

Action Steps..**168**
The 3 most important elements required for a healing on oneself
Your Guides
Who's Contributing to this
The White Brotherhood
The Purpose of Ego
Prior to God . . .
Meditation
After the Resurrection
The Story of how Elizabeth Healed herself
The Ring from Jesus
Meeting The White Brotherhood

Chapter 9
Patterns 199
Rewiring the Physical Form
Mastering Your Emotions
"You are all part of that Oneness"
Soul Memory
Dig Deeper
Your Tool Box
Judas
Mother Mary
The Energy of the trees
Think with your heart "In a more expansive way"
Marijuana
Judgment keeps you in continual reincarnation
Baptism
Autism
Personal stories: And the Oscar Goes To . . .
I'm OK With My Crazy!

Chapter 10
Emotions Are Your Tools.. 226
Be Patient
Excitement, Enthusiasm and Deep Faith
The Truth about "Sin"
Turning to the Christ Consciousness Energy
The 5th Dimensional Realm
Igniting the Christ Consciousness
Expectations
The Purpose of War
Obesity and Smoking
Treat Animals with Kindness
Alzheimer's
Cancer
Affection
Moms and Kids
Personal Space
No Names
What's Next??!!
AMEN!!

Introductions

This is not what you would call a "normal" book. None of what is going on here is. YET. And that is the beauty of it. This is something new here. Authentic and Accessible to all. Jesus has been quoted in the New Testament, but not to the extend of what we have here. What we have put together is not a story. It is a Factual dialogue of conversations that I have had with Jesus Christ. I have been asking Him questions over the span of many months, on a variety of topics, and in the process, He has been teaching me so that I can pass the information along to all of you, the public. YES, YOU CAN GET EXCITED! This is really happening now, in YOUR lifetime!! This is not just an interview with Jesus Christ. This is so much more!!!!!

In this book are the actual words spoken by Jesus. I have recorded all of our conversations and have transcribed them just as He said them. These are the official transcripts from our talks. Jesus is teaching. Jesus is answering questions and explaining concepts so we can understand them better. You may be asking, "Is this really possible?" "How did this come to be?" You bet it is! I will give you my introduction first, then Laurie will give hers, and then Jesus will explain it to you more in the book.

What I really wanted to do was write a book with my friend, Laurie Stimpson. Laurie is a very gifted Medium. We've known each other since 2005, I think. To trace back our friendship, we would have to start with being brought together by my aunt, who had gotten a reading from Laurie. I was then given her number. Laurie changed my life when she asked my ex-husband and I in our reading together, "Who is the one that doesn't want to move?" Those words spoke to my soul. It was like I was awakened to the facts that I had refused to look at up until then. I don't think she even knows how much of an impact that sentence had on me-until she reads it here. :)

For our book together, I thought Laurie could channel Spirit, and I would record it all and transcribe everything. It would have to be done over the phone because we live in different states but that sounded like fun to me!!! I remember the morning that I proposed the idea to her.

I had been on Facebook and a girl had posted a bunch of sayings by Abraham Hicks. I did not know who Abraham Hicks was. I made a mental note to find out. Then I called Laurie for some reason. I think it was to tell her about how I healed my postpartum depression (she had found the root of it during a past life reading she did for me). I told her how my husband and I had some questions about the Bible-like, "When was the 1ˢᵗ woman's movement from that time? How did it go from say, 15 wives—to only 1?" Cause that's not in there! It's not in here either though, hehe, but my wheels were churning at the possibilities of what I could find out! I pitched the idea to her. She thought that was great because she had wanted to do something like that but just didn't know who would want to do it with her! THEN she mentioned Abraham Hicks!! I knew that by her bringing that up, it was a sign for us to do it and wouldn't you know, I moved my leg and here a tiny white feather was perched on it! (An Angel calling card!!) So I knew that we were deciding to do something that had Heaven's Seal of Approval.

Laurie and I actually didn't start our project for many months. Time got away from us and we were kept busy with major life changes. Me with a newborn and my mom passing away from cancer and Laurie was still dealing with the repercussions that cancer had left her with.

I had been secretly hoping that Jesus would want to become involved with this book since I speak to Him pretty much all the time in my daily thoughts. He's my best friend in a lot of ways. Laurie had given me my yearly reading months before and Mother Mary had been the spokesperson. I remember how special I felt that she would be there for me in that way so I wondered if Jesus did anything like this.

It's not like Laurie and I said, "Hey, let's see if Jesus wants to do this." That never happened. It was all really very simple and that was pretty much the only conversation we had about it-the initial idea of it-before we started-except to set a date and time on the calendar to start. I just thought that we would see if Archangel Michael or Mother Mary would want to answer the questions that I had. I didn't know anything about Archangel Nathaniel so I would see if he wanted to come through. I just figured I would go into it with an open mind about who showed up and with what information they would allow me to have. I didn't really have anything prepared because I didn't know what to expect. I had to wing

Jesus and I's first conversation, much like I have had to recently do with my first conversation with Mother Mary for the second book in this series.

So many times, about so many subjects and experiences, I have thought to myself, "What would Jesus think about this?" I just wanted The Truth. Like many other people do. Many times I would get an answer to write about on my blog-some of that was turned into my first book, which Jesus references, titled, "Love, God" but to actually have a conversation back and forth with Him? That would be Awesome! To be honest, I didn't really think it would happen. I thought Jesus was much too important and—untouchable in a way-for this type of thing. You can imagine my surprise when Laurie told me that He would like to honor me with this just before we began. Me? Honor ME? Jesus wants to talk to me and answer my questions?!! THIS was BIG. BIGGER than I could have imagined!! Think about it. You are told literally MINUTES before you start talking to Spirit that it's Jesus that wants to talk to you. I freaked out-though you wouldn't really know it if you'd listen to the tapes—but wouldn't you? I mean, it's JESUS! All kinds of thoughts went through my head. "How do I behave around Him?" "I hope He doesn't think I'm stupid." "I hope He likes me!" "What if He asks me a question and I don't know the answer??" "Holy crap! This is REALLY happening!!!" "Be cool, Beth. Be cool."

Over the past few months, I have gotten to know Jesus pretty well. You will learn personal things about Him that you never knew before. He really is NOT untouchable. To anyone. I am just as worthy to be speaking to Him as any one of you and I had to accept my Self-Worth right from the beginning. Before all of this I thought of Him and God as my two best friends. Now I get to actually call Him up like one! LOL Yes, Jesus and I could chat about lots of things but I tried my best to get answers to questions that many of us have. Or maybe are afraid to ask Him. You wouldn't want to insult him, right? I found out that you can't. It's impossible.

There is a little about ALOT of stuff in here. There is information in here that will shock you, that will make you incredibly happy, that will be a Relief to hear. Concepts that you will have to take time to reflect upon and there are truths in here where you might have to put the book down and cry. I found moments where I would be standing in my driveway and I'd think about what Jesus had said and how that pertains to certain things both globally and personally and I would bawl. It wasn't until our last day that I actually really cried when I was on the phone with Him. What He said spoke to my heart and I felt the Truth in my Soul. (Don't look ahead though because I feel it will be special to you when you reach that point in your journey also). Throughout the book I have added my personal experiences that have accompanied these teachings so that they can be an example for anyone that may need it. Jesus thought that was a good idea too :) I have left out my personal opinions and thoughts that went through my head after Jesus said this or Jesus said that as the conversations go on because by me adding to it, it takes away from the messages themselves. I do not want my opinion to sway what You may be feeling and thinking. It is meant for YOU to be able to stop and reflect whenever you feel the need to. This is really about Your Journey. Remembering Who You Are.

When I first started talking to Jesus, I thought to myself, "How would Meredith Vieira or Diane Sawyer interview Him? What kinds of questions would they ask?" or "How would Brian Williams approach this?" But when it came down to it, I was myself. The information that Jesus gave me soaked in much clearer when I would type it out late into the hours of the night vs. when He would be telling it to me over the phone. Going back through and reading it from beginning to end, I am amazed that what He told me about Healing one week, there would appear opportunities in my life in between our talks so that I would know and understand how to use these teachings. That is why I am so excited to be bringing these messages forth! Because they work!!!! Over and over and over again!!!

My advice is to read this with an open mind. Start to observe what goes on in your life while you read this. Take notes. Keep a journal. This will take Effort on your part but it will be Worth it! You will be able to start to put these practices into action and JUST KNOW that you have help and guidance when you ask for it. Like Jesus says, the answers always come. It's just up to you to remain open and become aware of the different ways they do. Welcome to your Journey!!!!!

-Elizabeth :)

From my requests to know Truth from Jesus about many things, I learned how to heal.

You can too.

THANK YOU, JESUS!

This book is the result of a wonderful partnership with my dear friends Beth and Jesus Christ. What Jesus Christ has shared with us about spiritual teachings has given Beth and I greater faith, compassion, and depth of understanding.

We want to share what we have learned with all of you because of the impact these teachings have had on our lives.

This book came about because of love, faith, and reverence for the being we know as Jesus Christ.

Laurie Stimpson

CHAPTER 1

Self-Responsibility

April 16, 2013

Laurie: It was Jesus that was talking to me saying that that He wanted to talk to you. He wanted to be the one to honor you with this.

Elizabeth: Wow. That's big.

Laurie: Yeah, Yeah, well you honor Him all the time, don't you?

Elizabeth: Yes, yes, yeah, I was like, hoping that Jesus would want to be able to say something but I thought well, I didn't know if it would be something He would want to do so, yeah, let's go.

Laurie: OK. Alright. Cause I go kinda of-I may come in and out of it-I've never done on the phone like this before so this is new for me as well. Normally I just go into like a semi trance state where I close my eyes. So I'm going to try doing that. If I can't-if that's like too awkward with the phone then I'll go back and forth and I'm gonna record this as well so I will get my end of it-you'll get your end as well so one of us will get it. It's so funny cause I feel like this is different than what I normally do so I'm kinda laughing and it's different than giving a reading too. So. He's telling me not to laugh. He's saying, "Stop it."

Pause

Jesus: "Yes, it is I. It is I, Jesus. Do you believe me?"

Elizabeth: Yeah I do. Thank you! I love you!

Jesus: "And I love you as well. And it is true. I am here because of your desire to know Truth as you can understand it at this time. So you speak to me and honor me continually. Why would I not honor you as well."

Elizabeth: Thank you.

Jesus: "You're welcome. So. We are—I am ready for any questions that you want answered here and we, I say we because there are others here-that will not come through-that will also have information that I will relay to you so that we can ALL as a group of Souls-Beings here-Light Beings-assist you on your journey. So there are many others here but I will be the spokesperson for all."

Elizabeth: OK. OK.

Jesus: "So you ask questions."

Elizabeth: OK, um, well, this morning someone had said something and they were questioning whether or not, you know, what you looked like. If you were the white Jesus or you were Middle Eastern or whatever, and I kinda thought, "Well, it doesn't really matter." and that kinda led me to the next thing that was talked about was taking responsibly for your actions and if that was some main-a main teaching that you had for all of us. If you could kinda explain the Importance of taking responsibility for your actions and your words. So that you can help yourself—like the greatest gift you can give yourself and others.

Jesus: "Yes, well it is, you are right, it is what I came here to teach ultimately and it is the reason for taking responsibility for yourself is—the importance-there are many reasons but the most important being, because you cannot influence another's will. Ever. That's what creates karma-so when you feel that you are responsible for another individual by enabling or worrying or any such thing you are creating karma for yourself. Whether it be with that individual, or just for yourself for future lifetimes. This is the time, right now, we speak of your end of Mayan calendar-well-with these energies that are present, etc, etc, the New Age. What that is, it's the primary importance of this New Age IS entering into a knowing of each individual being responsible for themselves for the very fact that each individual HAS the ability to connect to their OWN SOURCE being God or the Universe, however you want to say it. You have everything you need Within you. And you do not need to find it from anyone else or to do it for anyone else. And by doing that you make your greatest connection to the Universe or God, and from There you find your Truth. What's Truth for you is not Truth for another because your life is unique to you. That's why it is utmost importance that each individual will BE responsible for themselves and themselves only but they must understand what those words mean. Many do not or they feel that if they are a parent they are responsible for their children. Yes. They are responsible but that they are fed and cared for and loved and nurtured. But when it comes to influencing the direction in life that they take, there is only so much that a parent can do. If a parent knows this about free will, understands it to it's fullest and practices it, and Is That in their life, they will be able to guide their children in the best possible way. BY being that example for your child. So I will stop because I gave you much that you may have questions that you want to have further explained."

Elizabeth: When you're talking about parenting a child. That makes me think of abuse situations where the parent is or an adult is taking/doing harmful things to a child, like, I kinda question, "How can anybody do that?" and, and I don't know.

Jesus: "So your question is, "How do you get involved?" because it would depend on the circumstance, would it not?"

Elizabeth: Yeah, I guess it would depend on the circumstance of getting involved. What do we say to somebody that has been abused or somebody that is being abused or even to the parent or the adult that did it or is doing it?

Jesus: "Again, we go back to self-responsibility and we go back to the fact that each person is here with their own unique journey, their own unique path. Therefore, when you speak to someone who has been, let's say one who is a perpetrator, in this case, the abuser, the abuser has come forth possibly, now these are—I'm going to regress for a moment and say that these are ideas that are avaunt-guard for many individuals because they go outside of normal thinking. They go outside of what individuals believe is the right thing to do but when you look at-everyone believes that they are responsible for themselves-even in regards to children here, that the child has CHOSEN that experience, OK? For some sort of lesson. The one who is the perpetrator in that case, is playing out a role. Does that mean you turn a blind eye when you see something? No. Because whatever is placed in your path-you must address. But if it is after the fact—and you are looking for healing, then there are many approaches you can take. By teaching individuals these Higher Teachings and Understandings and Spiritual Laws—that there is the Law of Cause and Effect. What you give out, you get back. And this doesn't pertain just to this lifetime. That's why there is Karma. So is that the one who is abused being abused this time because he did something bad in another lifetime? Not necessarily. That SOUL—that child-may have chosen that as a means to Learn Something and we don't know what it is. But it doesn't mean we ignore what is there, but we DO NOT JUDGE. We do not judge. Judgment puts you back into a lower vibration and puts you into that cycle of Karma. When you judge the child as having been victimized and that the abuser was evil and bad then you are in judgment. And as you know, as I taught, you are not to judge. Only God is the one to judge. Correct? And He does not judge. So, it's difficult to accept but it Will put you in a place of feeling more at peace with those circumstances in your lives that you can do NOTHING about. Only to be there as support. So you see, depending on what the circumstance is in which you find yourself, will depend on how you approach it but if you understand the bigger picture here, that each of us Chooses to come forth and to be In certain circumstances, to Learn certain things, it will help relieve some of that anxiety and sense of helplessness that people like you, who are here to help, see as being situations that are out of your control. So, if you look at it, and some will say that it's cold and callous, but if you can FEEL these TRUTHS within yourself, you will get the greater wisdom from it AND be able to assist others. Does that help you a little bit?"

Elizabeth: Yeah, that helps me because I have a friend that was abused when he was little and now he's turned to alcoholism and I'd like to be able to help him. I just don't know where my bounds are, as to trying to get him the help. I don't wanna push him when he's not ready, cause we all need to be able to do it when we're ready. Like, "we'll know"-ya know?

Jesus: "Absolutely. And in the case of this, I am sensing that your friend is not open to this, and your desire to help him comes from knowing your role here as one of being In Service. So you understand your role very very well. So whenever you see-because you're also an Intuitive, you Know and Recognize when someone is in need of help. Now you're going to take your intuitive wisdom to another level and you're going to also recognize WHEN they are ready for help and in ways which

4

you can help them. Maybe somebody like that, you are to be nothing more than to be there for them when they are in a bad state and not trying to change anything for them. But see them again, how I healed. See them as being WHOLE. See them as being the Wholeness. That is how I healed. When I would see someone who was ill, such as your friend, I would see them as the Eternal Being That They Are. And that is the picture I held."

Elizabeth: OK, OK, Yes, I understand that.

Jesus: "Yes. See, you understand that. I did not doubt that you would understand it. So, by doing that, you will get . . . first of all, what happens is you will hold the vibration of Reception and Allowance so the Universe and Spirit can work very easily. You will be very open to what it is you may have to do. Your friend might or might not sense this as well, and that is where the healing occurs. Again, he has Free Will. Maybe he is Not Done Learning that which he is supposed to Be Learning from his experience, experiences here in life, and you can only be here for him IN THAT WAY."

Elizabeth: Right, yes, I understand that. Yes, Thank You.

Jesus: "You're welcome."

Elizabeth: (Sigh) Let's see. This is fun talking to you Jesus. I'm talking to Jesus on the phone. (Laughter)

Jesus: "It's fun for me too. Yes. It is a Privilege. It's an Honor."

Elizabeth: Thank you.

Jesus: "It's a Joy. Yes."

Elizabeth: Oh you know what, my husband actually had a question. Life on other planets. Do the life forms on other planets respect their planets-like we need to respect planet Earth more. And are you Jesus for them, the same as what you are for us here on Earth?

Jesus: "In some Planets or Galaxies or Universes I am. I am a representation of the Christ Consciousness Energy and Christ Consciousness Energy is a vibration that permeates the Universe in Many directions. There are as many people as are walking your planet that is as many Universes or Galaxies that are out there with planets upon them. So each of them, in a different stage of evolution-depending on what stage of evolution they are in, will depend on whether or not I am there as assistance to them like I am for you on Planet Earth. In regards to how they respect their planets, very much the same depending on What They Need To Learn will depend on where they are at, essentially. So it is as varied as the people on your planet and that's the beauty of it all!!"

Elizabeth: WOW

Jesus: "Yes."

Elizabeth: So now this is making me, now I'm thinking your Crucifixion was painful and do you have to go to the other planets to have to relive something like that in order, you know, because it was said that you had your Crucifixion, because for the forgiveness of our sins. Now is that correct then?

Jesus: "Yes, essentially what the purpose of the Crucifixion was, that I was demonstrating to human beings in your particular circumstances, what you souls that inhabit the human form and are here on planet Earth, have a very unique process. Different than many other planets. There is something unique about planet Earth. So the Crucifixion was a way to demonstrate the range of emotions between the Crucifixion and the Resurrection. It is somewhat symbolic of what a human being will experience in their lifetime and how to go through each of the stages and remain constant within those stages. So yes, there were moments I lost my faith just like there are moments that you lose your faith here on Earth. But then you Find It Again. I went through physical pain, I was betrayed, I was put on the cross and felt the physical pain, as I said, I lost my faith, many of the things that individuals here—I was humiliated and such things but then I Came Back and showed that we have eternal life and it was such joy and within that I was showing human beings that when I say I came and relieved you of your sins, was showing you liberation from the ties to earthly existence through your emotional body-was you do not have to be tied to the emotional body any longer. You see, your existence on this planet, you are also in

6

evolution, you know that from being a cave man to where you are at now. Your technology reflects how you as human beings are changing. Your physical forms change also but they are the last TO change. You have subtle bodies that are all around you and one of your subtle bodies is an emotional body that has served the purpose of mankind evolving on planet Earth. But this emotional body is still necessary as you progress into what you call the 5th dimensional realm, where you all will be moving to but it is not a primary function. You are to be In Control of the emotional body as opposed to the emotional body being in control of you. So all of the things that happened in the Crucifixion were to open up that door way, bring in the Christ Consciousness because up until that point, Earth was not receiving Christ Consciousness Energy. I brought that in to Mother Earth herself when I bled and sweated upon the planet. What I brought in, the Christ Energy, Christ Consciousness Energy, through my own physical form, and all of this was brought in at the time to open up these doorways so that Humankind could then move into this next evolution of which you have been in for more than 2,000 years-according to your Earthly time. So, that was a lot of information, as well, going into several different directions so I will stop to make sure that it all made sense."

Elizabeth: Yeah, It all makes sense, it's pretty deep stuff.

Jesus: "Yes, yes, not for social tea time, is it?"

Elizabeth: No (laughter) You know, I was thinking the other day, I was thinking,what would it be like, you know, to just sit down and have coffee with you one morning sitting at the table. Like, what would we talk about? (Laughter)

Jesus: "What we are talking about right now. We might be talking about other things that aren't as so deep and profound because I have a deep appreciation for nature, of course, and if we were to sit and look out at even the snow that you say you are tired of, I would find probably pleasure in that as well. But we are doing the closest thing possible, you and I talking like this. I came because you have been asking to speak to me and we here In Spirit really—you and I are connected! You and I are very very connected. You know me and I know you. You are one of my soldiers if you will. I don't know if you like that word but that's what came to me. You're there doing my work. And it serves you and individuals like you that are there, that this planet is, and the individuals on this planet, are moving into a dimension of reality that is, will be-close-you will be moving to that Heaven on Earth that I spoke of."

Elizabeth: OK, OK . . . . yeah.

Silence

Jesus: "If you, at anytime, there are things that I am speaking about that are confusing to you, please, I can elaborate on them. You said that some of it was deep and I do want that you understand. The information would not be coming to you if you were not capable of understanding."

Elizabeth: Right, OK. Yeah, I understand

Jesus: "Good."

Elizabeth: My mind just drew a blank. Um, You know, I wanted to ask about is there a Mother God and a Father God, I know there's Father God but is there Mother God and is Mother God the same as the Blessed Virgin Mary and Mother Earth or is it somebody different?

Jesus: "If you think of, again, how do you describe God, really? Each of you has your own idea and you are limited in what you can understand entrapped in those human forms. If you think of God as being both Mother and Father God, would be the best way for you to understand it. Because you cannot have one without the other. You see it all over on your planet, you cannot have a male without a female or vice versus. You are dependent upon each other. So too is it with God or when you speak of God. If you think of God more as this Ultimate Energy that will help you to understand. It's not that it's a BEING as you have been taught in your bible studies. It is a Huge Energy that you are Part Of because it is all that is, and sometimes these concepts that you understand with the human mind are best left to saying to yourself, "Some of it's a mystery and I won't be able to explain it." Or to FIND the answer by knowing it within yourself. But in terms of Mother Earth and Mary, no, Mary is not the Mother God but she is connected to that same energy. She had to experience life on planet Earth. If she were God, she would not have come to planet Earth. She would not have needed to. And she is connected, very similar energy to the Mother Earth energy. In fact, sometimes those individuals on your planet that you call spiritual, that understand these things, will confuse the two energies But there is a Mother Earth energy that is separate from The Virgin Mary or Mother Mary energy."

Elizabeth: Will you talk about the Mother Earth energy because um, like over by our house here they're drilling and they're blasting Mother Earth. So they are cutting down the trees and they're making deep deep holes and every time I look at it I just get sad because I feel like it's painful for her. Um, is it really, is it-are we really just destroying the crap out of her? Not to use that language with you but you know.

Jesus: "No. If that were, remember, that there has been much disrespect towards the planet in which you live but there are many who do not disrespect it. Those who disrespect it are far fewer than those that DO respect it. So, that is a plus right there. The planet is here In Service also to Humanity. Without this planet, those who are destined to evolve on it, could not do their evolution. Now, it does not mean you can do whatever you want. But if you just TRUST that Nothing can occur if God or the Universe does not feel that it will be for the highest good Of All then Nothing can occur. If you can remember that, it will ease some of that pain that you feel when you see nature being altered in the ways in which you see it being altered. And remember, everyone on your planet has Free Will. EVERYONE. And you are interacting with each other continually. Earth is there kind of serving this purpose where you are upon it acting, it's the stage for humans. But you are guests there. And if more individuals understand that you are guests there because when the point were to come, IF the point were to come when Mother Earth said, "You have been disrespecting too much you are no longer welcome here." just like before, there were floods or there were ice age or the dinosaurs were destroyed, the same will happen to you. So when it gets to be too much, she's ultimately the one in control. NOT YOU."

Elizabeth: Right. Yes! And we should all remember that!

Jesus: "Yes. So, anything, if it is going on, again, when there Are oil spills or drilling and cutting down a healthy tree, these things that bother you when you see them and you know something, I'm going to ask you to do what I said for your friend who is the alcoholic and the one that was abused. See it all as being Perfect. When you see it as being in pain, then you contribute to the pain. When you see it as having a Divine purpose, and you are not in control, that only GOD Is In Control, THEN you will see as I saw and you will begin the healing. This is why you and I are talking today. You may think it is for others and it Will Be for others but it's to get you to the next level of Understanding because you are ready. So this is a very personal interaction today for you. You may realize it later on if you have not already."

Elizabeth: Well, I was kinda thinking, I don't know if it was ego thinking, that "oooh, He's here for me" but yeah. To be having your guidance and to be thinking of things as a whole and as love, that is really helpful. Definitely to me.

Jesus: "Yes, and by you doing that, you teach that to others who will teach it to others, who will teach it to others, and that is what is part of the evolution here that will bring you to that place that all of you are wanting to go. So your role here is very important. And what we are speaking of, you WILL put together and you WILL offer it to other people because they need to know. So it's not just personal, but it is personal. Because if you do not understand it, I need for you to ask for clarity. And if it's maybe in a few days, you know that you can ask for more clarity and I will give it to you because you are so important to what is going on here on the planet."

Elizabeth: OK, and I'll make sure that I listen to it again and make sure that if I have questions. Yeah. I understand that I'm one of your soldiers. I understand and I like that you know. I understand that I'm going to be, I FEEL like I'm supposed to be teaching people how to treat others so that they, it's like the chain reaction, so I understand that that's what I need to do and I'm really excited about it and I WANT to do it. So I want to be able to help so.

Jesus: "Yes, and that is the other reason why you are being given so much information is because you are willing. You understand your role here. Many have denied themselves that. You understand it, you are willing to do it, you are willing to go forward in any way that you see possible.

So, again, you made the choice, no one forced that upon you. You made the choice and you are moving forward with it."

Elizabeth: Yep. YAAAAY!

Jesus: "YAAAY, Yes. Yes, I agree."

Elizabeth: Um, what do we wanna talk about now?

Jesus: "You, you ask me."

Elizabeth: Um, I had put the question out on Facebook as to if anybody had a question and one of my friends asked, her question was: We all one day want to die peacefully, but unfortunately we cannot control cancer, car accidents, etc. things that may cause us to have a painful death, but I have always wondered is it painful entering Heaven?—Michele N.

Jesus: "OK, no, it is not painful, she says, 'entering Heaven'. I'm not sure what she means by that but we'll say that is it painful leaving this planet? No. Some of you, however, Choose that. Remember going back to Free Will and what you Chose coming in. You knew it coming in that you were going to have Free Will. You set things up to learn certain things. So those of you that are experiencing painful deaths, it is part of your journey. And yes, that can seem like a cop out for many, but it is the Highest form of thinking that you are all capable of right now. So, hold to that. So your friend, speaking of those who suffer, can you ever have a peaceful death? Yes. If that is what you choose. If you do not choose that than you will have a different kind of death. But often times when someone is about to die, they are, their souls leave their form BEFORE there is even any sort of impact of some sort of pain. So, those that die instantly or in tragic accidents or anything of that, often times they are out of their bodies before the force comes that causes the pain. So, does that answer the question?"

Elizabeth: Yeah. That completely answered it because that would have been the answer that I would have given her. (Laughing)

Jesus: "OK. Very good. See?"

Elizabeth: I just want it to be right so . . .

Jesus: "She'll believe it more from me than from you though, huh?"

Elizabeth: Right (Laughing)

Jesus: Laughing (He's laughing!!) :)

Elizabeth: Oh, here's a good one. Is it common for angels to take human form and walk around? You know, just be like, blue jeans and a t-shirt and just be like randomly helping people out. Do they do that? (I was thinking of the TV show Touched by an Angel)

Jesus: "They are not necessarily angels. The angels are the closest strata of Beings, they are closest to humans because they are the closest realm, let's say, to Earth. Angels-generally there is only one group of angels in that strata that will incarnate. Those are the ones that you would laugh at, but they are the ones who are working on their wings so to speak. I am using that very metaphorically here but they are rising in the levels of being angels. So which is a whole nother (flip tape) . . . often times, those that are incarnating can be of another type of spirit guide that would not be considered an angel. They are a different type of spirit guide who is there from another realm, that is also close to Earth, but it is a realm where often you get your particular guide that will be with you but it is the first entry point that you go to when you leave Earth."

Elizabeth: OK . . . OH!

Jesus: "That's where you meet those that have died, they can come to that realm and you can meet there."

Elizabeth: So that's my next question. How many levels are there to Heaven? And um, so my understanding, I think, is that like, Hell is the very last level. But I guess, is there many levels to Hell then too? And I wanna ask you, Is Satan really a bad guy?

Jesus: "No. OK. Let's answer the simpler ones first. So, there are, let's put it this way. Hell as you know it, does not exist and Heaven as, let's say the popular understanding of Hell and Heaven do not exist. Heaven does have many different levels, of course. As does Hell-Realm. Hell is not inescapable. Nor is Heaven your final resting place because you are in constant evolution. When one speaks of Heaven and Hell, they are states in which you go to after your earthly existence depending on how much you are. So, how much you have judged yourself, what kind of soul, where you came from before, so it's a very complex understanding but let me just say that there—just make it simple for the moment-that there are many levels in Both areas. Do you want to ask more before I begin to speak about Satan?"

Elizabeth: No, go ahead, tell me all about him.

Jesus: "Satan is the good guy. Satan is the bad guy. Satan is your opportunity to . . . he is there to make chaos out of order. When Satan, or what you understand is Satan, comes, it's the dark. You cannot have the dark without the light, correct? Or the light without the dark, I'm sorry. You cannot have the light without the dark. Satan, is—again, a popular understanding, a popular figure, is not quite that. Satan can take on many forms. He is there to, to bring, he is the one to bring you to that understanding of what we talked about before, of each of you being—having Free Will. You all have choice. You can choose to see it this way or you can choose to see it that way. Satan can only do your bidding. He cannot intervene. But if choose to dance with Satan, so to speak, it is because there's something there for you to learn. So, he's not in our view, bad. He's there to keep balance for the ENTIRE Universe. You will fear Satan because as human beings you fear Satan because you fear conflict, you fear pain on your planet, you fear going in deep and understanding what is within you, the very deep parts of you, as human beings. So that's why you fear Satan. Not everyone fears Satan. Many understand Satan in many different ways and those are your true warriors that are on your planet. Does that help you a little bit in understanding Satan's function for you?"

Elizabeth: Yeah, that helps me cause everybody makes him seem like he's a bad guy and he makes you do bad things and that's not true because it's all of our free will and we are the ones that decide whether we are going to do something bad or not, right?

Jesus: "Absolutely, absolutely. So he is just there balancing the scales. Teaching. He cannot come in if you do not allow him to come in. And remember, judgment is the easiest way of connecting to Satan—he loves judgment."

Elizabeth: Ooooohh. That's a good one for people to know.

Jesus: "Yes, because when you judge. So you judge the abuser. You judge the abuser. You've allowed Satan to come in because Satan says, "Oh, OK. Let's see what you really understand about this." then you find yourself in situations . . . because you are responding to spiritual law here. When you judge, remember—cause and effect, when you judge, you receive THAT BACK what you have GIVEN OUT."

Elizabeth: OK, that makes sense. And our thoughts are all, like, we're all just putting out energy and our thoughts manifest into whatever we're thinking, so if we're in a bad mood, like if we're thinking bad things than that's what we're gonna get. We're gonna get more of the bad.

Jesus: "Yes, absolutely and it's not easy. I understand, I have been there. I understand the human condition. Of course I had skills that I had developed in human form but all of you are capable of doing these things and that is what you're all here to learn to do this time around. Many of the things that I did."

Elizabeth:Yeah, that makes sense, it kinda seems that you've covered a lot of bases. How come there isn't a whole lot written about you in the bible of your early years? There's not a whole lot in between there.

Jesus: "Well, that is because those years really were years that I spent, in um—in various forms of learning. And there ARE things written about those times but they have been lost to the ah, to different circumstances. Some of them will be found again. Some of the information will come through in situations like this thru a Medium who can access it, but it was a time where I was taking and Understanding what it was that I was supposed to be doing. I was in preparation FOR the Crucifixion. Even though I had all those abilities at a young age, I was able to do them, I needed preparation at a different level And for a while I did disappear. I did Leave Here-Planet—and was gone for a while and that is the other reason."

Elizabeth: Holy smokes.

Jesus: "Yes. But I'm able to do that. Or Was able at that time. Yes."

Elizabeth: So, we're not talking just like meditation, you know, like leave your body, are you really saying that your actual physical body was gone also?

Jesus: "Yes."

Elizabeth: Did you tell anybody where you were going? Like did you tell your mom?

Jesus: Pause. "You make me laugh. Yes I told my mom, she gave me permission to go."

Elizabeth: Laughing

Jesus: "She signed the permission slip for me to take a field trip."

Elizabeth: That's funny (Laughing)

Jesus: "See, I do have a sense of humor. It was part of the plan. It was part of the plan because of . . . it was just part of the plan. There is a bigger picture here and with more time, as you and I converse more because we will be doing this again, I hope, it seems something that you want to do, you can ask more about that. Where I went and what I did because that time period IS very important and unknown because it was too far out for anyone to really accept and understand. So it was, that information, a lot of it was destroyed over time or none of it was even recorded. I was an unknown. So, yes, my mother knew where I went because she knew my higher purpose here. She, my mother, was more evolved than myself in many ways. She-I came to Her because she needed to teach Me. So she is the one that taught me, as a child, who I was."

Elizabeth: So you did or didn't have the understanding that you were the chosen one?

Jesus: "Not until I was able to begin to understand her words and then she began to explain to me who I was and what my purpose was here and she was the one that began to guide me to use what I brought in. I knew much because I was very skilled even though I was in human form, I was aware of what was outside the human form because I did come here with a very high purpose. And you know that, but I was still In human form and having to have to go through things. My mother was the figure who was chosen because of Who She Was. And she knew who she was from a very young child. She knew that there would come a time because this has been part of-it had all been planned. So my mother and my father knew that they would be the means for me to come here to Earth."

Elizabeth: Wow.

Jesus: "Yes."

Elizabeth: That's amazing!

Jesus: "So, and my father. And you know, my father is not given credit where credit is due. But my father was also an extremely evolved Being with many Gifts so they were the ones who taught me much and helped me understand who I was and why I was here, and . . . but it was all meant to be that way."

Elizabeth: OK. So, yeah, I was thinking, your father Joseph, there's not really much about him. Just that he believed Mary and just, you know, I keep thinking about my husband Kevin and how he's such a good dad to my kids, like surely Joseph must have been an awesome father too.

Jesus: "Yes, I mean, he was human. He was human but he had great understanding of his purpose and remember, so much has not been told. You have one book that is very limited in what it has spoken of and yet there were many lives and Many Lifetimes and much was written symbolically. Not literally. But yes, knowing what the history, and my history was and others is good but we, I would suggest that people just use their—expand on that and do not take it so literally. But I think you know that as well."

Elizabeth: Yeah, I, yes. I was thinking that earlier today. Is that it really, I could try to discredit some of the bible but you know, it doesn't really matter that I should even do that because it just doesn't, I don't need to.

Jesus: "Exactly. Exactly. It's serves no purpose. Yes, so it is a good idea, I'm going to suggest to you so that you can move forward with all of this, that you continue to ask others to ask questions and get this compiled together so that you have it in a format that is easily accessible to individuals because the Truths Here are, whether they are accepted or not, they are still Truths. And the more that have access to it, the better. So, and the more that can ask questions on a regular basis, the happier we will all be."

Elizabeth: "Yes, that's why I put it out there on Facebook cause I thought I've got a different kind of understanding than what people have and everybody and I don't wanna sound like I'm coming from my ego but they're not at where I'm thinking, so I figured I'll just let them ask questions because that's the kind of questions a lot of people want answered. So."

Jesus: "Absolutely so you are doing a fine job."

Elizabeth: OK. THANK YOU! (in a cute voice)

Jesus: Laughing . . . "So what else do you need from me today?"

Elizabeth: Um, I don't know. I think we covered a whole lot of stuff.

Jesus: "Yes, we did. And as I said, this will not be the only time that we speak. This hopefully, as I see that you are projecting, and what you have told me that you want to do, this will be something on going. So, the Medium, she is willing to participate in this as well. So I believe that you and I will be speaking on a regular basis. So, you keep that in mind and others may come in but at any point that you prefer speaking to me, you just tell me that and I will come forth to speak to you through the Medium."

Elizabeth: OK. Um, that's really good news. I'm happy to hear that. So thank you for spending time with me doing this for everybody so.

Jesus: "Yes."

Elizabeth: Continual teaching that you're doing.

Jesus: "Yes, absolutely,absolutely. If we are done then, or do you have something else?"

Elizabeth: Well, I just wanted to hit on, you said that you really are connected to nature, and I like going outside and taking walks. And I've been trying to kind of encourage the people that I know to get outside and you know, just hug a tree or just you know, stand and watch the birds and listen and do that kind of stuff. So . . . just wanted to tell ya that I guess. (Laugh)

Jesus: "Thank you. And yes, I see that you do that because you know of course, we can, here In Spirit, we can see anyone, anytime, everyone, at all times so we are watching you so if you feel like you have 2 eyes on the back of your neck, that's me. I'm kidding now of course. But yes, because they say you're too serious. I'm too serious portrayed as so serious all the time and I can be very serious but I'm also very humorous at times so I like to bring that out with those that appreciate it."

Elizabeth: Thank you, I can tell that you are humorous. I woke from a dream one night that I was dreaming about you and I guess I told my husband that I was playing with you so, if you're playing, we should all play more, right?! I mean . . .

Jesus: "Absolutely, absolutely. Yes, through play you release much energy that is of a very high vibration."

Elizabeth: K. Good. Well, Jesus, I thank you for your time.

Jesus: "Yes, I thank you and I'll give you my blessings and we will talk as usual very very soon."

Elizabeth: OK, thank you. Bye

Jesus: "Bye."

After I was done talking to Jesus I looked out my bedroom window. I was in such a state of Gratitude. The clouds were parting to form the shape of a bird using the blue sky. Like a cookie cutout. It was a bird flying. It was so perfectly shaped! I then noticed a little bird sitting on the tree branch just outside the window. I studied him very well and then ran downstairs to get my grandfather's old bird book. The little bird was a Golden-Winged Warbler. I had never ever even seen one of those before! I went outside and stood under the tree and he sang to me. I knew that this bird was from Jesus. As was the bird in the sky through the clouds. I then came inside the house and went to where my baby was playing underneath the living room windows. I looked out at the sky and saw 2 clouds that were starting to come together to form a heart, like when you put your hands together to make one. I started taking pictures as the 2 got closer. And then it happened. The cloud on the left turned into the face of Jesus. I was in complete awe and very excited!! I started to yell to my family to come to the window and look for themselves. There was no mistaking that this was Him. I was so happy that my kids and husband were in the room with me to see it :) Things were moving at such an exciting pace!! I pretty much was jumping around when I told my 8 year old son, Adam, that I had just been talking to Jesus on the phone! And he was so cute. He asked, "What is Jesus' phone number?" I didn't know what to say so I said that it was Laurie's number. Then about a half hour later, Adam got his answer. I had to drive my daughter into school for volleyball practice. As I turned on the key in the ignition, the song that was playing on the radio immediately got my attention. It was Mariah Carey singing the song that had been sung by The Jackson 5—"I'll Be There". The words that she sang were, "Just call my name and I'll be there." THAT'S Jesus' phone number!! It's His name!!

CHAPTER 2

Beginning to Heal

May 2, 2013

Jesus: "Yes, I am here present with you. It is I, Jesus, and yes, are you ready for me today?"

Elizabeth: Yes, I'm ready for you today. I was a little Unready last time. I was really really nervous and I don't think I was quite prepared as I should have been so I'm sorry.

Jesus: "Not at all. It was informative. It was as it should have been. Your nervousness does not influence the information coming through. It takes some practice understanding—feeling ease to interact at this level. Plus you are in human form and feeling the emotions with such intensity of being in human form. So, it went all well from our eyes here on the other side."

Elizabeth: Oh, good.

Jesus: "Yes, it went quite well because we know what you are doing and will go forth with this and we are sure that you will succeed at that which you are doing."

Elizabeth: OK well thank you to you and everybody else that's here with us, for helping us do what we're doing. I'm gonna ask you. Is the purpose of this that you want me to write another book? How do you want this information to be shared with people?

Jesus: "That again, when humans ask these questions, they are thinking with their ego mind, which is fine. This is not a bad thing. You have it for a reason. But you are thinking with your ego mind and asking us what we want you to do with the information. The information is for EVERYONE. We are hoping that you will know HOW to put it together if that is your desire. Who should reach it or who should receive it is also really not in your hands. And you know that. So what we're saying is that the earthly part of it, you decide. What feels right for you, you will follow through on that because what you'll see, it's not so much what we want it's what you want. This information is available for all who seek it in one way or another. There are many who receive it by their own reflections, by their own journeys or in many through poetry and literature or music. On their own, basically. So HOW it is presented makes no difference to us. What you are doing is affirming your ability to gather information, and then give it to others and what we're seeing is that you have a desire to assist others and this is one of the means in which you have chosen TO assist others. So, do you see it from that perspective? It's a little bit of a different twist."

Elizabeth: Yeah.

Jesus: "If you do nothing with it, we don't care. Because you have Free Will."

Elizabeth: Yeah, well I really want to do something with it cause I really want it to be out there and available for people so . . .

Jesus: "Yes, absolutely and the potential for it reaching many is there. Again, it's so much of what you put into it and your desires for assisting others that will be the impetus behind your decisions that you make regarding how to put all of this together as you say."

Elizabeth: OK. I had a bit of a, I don't wanna say it was a nasty email but from my brother-in-law it just made me . . . it hurt my feelings but what do I tell people that say, "Well, you're not really talking to Jesus." I probably don't need to say anything, do I? (Laughing)

Jesus: "Yes, you answered your question. Yes, it is difficult because there are many who's frame of reference is different than yours and who's abilities to, not abilities because it's not an ability. Their ways in which to receive guidance comes from a different stream of human existence let's say. So, for someone who does not believe, there is very little that you can do to convince them until they've had an experience on their own. It's not-it's unimportant really because ALL serve a function and ALL are on their own personal journey. So, yes, you are right. Do nothing. What you want to really do is pay attention to how-always, this is for anything-pay attention to how YOU feel and ask yourself, "What do I need to know about the way that I'M feeling about this?" In your case, 'Why am I needing to protect this so much?" "Why am I needing to have the confirmation come From this other individual? Why is that I want him to believe just like he wants me to believe his way?" You see, so it kind of is the same thing. He wants you to believe his way and you would like for him to believe your way and there's very little you can do about that except to accept where you are at and to have Faith."

Elizabeth: OK, yeah, cause it was Faith was what he questioned. I think I was just more insulted by what he questioned my Faith when he doesn't understand and try to know me anyways. That was just my own deal I guess so I just gotta get over it.

Jesus: "Exactly, your questions are very valid and pertain to the Whole Here so when you ask something that is occurring for you in your existence, in regards to our experience here, you will see that there are others with that same question and having that answer is a very much-it's a much greater insight into the workings of Spirit and Humanity than some sort of yes or no answer. So, yes, your personal experiences will play into what you are-what you are both, you and the Medium, are doing here. But with both you and the Medium paying attention to what is going on in your lives and how it reflects back on what the teachings are will show you-because you are asking the questions and does not mean that you are outside the realm of understanding. There is more for you to understand. So you are having the experience so that you can better understand and take the information into that arena of True Understanding and not just pedantic information given out by one who has not had the experience you see."

Elizabeth: OK, yeah, cause I think a lot of the people go strictly by the bible and they close themselves off to So Much that's out there . . . I wish that they would open up but I can't make them so yeah.

Jesus: "No, and that's their journey and this is the way it is designed here on Earth. It is just that way."

Elizabeth: OK, I'm going to ask. I'm gonna ask you straight up. The issue of Homosexuality. A lot of people are saying that homosexuals are gonna go to hell and they're using the bible as a reason behind it and I would just like to Officially have your stance on that, please.

Jesus: "First you must believe that there is a hell for a soul to be condemned to such a location. And there ARE various levels of existence beyond your earth plane that a soul can go to and one would be something of a hell but a hell is a place that has been described to you by your teachings on Earth, a place that you cannot remove yourself from ever and it is dominated by Satan. What Is Not Told To You in regards to what was the initial information, regards to what is considered hell, is that Love and Good overcome everything. And those who are in a state of Hell will stay there as long as they believe that there is such power as represented by Satan, himself. That is the purpose of Satan. So, to be a representative of the hellish experiences in the Universe. So to say that there is not a hell is wrong but to say that there is a hell from which you cannot exit is where there is misinformation. In regards to homosexuality, let me ask you this. Why would that person go to hell?"

Elizabeth: I don't think that they would, personally in my own viewpoint. I don't think so at all.

Jesus: "But why does one believe that? How do you understand that?"

Elizabeth: They understand that, oh, they believe that only a man and woman should be together.

Jesus: "But, OK, so, and Why would this send them to a state considered hell?"

Elizabeth: Because they're claiming that the bible says that it's wrong.

Jesus: "OK. And this bible, here. Bible. It's such an important book of information is it not for so many?"

Elizabeth: It really is.

Jesus: 'But"

Elizabeth: They're not making up their own decisions. They're letting— they're not trusting their own feelings on it, I guess.

Jesus: "Well, OK. If one knows that there is Only Love, true? That ones who are beyond this earthly state, even in your earthly state there is much Love, much much Love. Much more than there is evil. But there is-it is only a state of Love, in different degrees of Love, is the best way of describing what it is like to be out of human form. So, If they believe. OK, because to try to understand the way they believe, I do, but I don't want to go in that direction."

Elizabeth: OK, that's fine.

Jesus: "Believing that, No, hold on. Believing that one should end up in a state of hell due to their sexual preference IS NOT the criteria for being in a state of hell. Being in a state of hell, the criteria comes down to believing in a power Other than Love. Essentially. Does that make sense? So, if one were to choose, so, you see, the bible was written by man, not by God. It is man's interpretation of God's word. Is it not?"

Elizabeth: Wow. Yeah.

Jesus: "There are, there is much missing. They—it was written in a language and in a time that is completely different than the one in which you are living,currently, so the information pertained to, it was again, a means of having. OK, at one time, the reason that God's word about same sex population as being Not a good thing was because the human race needed to procreate in order to increase on the planet. For the souls coming forth. It was the design of things at the very very beginning, you see, of your planet, when man appeared on your planet. So certain elements were necessary for it moving forward. So, the information that was given initially has been interpreted and misinterpreted along the way and was also used as a means for giving humans an understanding of how to stay on Earth so that they COULD procreate and continue on, on Earth. If there was much same sex population, there would not have been as many births etc, etc. So, it was not Truly God's Word that came through because God would not have said anything like that. They were humans taking God's word and switching it around a little bit so that they could also make sure that there was the continuation of the species."

Elizabeth: OK, so, how much, I'll ask you this—how much of a ratio is opinion, just man's opinion in the bible?

Jesus: "That I cannot say because I'm not very familiar with it, there is much there that is of value. You have what you call the New and Old Testament but that is just a SLIVER of information that was available at one time for human beings. You have many-much that has been in present day that has changed in regards to this book and this book was put together as a means of controlling when the church you call the Catholic church decided it was going to, wanted more control. This was one of the means in which it controlled its masses. So, the information, yes, there's some value to it but it's not all clear information."

Elizabeth: OK, OK.

Jesus: "So it cannot be discounted but remember that God is only Love and if you look at what they call the Old Testament, they treated—God was viewed as being spiteful and vengeful, was He not?"

Elizabeth: Yeah, that was going to be one of my questions. Is that people fear God, but I feel like there's no reason to fear Him at all!

Jesus: "Exactly, so who created that?"

Elizabeth: Man.

Jesus: "Exactly."

Elizabeth: OK

Jesus: "I personally would suggest that you, if it feels necessary to read the bible, yes, read it, but read it with as open of a mind as possible. However, the information in there is so much pertaining to a period of time in which you are no longer living. Culturally and the way human beings saw the world even. You have to understand that human beings at one time did not See Color as clearly as they do now. Images had a more blurry effect. Many had eye problems. But it was the norm. Because things were not as defined and then you have gone, you are in a period of time now where everything is very crystal clear because the soul that is in the human form is very very encased in that human form because you have reached the point of, well you are coming out of it, but 6 months ago when you spoke of the Mayan calendar and such-that was the ending of a period of time when Humanity became it's Peak of density in the human form. Now you are moving back out so you will see that people will SEE differently, HEAR differently, have different NEEDS that will be present for them to Stay Here On Earth. That is the point. It's a very complex matter, this discussion of the bible because there ARE things of great value in the teachings there but remember, much of it was parable, much of it was metaphor for life experiences-much like you would watch a movie today or read a book based on something knowing full well that that's not actually how it is but it is something that would represent either an ideal state or a possible state."

Elizabeth: OK. Well that helps. So, of the New Testament. The words that were written by Matthew, Mark, Luke and John and they are quoting you, do you know if those are accurate quotes?

Jesus: "Yes. Some of them, yes. Again there was, that part of the bible is more accurate, due to the fact that that part there is based in time reference to where you are now, it's only 2,000 years ago. And again, much has been left out, but 2,000 years ago is much closer in the way human beings were than it was when the Old Testament was written."

Elizabeth: OK, I wanna ask, something that might have been left out. Were you married?

Jesus: "Yes. In the way in which you would understand marriage, yes."

Elizabeth: And was it to Mary Magdalene?

Jesus: "No."

Elizabeth: (Gasp) REALLY? Did you have children?

Jesus: "Yes."

Elizabeth: WOW! Do you have any living descendents now?

Jesus: "Absolutely."

Elizabeth: That is so cool! I'm so happy for you! (Laughter)

Jesus: "I led a fairly normal life. (Little laugh) Let's call it fairly normal. You see, my life on Earth was not normal but there was a long period of time where I did live a fairly normal life and then at the time when I knew I must come forward with God's message and bring forth the Christ Consciousness, which is why I was brought to Earth, than I became known as some what of a Rebel and that was when I had to abandon my family and my children."

Elizabeth: (Pause) Wow. I'm sorry.

Jesus: "Yes, I was very very young with children and it was what you call an arranged marriage."

Elizabeth: Ohhh, OK, well that's interesting.

Jesus: "Yes, there was a reason for that. It was necessary to keep the bloodline going."

Elizabeth: OK, now I wanna ask, So, you're saying the bloodline. I wanna ask, was Joseph your biological father?

Jesus: "Yes. Yes, you cannot come into the world, yes, you can, and I would have been able to, but then it would have defeated the whole purpose of my Being Here and going through that which human beings go through. You see, in order for me to do what I did, I took on that task. I was God's messenger. I am His son just like you are His daughter, we are all His children. So, because of my abilities, that I had spent time on Earth prior to this, so as I was CHOSEN to bring forth the Christ Consciousness, then I was, I had to come in as other human beings would come in. So when they say an Immaculate Conception, I know that is where you're going, they are speaking of a certain amount of purity that was in this Process Here, that is different than the process that is, occurs for human beings. So. Let me explain a little bit. There were essentially—I came forth as one human being with a soul. At the time that I began to know that I was to begin to out into the world-let's say another soul-like me—came in. I am trying to explain concepts that-essentially, there were 3 of me that came into the body of Jesus."

Elizabeth: Three souls that joined together? OK.

Jesus: "Yes, well, they did not so much join together as one would depart and the other would come so that's what was considered being a pure and immaculate conception but For Me To Come In, the final one that came in, that are 3 aspects of this role that I have, I had to—let's say that there were 3 Souls because that will be easier to understand. Three souls at three points in time that entered the body that was known as Jesus."

Elizabeth: Oooh, so, kind of like taking turns?

Jesus: "Kind of, yes, that's the best way of explaining it."

Elizabeth: Is it like the Father, the Son and the Holy Spirit, like the Trinity or just different souls.

Jesus: "Ugh, more like different souls but not quite different souls. That's where it gets a little complex. They are a unity of souls that IS the Christ Consciousness but each one came forth needing to learn certain things but they are all the soul and body of the Christ Consciousness and the final one was the full Christ Consciousness that I was able then, as Jesus, to bring forth. And that was my task as both a human and as a spiritual being. This had never been done before and I was the first to do it. So, you can say that I had a soul that was split in three, actually there are many aspects of the soul of the Christ Consciousness but you could say that what was brought forth was split into three and then unified at the end at the time of the Crucifixion."

Elizabeth: OK. Wow.

Jesus: "You see, I had to go through also what human beings go through otherwise I would not have understood What it means to be human and what we need as humans."

Elizabeth: Yeah I understand that but thank you. I thank you to infinity for coming here for us and leaving your family and that would be so difficult and the Crucifixion and you know, giving up your life for all of us, that is a huge big thing and I thank you so much for that and thank you for all the people that don't thank you for it too. So.

Jesus: "But you cannot thank for them. You want to much, but you cannot thank for them cause gratitude comes from you. And know that this is something that you very well understand and without this process intact, Humanity was ready for this experience to occur, this moving forward, the bringing in of the Christ Consciousness. It wasn't to Save You, so much as to Congratulate you, you human beings and it was God, Himself saying, "Yes." it wasn't about saving. But it was about moving you forward in your own evolution. Does that make sense?"

Elizabeth: Yeah! That's a really good way to look at it!

Jesus: "Yes, so without it, without the Christ Consciousness, there would be no forward moving, reconnecting with all that is, that Oneness that is God. Humanity would not-this is a great experiment here on Earth-human beings-it's unique in the Universe although there are many many many many many a multitude of planets and universes, it's immense, immense and we cannot possibly, you cannot possibly understand how much there is-being in human form. Yet, without Earth itself, this is why humans have an understanding of their importance here because they are the first ones to have certain conditions that are such for this experiment, this seeing how we can be-Create a Heaven on Earth. That's the whole point of all of this and because those who have inhabited Earth have done such a wonderful job—it's the best way of saying it—at creating this and moving forward and understanding that they open up the doorways for this great-great things like the Christ Consciousness being ALLOWED to come in and assist them. Without Christ Consciousness, Humanity would still be in certain conditions of hopelessness and there would be those only exclusively, an exclusive number of individuals with the understanding like there was at the time I walked there. It wouldn't be a general understanding. Most would be in human form in ignorance and believing in revenge and spite and all of that as a means of existing. Instead, there was another, an added layer of Conscious if you will, that humanity was then Gifted With BECAUSE they are ready for Christ Consciousness. So now Humanity, at that time that I brought it forth, that I Opened the doorways through my own experience, you all repeat in your own personal lives, much of what I, and you do it with knowing that there is something there for you to achieve and that is the Christ Consciousness and that is bringing in that Love and that is why you are unique in all of the Universe. There is no other planet that has made the progress that Earth and it's beings and inhabitants have over time."

Elizabeth: WOW. I don't know what to say about that . . . YAY for us!!

Jesus: "Yes, instead of looking at yourselves with disdain and that you have not succeeded and such, it would do you all well to look at yourselves in the way in which we see you and that is the great amount of success that you have all had in moving forward."

Elizabeth: OK, alright. That's great for people to think about.

Jesus: "Yes."

Elizabeth: I kinda wanna talk about what else is left out of the bible but I wanna ask things that what people have been asking me to ask you so. Ms. Iyanla Vanzant wants me to tell you hi because I was at her Wonder Woman Workshop this weekend, 2 weekends ago, well, you know I was (laughing) cause I was talking to you (He's Laughing along!! :) But um, those ladies there, her and her God Squad, as she calls them, are just doing some unbelievable, amazing things to help women and I just watched everyone around the room when they were surrendering to you and I just was in awe. How does that feel? How does that make you feel when you see people loving you so much like that?

Jesus: "That's an interesting question because it's not how I Feel that is important. It's how YOU feel. Then I know that, because I know this anyway, but it's ah, you asked the question in such a way, I have to answer it so that you understand that it's not about me or it's not about anyone who has attained the level of enlightenment that I have attained which are many. And what it is is that we feel great Satisfaction in knowing that there, that we are ALL moving in that direction and it's JOY would be the greatest feeling is Joy. Joy not for US but joy for YOU. I am like a mother or father when you love your child unconditionally and when they do something, they want something, or they attain something that you know they are capable of attaining and they do it and the great joy that they Find in that, that is how I feel. That is the best way of putting it. You are happy FOR THEM."

Elizabeth: Alright, I can understand that cause I surely was happy for them. It was awesome!

Jesus: "Yes, so you see, you were feeling as they were feeling, and then everybody was feeling, you were all feeling this in that the vibration of that, you know, feeds and grows and assists the Universe and your planet in moving forward in the direction that it's going. Of bringing Heaven on Earth."

Elizabeth: OK, we'll just keep showing love towards others, OK.

Jesus: "Yes."

Elizabeth: Where do we draw the line when somebody is being a poop head to us (Laughing) like about, where do we draw the line of being nice or saying, "I've had enough of this!"

Jesus: "Well, that again, is a personal preference, that is a personal experience. So you are in interaction with each other to teach each other. You learn and you teach and you teach and you learn from each other and if you understand that all of you are here and all of those who are around you, you have basically asked them to be actors in your play. So, you are the Director and you are the main star in your life. So when someone is irking you, you say to yourself, "Hmm, I put you in here for a reason, I'm going to find out what it is." The reason must be something for my Own Enlightenment. Everything is meant to reach you towards Enlightenment. Bring you to Compassion and bring you to Love. Everything. 100% of your experiences are meant to bring you to that. But you've got Free Will. That lovely Free Will. It is both a, it's a double edged sword at times for humans because it gives them conscience or should give them conscience and at times it doesn't. So you have Free Will. You have the Free Will to decide HOW you want to interact. But if you go back to the metaphor that I have given you, being that you're the star of your play, you are the Lead role and you are the Director as well and you are deciding who's there and you put the people in there and you ask them to perform certain functions because you want to reach that place of Enlightenment and the best way and the only way really to reach Enlightenment is not to go sit on a top of a hilltop and meditate. It is a way of reaching a Form of Enlightenment but the whole shebang is done Through Finding Love Where You As A Human Being Cannot Find Love. Where the ego has, or you call it Satan and Satan is ruling or the devil or whatever is ruling and telling

31

you, "Do not love, do not love—that's the other person." That's when you stop and say, "This is for me. I've created this. And I want to know what it is that I'm trying to do here." Then you'll know what you need to say and what you'll need to do. Are you always supposed to be nice? Is that your question?"

Elizabeth: Yeah, I guess so. Yes.

Jesus: "That's impossible. That's absolutely impossible. You're in human form and you don't know who chose you-well you do know because you are interacting with all of those that have asked you to be actors in THEIR play. So, all those that you know are there and they may need you to do certain things so that THEY can find Love and Compassion also."

Elizabeth: OK! Alright so, from now on if I get upset, I'll bite my tongue and I'll think about what do I want to say and I'll pray about it and then I'll wait for my answer. Well, I'll know. I don't know.

Jesus: "Yes. And if you are impulsive and don't bite your tongue and don't sit and pray and you say something snippy, THEN say to yourself, "Oh, what's in that for me to know?" Because maybe the other person needed you to be snippy."

Elizabeth: OK!! Alright! Alright! YEAH, that is so nice cause I don't like being nice all the time (Laughing/Relief)

Jesus: "No, and it's an impossibility. It's not an impossibility, let's put it this way. It's impossible in human form because you are here to really deal with that demon but you will get to a point where you-let me put it this way—you're understanding of what it means to be nice is a bit—and most of Humanity's—is a bit off. Not a bit, it's very largely off. Are you being nice to somebody if they are behaving inappropriately towards you and being disrespectful to you and consequently to themselves because we are all One if you don't say anything and you continue to be nice and you allow the behavior? That's what so often occurs. Don't say anything because you don't want to offend. Well, where's that getting you? No where."

Elizabeth: Yeah.

Jesus: "So, I wasn't nice. You know there are many stories about me and you don't know the half of it. I was human just like all of you. That is not what will condemn you to your hell that you speak of. What will condemn you to your hell is judgment of self, judgment of your OWN behavior and actions and not doing what I've just said. When you can Love and be Compassionate towards yourself All The Time, even when you have done something that you say is bad and you still can maybe not understand but have Compassion towards yourself—that is the key to unlocking that ever, that vicious cycle of continual judgment. Compassion. Because it is judgment that puts you back into that hell that you speak of."

Elizabeth: OK. My husband wants to know, "If we are not supposed to judge people than how do we get them the treatment that they need?'

Jesus: "Treatment? What do you mean by treatment?"

Elizabeth: Well, if someone that we know is acting kinda crazy and maybe they need to go talk to a therapist or something, if we're not supposed to judge them going, "Oh, they're kinda acting a little loopy." I don't know . . .

Jesus: "But see you're understanding judgment in human terms. When I speak of judgment, I speak of judging anyone's behavior as though it were, you are superior to that behavior because you do not do it. Judging . . . if you see someone is in need of assistance, it's always best to . . . that's why it's so important for everyone to understand that they have Intuition and they have Guidance and open themselves up to all of this because then you make decisions that are based in what is in the highest good of everyone. Maybe the person who needs to be committed to an institution needs that as their experience here for Enlightenment and has chosen that as their path. Or maybe not. But in order for you to know what to do in ANY situation, it is best always to be in that state of asking. And when we speak of judgment, we speak of when you do something when maybe things did not go in the direction that you wanted them to go, and you say, "I meant well, but look at what ended up happening." Then you judge yourself as being—as having failed. And then when you do something that is very human. So, let's say you do bad things. Because EVERY ONE of you down there is doing bad things. EVERY ONE OF YOU and when you judge your behavior as "bad" you continue the cycle. That's what I mean by judgment. Not by evaluation is what you're husband is saying. Evaluation. Not that you are evaluating a situation and looking to determine whether or not someone needs help of what kind of help. That's a different story."

Elizabeth: OK, so we need to be Easier on ourselves and start thinking more positively and not putting ourselves down so much.

Jesus: "Yes, because there are no mistakes. This has been said time and again. THERE ARE NO MISTAKES and all the atrocities that have occurred on your planet, all of them, there are just not the holocausts, there have been holocausts since forever. People are dying. There are holocausts going on right now in your world-you are just unaware of them because you have a media that prevents you from knowing Truth. But that being said, that is another story. In those experiences, if you believe that each of you have Free Will and that each of you have CHOSEN what you are currently living as your life, that gives you Freedom and you are responsible to yourselves and yourselves only and this is the bottom line. So whatever you find yourselves in, whatever circumstances or situations, you know that you have been a willing participant in creating that. In creating it for some reason. Maybe you don't always understand. So say these atrocities like the Holocausts where many were victimized, that was an Opportunity for the GREATEST, the GREATEST amount of Enlightened Souls to do their work. And it did occur."

Elizabeth: OK, Alright.

Jesus: "There were more souls that reached Enlightenment during your so called Holocaust than in 200 years time or more, since the Holocausts of the Native Americans and such. It has been going on, it is an Opportunity for Enlightenment."

Elizabeth: OK.

Jesus: "And there are those that do not want to hear this because they feel that these words mean that it's OK and we condone that behavior. That Is NOT IT. We DO NOT condone bad behavior but you cannot clean up anybody else's backyard. You can only wash your own dirty laundry so to speak. You MUST take care of yourself and yourself First. For no one is blameless or faultless. You create through your thoughts—as you know-and you all are contributing to many of the Holocausts by fearful and negative thinking anyway."

Elizabeth: Ugh, see, I was just telling my cousin the other day to stop it! (Laughing) OK, Alright.

Jesus: "Yes, and remember you have each chosen your personalities as well that will suit you for the purpose of what you are trying to do here. So it seems like it is very random but it is not. IT'S ALL PLANNED OUT. No two individuals are alike on your planet. You have similarities. But no two are alike. And all of you are there with your own unique expression, each looking to do the same thing and each assisting each other."

Elizabeth: OK, and I think you had said the last time that we spoke, is that God doesn't let anything happen if it's not for a greater good. Is that correct?

Jesus: "Yes. Yes. Cause it's all planned."

Elizabeth: Yeah because that alone, that's just an eye opener. I thought about that about the 9/11 attacks and I just thought, Wow, that, it makes it-it makes it Heal. Like, OK-not—ya know?

Jesus: "Yes."

Elizabeth: It's hard to describe but yeah, OK.

Elizabeth: Um. Well, my friend Denise has a question. She wants to know, "What is the easiest way to calm your mind to reach your highest good when there is so much outside influence affecting you." And she's sitting here with me, listening . . . hehe.

Jesus: "So, please repeat that."

Elizabeth: (Repeating)

Jesus: "Oh, that is very much an individuals own personal way of doing it. Each of you, calming your mind, depending on what kind of mind you have. Each of you will find ways that are unique for you. There of course is meditation and to calm the mind completely, as they say in meditation, takes great practice. And it serves a purpose because it allows you to connect to Oneness. But what I want to stress here with you is that, each of you finds this in your own way and the best way is the way that you find for you. Now that is a very broad answer but if your friend was asking me specifically, what's the best way for her, I would give her indications as I would see that were for HER to know. And each of you have your own unique way of doing that. I don't know if that's what she was asking."

Elizabeth: Is that what you were asking? Yes, she's sitting here with me listening

Jesus: "Yes."

Elizabeth: I guess we could probably say, with me, I like to run. Some people like to cook or do other things

Jesus: "Yes. Yes."

Denise: So, Dear Jesus, what would be your recommendation for me?

Jesus: "I would have you understand, to be aware, what it is that first gives you, what you do that, when you are doing it, you feel most connected. Because it's what are you feeling in that moment. And it's as my friend here has said when she is running, she feels the greatest amount of connection. Find that. But yours really is a particular and unique process. One of discovering and understanding of your emotions and how you use emotions as a guide to find who you truly are."

Denise: OK.

Jesus: "Does that help?"

Denise: Yes it does, thank you.

Jesus: "You are welcome."

Elizabeth: Alright, let's do another question . . . My friend Mary from New Prague wants to know, "When are you coming back to visit us in person so we can visually see you? Yes, I know that you are always with us and answering our prayers." She also wants to know, "Do we know our friends and relatives when we go to Heaven?"

Jesus: "OK. Do we know relatives and friends when we go to Heaven?"

Elizabeth: Yep.

Jesus: "Was that the question? Yes. You're relatives and friends are there waiting for you as they are the bridge for you to cross. They assist you in your journey to the other side and "When will I be coming back?" That is to be determined. But it will, the soul that I am, but I will not look like I did the last time, obviously, but there will be a second coming and that cannot be told because if you were to know that, many humans would not, it's as tho if they knew, certain things they would no longer make the effort towards their evolution. So, if they knew that I were coming back, then maybe they would sit back and say, "OK, Jesus will take over." Once I get here. I'm kidding of course, I'm kind of trying to jest with you a bit. "Let Jesus take over." That's what they always do, right?"

Elizabeth: Yes

Jesus: "But, there is, but the conditions have to be right for that second coming."

Elizabeth: OK, we'll take it as that. I kinda was thinking, well, we don't really need to know that-the future is day to day I guess so.

Jesus: "Yes."

Elizabeth: My friend Tim wants to know, when will he meet his new wife? His wife. He just wants to meet somebody and be happy. And I wasn't gonna ask this cause it was personal, but then I thought, "You know what? A lot of people want to know when they are gonna meet their spouse." So, what kind of general answer can you give to that?

Jesus: "So your friend, Ken, you said?"

Elizabeth: Tim.

Jesus: "Tim? I'm sorry Tim?"

Elizabeth: Yeah, Tim _____.

Jesus: "I would say to him, his focus is, again, this is something different then as you said, it's a personal thing but his focus is not on . . . I cannot say when."

Elizabeth: I didn't think you could!! (Laughing)

Jesus: "Because he is creating, again this goes back to the Law of Attraction and what is he creating and what did he come here to do and where does he have his faith and trust. He is very much feeling very lonely and he would be-in order to bring someone into his experience as a spouse or a partner, it would be best if he understand his loneliness so that he can then change his vibration. Because that's really what it is."

Elizabeth: OK, YES! That can be great, a lot of people can . . . that's a good one, thank you!

Jesus: "Yes. You're welcome."

Elizabeth: Let's see . . . Melissa W. would like to know, "Why do we hurt so much and for so long when we lose someone we love when we know that they are going to Heaven and they can be free from their pain?" So, our human emotions.

Jesus: "Yes, all human emotions because in this time period that you are in and have been for since, for some time now, it is meant for you to deal with the emotional body. So emotions have become very much, they have intensified, let's put it that way. They have always been there for humans. It is the human condition. It is what sets you apart for Humanity. The condition of being in the human form. It sets all of us, when we are in the human form Apart because the intensity of the emotions—good and bad as you call them. So, the grieving process is one of the greatest opportunities of Reconnecting with Oneness. It is the emotion that most would, well, they all are meant to bring you back to-as I have said before-compassion, love of self and back to knowing that there is only one-there is only the Oneness that we all come from and grief in human form is probably the greatest one because there is a sense of loss of never having again and never seeing that and having that space ripped out of you-some would describe it, there is a hole inside of them and that hole cannot be filled by the other human being. It is a call for you to redirect your attention and your energy towards reconnecting with Oneness."

Elizabeth: Oh, OK.

Jesus: "Again, all emotion is that but grief is the greatest and strongest."

Elizabeth: Well, I know Laurie wanted to be going at 3: 30 so we'll have to be closing now and maybe if you could give us a special prayer to say?

Jesus: "Sure, let me think. You are all better with prayers in that sense than I am. Let's-let us do this. Because this is something for you and your friend, and the Medium as well, why don't I . . . . I want to, not that I don't want to bless the others but I want to bless the 3 of you in a special way and all of those who have contributed to today's messages by their thoughtful and insightful questions and a prayer would be . . . the best would be something along the lines, again, I am not as good as you are at putting these things together but . . . you see? You know why?"

Elizabeth: Why?

Jesus: "Because you in human form have a Need that is different than when we are out of Spirit. You, when you pray to us, are praying for connection and therefore it is driven By that strong desire for connection and the emotion put into prayer, if it is, from our perspective, if it is a prayer that I give you, it will not maybe be the emotion that you need or another needs. Do you understand? So when you find your own words for prayer, that is the best. That's why when you say, 'can you give us a prayer?' I stumbled because of my understanding and how I want you, because of who you are, to understand the power of prayer comes not in the words but in the vibration being spoken, or felt, at that moment. So you could be saying gibberish but if the vibration is one of love that is your prayer."

Elizabeth: So, it's personal, that's why chanting and all the other different ways that people do their own prayers, that's why they all work!

Jesus: "Yes."

Elizabeth: OK.

Jesus: "So, I'm sorry that I cannot, but I'm blanking on what to give you and I don't want to give you something that has no value."

Elizabeth: No, that's totally OK cause you've been with us today, so that's good enough (Laughing)

Jesus: "Yes, yes, and if the next time I find some words that have special meaning for you or someone who has written in, than I will give that to them. A special message of love, yes, I can do that, that is different."

Elizabeth: OK, alright, that sounds good. Well, thank you!

Jesus: "You are welcome and I thank you. This is a very beautiful experience and I see it only growing and in your generosity and wanting to help others."

Elizabeth: Awesome, thank you.

Jesus: "Yes, I will now leave and let you speak with the Medium. Goodbye and we will speak soon."

Elizabeth: OK! Love You!!! Bye, bye!

Jesus: "I love you too. Goodbye."

Elizabeth: K. bye

CHAPTER 3

Faith

May 9, 2013

Jesus: "Hello my friends, we are gathered here-"

Elizabeth: Hi!

Jesus: "Yes."

Elizabeth: (I interrupted Him-I was excited!) Hi, I just wanted to say hello back (Laughing)

Jesus: "Laughing. Yes, so, today we are once again coming together for Instruction, for Understanding would be how you would best describe what we are doing here. It's important that you—how do I put this-what you are seeking to understand—you and your friends—are laws of the universe and they are very simple yet for you as humans, at times, difficult to implement. So, it makes one question, in human form, the validity's of these teachings and these understandings. So, fortunately, there are those on your planet who have much experience but this information is for everyone. So, hopefully today we will go deeper into Understanding so that I can help all of you reach the, the Awareness that you are so seeking. So let us begin with your questions, for those will bring more insight as we move along."

Elizabeth: OK, well today I wanted to talk to you about healing.

Jesus: "Yes."

Elizabeth: How did you heal people and how can we do it ourselves and also, can we manifest things like cancer in our body just by talking about it and thinking about it.

Jesus: "OK, very good. For it is a very complex issue seen from the eyes of the human being. It's not something that is, you are able to easily take from the philosophy if you will-it is not a philosophy-from the Concept of this for it is law. Healing is based in a law. So is disease. The manifestation of healing and disease are both based in universal law. Let us begin there. You understand what I mean by Universal Law, do you not? Or should we touch on that topic first?"

Elizabeth: Well, I understand it but other people listening to this might not understand it so if you wanna just clarify that for them?

Jesus: "Yes. So you are living in a universe that is dictated and held together BY universal laws. Just as you have natural laws on your planet. Those of gravity and those that are shown to physics. Those are what you call your natural laws. Your universal laws are many but there are primary universal laws and one of them is Cause and Effect that many understand. The Laws of Attraction-that has been widely spoken of, of late and others-Laws of Compensation, Laws of Divine Return, there are many laws and these are laws that hold together the fabric of the universe. They give definition to All Beings Existence. So without these laws there would be chaos. Chaos does exist but from chaos is born then the Need for these universal laws. For they give you, as the Divine Being that you are, the possibility to Transcend the human form and to exist in your divine, as a divine being also in human form. When you are outside of human form, you do not have disease or you do not need healing as you understand it here. So, once you know and accept that there are universal laws that are just there as there are natural laws, that gives you a foundation from which you begin to understand the laws of healing and disease as you have asked. Let's begin with whether one can create a disease such as cancer. Everything, Everything in your existence is created By You. You the individual—on the planet. Disease is created by your thoughts and your feelings. Now, many struggle with this. For they want to understand so as to eliminate the need for disease in their earthly existence and to understand that, you must begin with understanding how you are, as a human being, everything goes back to the individual himself. So, we will speak to you, you are walking the planet as a divine being, encapsulated in the human form. You have free will. Remember free will is what was given to you so that you could then say, 'I will do this or I will do that." In that, you were also given the ego mind, you were given the different bodies and such, as you understand yourself. So, you come forth with this Foundation for creation. If you think of your existence here as a Unending Creative Experience, as it is in the universe when you are outside of your physical form, there is Only Creation. So, what are you creating in every moment. Your way in which to gauge what it is you are creating is through understanding yourself and what it is you are thinking and feeling at all times. This is not easy. There has to be, for a disease to exist within the physical form, there has to be a belief that disease exists. If there is not a belief, a fundamental belief in disease existing, it cannot exist. It is created by the individual, so each of you will have similarities and each of you will have ways in which you manifest your own discomfort in life through your thoughts and your feelings. So, let's stop there because there is more to this but I feel you need to ask more, some questions for to go deeper."

Elizabeth: Well, that makes sense, I just feel that people might question, well then how come children have disease then?

Jesus: "Yes, so this is where it becomes more complex. So why does a child come in with a disease? Remember, you have to remember that you are not, even as a child, you are not without free will, you are just in an immature form. At all times you have free will. You Chose the Form that you came into for a specific reason. Only you can fully understand that and as a your individual experience. So a child coming in with disease already present or created had very likely Chosen that means to Gain Understanding for their journey here. So, are they consciously aware of their process? No, because of the Forgetting when you enter the human form but Prior to entering the human form, there was a decision to go a certain route and create certain things that were already present for that. For whatever it was that they needed to learn or for those people around them that they need to learn. What Human Beings fail to understand is that you are on this planet to learn. Not on this planet to have fun so to speak. The potential for that is always there. Opportunity for living at peace in peace and harmony is always present yet you are living in an environment which is being constantly—is in constant motion and constant change. So those who are children with diseases, have chosen that path for their own enlightenment, would be the best way of describing that."

Elizabeth: OK, and for that of their parents then also.

Jesus: "Yes. So, it's difficult for humans to grasp these concepts because of their belief patterns and indoctrination when you come into physical form. You are bombarded by the-what is already present here on your planet—you come into an environment that is already set for you. You have unfortunately—you forget because if you remembered you wouldn't go through the toil of understanding to achieve enlightenment. If you can understand that the only way to Enlightenment is to go through this process—as you are designed-those who chose this process—it is the only way to achieve the enlightenment that they are looking for. It is Just That Way. It's just set up in that way. It's as though, to make the same comparison to one who wants to become a doctor and chooses to become a doctor and follows the path of what it is to become a doctor in terms of schooling and such. It is just that way. Without going through that process, one cannot become a doctor. Correct?"

Elizabeth: YES

Jesus: "So it is the same with Enlightenment. You cannot become Enlightened without going through the process of Earthly Existence. Earth was created Specifically for certain souls to inhabit in order to reach enlightenment in this specific way."

Elizabeth: OK.

Jesus: "So, some things remain a mystery and that's where Faith comes in and your Trust in Faith and that is really the fundamental Flaw in human character is-and where one who fails to reach Healing of any sort—whether it be physical, financial, spiritual or anything is that there is lack of Faith and without Faith, nothing can be achieved of any value and you are really here—each of you-to Reconnect With That so that you are living in a state OF constant Faith and Trust—that you are NOT alone and that you are being guided at all times and that everything that is occurring is for you-specifically for you-to learn from in the way which you have chosen at some point in time."

Elizabeth: Good stuff. This is good stuff.

Jesus: "OK, good. That's important. Because what we are talking about may take a few sessions to really understand and then it will take your efforts at applying some of what we talk about in order to bring about that which you are looking to manifest."

Elizabeth: OK . . .

Jesus: "So, ask more questions because there are many aspects of this that we must delve into."

Elizabeth: OK, so if to heal ourselves is to have Faith, can we heal people that have little Faith?

Jesus: "Yes, yes, it is so very unique to each situation and each person. At what point does one of little Faith—when you are able to intervene—does it shift over TO Faith. You see what happens many times, individuals have been healed but they continue to Believe that they are ill and have a certain disease and that is perception. Their perception of their world and their existence Gives Them Back what they are asking for. So again, what you focus on-your perception-so your focus—will be what you are then creating. So, many different elements come into the concept of self healing through spiritual means and it all takes understanding, patience, practice and once again Faith. Faith that this does. I would say to you, "Have you asked what you would do with someone who has no Faith?" You were somewhat going in that direction-one of little Faith, what would you do with someone like that? How would you help someone who is of little Faith, but wanting to have Faith?"

Elizabeth: I would try to do my best to help them to . . . I don't know, I guess I would try to do my best in guiding them but I guess it would be specific to whatever circumstance that would be.

Jesus: "Yes. So I put this question forth to you because I want you to ponder it for the next time that we talk so that you say—because this is why you are here-each of you that I am speaking to—you have all come here for your own purpose, but in your case, you have come here to help those who are less Enlightened if you will. Those who are Newer to this journey. The ones who have come along recently-the newer souls-you are here to help them FIND Faith. For you have no problem with Faith, do you?"

Elizabeth: No, not at all.

Jesus: "Not at all. Yet your friend the Medium has problems with Faith, does she not?"

Elizabeth: Yes, she does.

Jesus: "So, yet. So there's an example. We are—I am bringing this up because this is what you are here to do for other people is to find—and each will be unique in their ways—that is why you put together the information that you put together and published it in such a way so that it would reach a larger audience because your purpose here, and you know it, is to instruct, or is to assist others in finding Faith."

Elizabeth: Yeah, I like that too.

Jesus: "Yes, so that gives you some direction because yours is unwavering."

Elizabeth: Thank you, Jesus! It's so nice to hear you say that!

Jesus: "Well, you are here on the planet assisting us and when there's information that can be beneficial such as this, we want you to know that."

Elizabeth :OK. Thank you.

Jesus: "Yes."

Elizabeth: Thank you for mentioning my book too, I'm quite proud of it. (laughing)

Jesus: "As you should be, as you should be and that is just the beginning for you because you are of great Faith. Again, let's go back to Faith because here is the fundamental Truth laying behind creating Anything-whether it be disease or healing or abundance-but abundance really is ALL things good, not just financial abundance. So, Faith, without it, it cannot, it becomes a greater struggle. So, you may be asking yourself, "Well, why do some have Faith and others do not?" That is something that may come to mind. You will want to ponder this over-from now until we speak again so that we can delve into this so that you CAN help those that are in your lives because they are there for you to help them Find Faith because you have designed it all in that way."

Elizabeth: OK, well when you talk about people being in my life that you know, Lack Faith, it makes me think of a friend of mine that her mother lost her children and so they, and she's had several miscarriages so um, you know, she kinda wonders why God would do that to her if, you know, I don't think she necessarily Doesn't believe in a God, but she doesn't have the Faith so.

Jesus: "Right. So, again, it is something that cannot be given to another. There is no instruction for it. There is no rule book. We cannot put together a "How To" pamphlet here. We can Only Assist Others by indicating to them where—how they can find it within themselves because that is the journey. All of you are on that journey looking for that and when you find that Faith and you have that Faith and Trust then you walk through life with greater ease."

Elizabeth: See, now my Faith, a lot of times, I'll ask for a sign and I'll get a sign and I had a question actually to you is, "How do we know that it's you that's giving a sign." But you know it's in your heart, I guess is what would be the answer I would think.

Jesus: "Yes, you only can know because you Feel It. That's what we were talking about earlier, in terms of your thoughts and your feelings. That each of you must learn to know yourself. You had a man on your planet who said, "To thine own self be true." What he meant by that was, know thyself and become very familiar with who you are and when you do that you are connected to your-not your self, so much—as your feelings. You are aware of what you are feeling. It is through that journey There that you begin to connect to these higher vibrations of Faith and Trust and Love and Compassion. But it is only through knowing yourself and being true To Yourself that you can find that path."

Elizabeth: Self-awareness. OK.

Jesus: "Yes, self-awareness, always. So, again, it goes back to those who are struggling-have-each-of you has chosen a different way in which to find enlightenment. You have all had many many lifetimes here on this planet-this is just a stage for all of you to come forth and act out your individual experiences for your own benefit and for the benefit of others but primarily for yourselves. So, you are, I came forth to Demonstrate that what I could do, Everyone could do. And as I spoke to you the last time, this is something also, that I do now—I did that because I opened up the possibilities for this happening. So, in your earthly existence, 2,000 years is a very very short period of time yet much has occurred in that 2,000 years that evolution has taken on-gone forward by leaps and bounds for you-yet in many ways you are still very immature. So, Now is the time to open up to the possibilities of manifestation and manifesting those things that you desire. Now in this whole process you have to understand that you are working with your conscious mind AND your sub-conscious mind and this is another tricky area because what is in your sub-conscious mind are those things that you are not aware of consciously but they have more control and say over what occurs in your life than what you have consciously. This is why people will do affirmations and doubly try to affirm certain things and things do not go in the direction of their affirmations because at a sub-conscious level there is a block and that's something-that's why it becomes very tricky and it can seem so far fetched and difficult to obtain these types of manifestations that we are talking about today."

Elizabeth: OK, They're blocking themselves.

Jesus: "They're blocking themselves but they are not able to see it. So again, it's taking the time necessary to understand yourselves, being aware, trusting in guidance and seeking answers From guidance because we are ALWAYS there to help you as you see continually. You ask for a sign and you get the sign."

Elizabeth: Yes, yep. And everybody needs to start asking. And maybe people are just afraid of opening up that doorway to you and Heaven, I don't know.

Jesus: "Many feel undeserving, many feel that—they lack the Faith. We'll go back to that. They lack the Faith that there really is an existence beyond the earthly plane and that I truly exist beyond the earthly plane amongst many others."

Elizabeth: OK. Well, I'll do my best to try to help people open up so.

Jesus: "And you have those around you who are in need of that so practice with those who are there by you and see how it works. And through that you will get a better understanding of how you will then be helping those that are not so close to you."

Elizabeth: OK, OK. Now I wanna go back to the healing part of it. Um, because I healed my son Adam, he had these contagious warts on his legs but I did a Qi Gong kind a thing and it completely healed him! So is it because of my Faith that healed him, well I know it is that too, but like, I already had the mind frame that "this is going to work."

Jesus: "Yes, absolutely."

Elizabeth: Was it anything that, did it have anything to do with kinda erasing them out with a white light coming from my finger tips and adding energy to it-any of that or was it pure based Faith.

Jesus: "It was both. It was ALL of it. The-so you had the Faith— you had the belief that they could be healed in such a manner and then you followed your guidance because that was guidance—this will help in the end to be healing-and you did what you did with your hands in order to enhance the healing. You worked with Energy because that's another aspect of it. But you could have worked with energy in continuation but if there was no Faith or there was even the slightest bit of doubt, it would not have worked more than likely."

Elizabeth: OK, OK, alright. Cool.

Jesus: "Yes, you are living in a time when everyone is-you are here to take responsibility for your own lives and to come into your own power, as you say. To Acknowledge yourselves as Divine and Powerful Beings and because of that, that is why there are things occurring for so many people that Need Healing so that they can begin the process and Claim Their Own Right To BE Powerful Beings. That is really what it is. That was the doorway that was opened a few months ago. The doorway of Claiming your Own Power as a Divine Being."

Elizabeth: I love that you say that cause it was just what I was thinking before you started sayin it! (Laughing)

Jesus: "You see, we are on the same page."

Elizabeth: Yeah, we are. Yeah we are. So we all need to find our own Power and we do all have this ability to be able to heal and send out energy through our hands and you know, we should all use it!

Jesus: "Yes, Absolutely. The more you use it, the more you develop the Faith, the more you practice it, the more your Faith will and Belief and Trust in all of this the more it will be it and you will understand. Now there are those who have greater blocks to this than others. And I will keep referring to the Medium because she is a good example and one that will be good for all, for herself and for you and others to—who are wanting to understand this because of on the one hand, she is, has great Understanding. But yet, there are blocks that she is unaware of. So this information today, hopefully will reach her as well, and she can utilize it but you are there to assist her in Remembering so that you can help her in this process. As she has helped you in various processes as well."

Elizabeth: Yeah, I feel like we are very much a team.

Jesus: "Yes, absolutely."

Elizabeth: OK, Good cause I just sent her a thing on being powerful last night. (Laughing) (and after this session she told me that she hadn't even opened up that email yet when I asked her what she thought about it! So SHE didn't even know!

Jesus: "OK, perfect. Because that is what it is. There is a reluctance on Human Beings parts to Take their Birthright of Divine Beings and that is the Power and about being Powerful. There is a reluctance is actually not a strong enough word-there is a Refusal and for whatever reason-each individual has the reason WHY they refuse to do it. Some of it is because they feel unworthy and that it's not for them and these are-whatever it is that is for the individual, it is their block to their own healing. Because once you have accepted that you are a Powerful and

Divine Being-AS I AM-ME JESUS-that you are all the same AS ME-Then Nothing can stop you!"

Elizabeth: OK, I'm gonna get personal now and say that I was just thinking along the lines of being sexual and I'm coming into being OK with that and I don't know if maybe people are raised to not be OK with it but I am OK with it now and it feels really good. Like I wish people would be more free in that and not feel like they are doing something bad or you know, wrong or that they are not going to be frowned upon for it. You know what I mean?

Jesus: "Yes. Sexuality is another topic of much complexity for human beings because Through the sexual experience there are-through what you would call your orgasm is the sensation-it is not just a function of the body-it is a function of the spiritual body as well. (flip tape) It becomes very very complex in the human form but it's meant to be that way—it's another tool that assists individuals in their enlightenment."

Elizabeth: Ooooh, Really!

Jesus: "Yes. If you think about all of the ah, between the finances—money and sexuality—they are both ego based but spiritually based because everything is spiritually based. So, but they are the areas in which Mankind is using these areas for Enlightenment-in whatever ways. Remember, we've talked about this, to not judge anything. Do not judge anything you've done or judge anyone else. And when you understand that these are the two areas where man has the Greatest Potential or Opportunity to exercise free will. Free Will, yes, you can exercise it every moment of everyday but in this area it is just extenuated and that is why it is-these two areas are the greatest for enlightenment."

Elizabeth: OK. That can make people feel good about it.

Jesus: "Yes, yes but yet there are so many strange emotions-perversions-regarding the both money and sexuality for human beings. So it's interesting how it is being utilized by many in ways in which guilt is associated with it."

Elizabeth: That's a good word to use for it, yes.

Jesus: "Yes. So, it's really the vibration of Guilt, that one would want to look at."

Elizabeth: OK. Alright. I don't know what else to say about that. (giggling)

Jesus: "So, in regards to Healing, going back to what it is that we will be discussing, is that Healing really comes down to many different factors and one who has disease in their body would be very-it would be very beneficial for that individual to begin a process of self discovery. Number 1. Begin to understand who they are. And that is done in many different ways but most will do it through a form of meditation. Now when someone says, "Know who you are." they immediately, most individuals think immediately of who they are as a human being—not who they are as a Divine Being. The way, what I am saying is you must—a journey of self discovery in Who You Are As A Divine Being and by doing that, it's setting that Intention. How you have to do, you will be guided as to what you need to do to go Within to begin that journey to understand the manifestations of disease. Other areas that you want to consider in terms of someone who's already with an aliment. To review where they are holding onto anger, hurt and basically, unforgiveness. Where is it that they are refusing to forgive and to let go? Because they are standing in judgment of another or themselves. It is what is the greatest creator of disease on your planet is unforgiveness."

Elizabeth: Yeah, OK, sorry, I was just looking at the baby. Um, Forgiveness is the greatest creator of disease—UNFORGIVENESS, OK. So we got to get the base root of that to be able to get at to what that's creating . . . OK.

Jesus: "Yes."

Elizabeth: Sorry I got distracted there.

Jesus: "It's OK. That is not a problem. I understand. Again, we are doing this in segments and there are no rules here. We do what we can with what we can at the time, right?"

Elizabeth: Yep.

Jesus: "So, you have—today—only the top part or the—I don't want to say the tip of the iceberg because you got more than that-but you've only begun this Understanding here. You have to take it deeper because the information that I've given is they are all words and for those who do not believe and are struggling with that—in having that-but yet the desire is there for something—that is what you want to really focus on because that is where I want to be taking you in the coming sessions that we will be getting together."

Elizabeth: OK, filling the vacant whole.

Jesus: "Yes. The How To Heal—Truly. Because when we speak of healing, we speak of healing in everything. You are healing—it would be more a Remembering of who you are and why you are here."

Elizabeth: Would I, is the purpose, that I would be starting to heal in Your name? Like, "In the name of Jesus Christ, I heal you."

Jesus: "YES."

Elizabeth: OK, That's a huge responsibility there, Jesus! (Laughter)

Jesus: "YES. But you are up to the task."

Elizabeth: OK. So when I do that, is it just going to be my Faith, and those words that will heal people and if I lay my hands on them or do I need to do anything specific beyond that, as far as like a special visualization, thinking of colors coming from my hands, anything like that?

Jesus: "You will be guided. Each one will be different for you. So, as you do this, start with what you know and then pay attention to what is being channeled to you as information about what it is that that individual may need to enhance the healing."

Elizabeth: OK. Are we talking about not just physical healing but emotional healing as well?

Jesus: "YES."

Elizabeth: OK.

Jesus: "Yes, when we speak of healing really, here, healing-when you heal, truly you are healing the emotional, not the physical."

Elizabeth: OK.

Jesus: "When one is healed—all of those that I healed were open to and Willing to know. There was not resistance to their experience. They need not have resistance any longer. So When the healing occurred, they were Transformed because in that moment, in their consciousness, came the memory of who they were. That's ALL that I did. I Reconnected them to their Source. And they were open and willing to reconnect. They felt it. And it was A Feeling as opposed to anything intellectual. And that is why it is so difficult for you to do this as instruction as opposed to: Practice. And just doing it in a way that Shows others."

Elizabeth: OK. Are people going to be coming to me then for this?

Jesus: "If you so desire."

Elizabeth: OK. I would like to be able to have people come to me. I feel like I bump into people that I'm meant to bump into and you know, things happen like that way.

Jesus: "So, you—begin with the ones that you have around you. And know that they are-all you have to do is ask. Remember that is the other thing. If you are attempting to heal someone and they are-you have not asked them then it will not work."

Elizabeth: OK. So I must ask their permission first.

Jesus: "Yes. And then it would be important for you to set up possibly a time so that you can be in a one on one situation with this individual and then begin to play. And say to them, "This is something new for me as well, let's just see what happens here." So that you don't feel that responsibility of failing because you don't want to-yours is not from lack of Faith that you feel that you can fail. Yours is from a desire to help another. You understand why a healing would not occur-for the most part—and yet, you don't know, you are not able yet—to identify those individuals who are not ready for healing. So you will be trying to heal those individuals who are not ready for healing and you will feel, at times, sad because you are not able to assist someone and we do not want you to feel that there is a failure on your part. That it is a combined effort because when you are working with another and you are looking to perform a healing, that other MUST FEEL The Connection for it to work. This is not explained in the information that has been passed on, but there will hopefully—there is this information put down in what you call scripture in books that are still hidden to Humanity that will hopefully come to light at the time that they are-that Humanity is ready to hear them."

Elizabeth: I sure hope so.

Jesus: "Yes."

Elizabeth: You aw, wanna give us any directions as to where to go for these things? (Laughter)

Jesus: "No, because they are in the hands of some individuals that ah . . ."

Elizabeth: (I cut Him off) Oh, are we talkin about The Vatican, Jesus??

Jesus: "Some of that is in here and some of—there are others as well. So, yes, it is too complex and it's not-remember, everything is as it should be."

Elizabeth: OK, so I'm not gonna be mad at The Vatican for not sharing what they know.

Jesus: "Exactly. They are performing a service. Remember, anything that you have in your experience that you do not like-what should you do?"

Elizabeth: Um . . .

Jesus: "I'm testing. This is an exam. It's your first essay question."

Elizabeth: (Laughing) OK, repeat the question then please.

Jesus: "So, you have something in your experience that is uncomfortable for you that you dislike and you would like to not have it be that way. What would you do? What is your responsibility?"

Elizabeth: Um, I would think that I'm not going to worry about it cause it's out of my hands.

Jesus: "OK. But say it's something that is important to you. So can you just not worry about it and let it be out of your hands completely? What if it is something that-what if there's something more there? What if nothing changes then and you stay in that condition for a very very long time?"

Elizabeth: Well, then you've gotta do something to change that.

Jesus: "Do you have to do something to change it or do you have to begin to Understand it and Why it is in your experience? What is it trying to teach you?"

Elizabeth: Well, you'd have to use an example. Like give me an actual example. (Laughing)

Jesus: "OK. So, say you have a person in your life that has to be in your life. Say you married someone and his mother is a royal pain in the neck, OK? And that person is in your life. And you have to interact with her or you have a boss. A boss would be a better one and you have to keep this job because you are supporting your family so you have to coexist with this other individual. What would you do? Let it go? But it irritates you in continuation. So what would you do? What would be the way in which to find Release and Enlightenment? And to know yourself."

Elizabeth: I would try, I don't wanna use the word, tolerate, but I would try to be as nice as I could.

Jesus: "Oooh, my."

Elizabeth: Uh, o. (Laughing)

Jesus: "Well then have fun. (chuckle) What I am trying to get at-and you know this-when you have experiences in your life-anything—an individual or an experience."

Elizabeth: (Blurting out) They're teaching me something about myself.

Jesus: "Yes. Otherwise, what is not in your experience? That is what you want to ask yourself all the time. What is it that I need to know about this?"

Elizabeth: OK. What do I need to know about this?

Jesus: "Always. Asking "why" closes it off. Asking, "what do you need to know," as they say, "getting curious about it"."

Elizabeth: Getting curious, alright cool because I don't know why that confused me because I did do that a couple of different times already within the last few months. "What's in it for me to learn?" Sometimes when I'm talking to you I kinda blank out or something, I don't know.

Jesus: "Yes, I knew that you knew but I wanted to explain this because it is another aspect of Healing that is very important for all of you to understand. "So, this is in my experience and what could it be trying to show me?" And do that with Gentleness and you'll get your answers and Then when you no longer have NEED of that experience because you have then HEALED what was causing the experience then you will no longer manifest it in your life-or it will manifest but you will not be bothered by it."

Elizabeth: OK, alright, that makes sense. I mean, even though you still gotta work with the boss, OK, alright.

Jesus: "You understand."

Elizabeth: Yeah, I understand. (laughing)

Jesus:—He's chuckling :) "Yes. So, that's because-you said at the very beginning we were going to be talking about healing and that is the topic because you are-hopefully through our meetings, we can come to some place where we can offer more information about healing than has been known before."

Elizabeth: Yes, I hope so.

Jesus: "So what else?"

Elizabeth: When you were talking about that the other person has to actually be willing to able to be healed, it made me think of my Mother.

Jesus: "Yes."

Elizabeth: And I don't want to hold guilt over not being able to help her because she didn't Allow me to help her.

Jesus: "Absolutely. That was HER CHOICE. She had FREE WILL. Had she used her free will to open up to the possibility than who knows what might have happened."

Elizabeth: Right.

Jesus: "And she was unaware of it. She felt she was being open to you. Because that was her makeup. That was how she was—designed it for herself as well."

Elizabeth: OK

Jesus: "She was not ready this lifetime—for Enlightenment at that level let's say."

Elizabeth: OK, she'll get another crack at it some other time, right?

Jesus: "Yes."

Elizabeth: (My friend Denise was asking me to ask Him if she will have to reincarnate another time) She'll have to reincarnate then to learn that some other time, yeah.

Jesus: "Yes. Absolutely."

Elizabeth: I wanna ask about . . . healing . . . I wanna ask about demonic possession.

Jesus: "OK."

Elizabeth: How-where do demons fit in to all of this?

Jesus: "In regards to disease and healing or just in general?"

Elizabeth: Well, how does somebody get possessed? And how do you know that they are so that you can actually help them get that out?

Jesus: "Well, again, it's only through-by allowing it to occur that one becomes possessed. Because one is—Believes in the power of That because . . . there is great fear to begin with. There is great fear and then one has the belief in the power of the lower vibrations over the higher vibrations and that's how it occurs basically because the individual that is possessed has a deep fear which leads to a belief that they have no control. That they are at the whim of God and all non-physical, well even physical but they are at the whim of all other Beings and then they are, they have no choice and no power of their own so that's how come the allow it. If they understood they have the power to just say no, than it would not occur."

Elizabeth: Well did God make demons then?

Jesus: "YES!"

Elizabeth: Interesting

Jesus: "Well because they are necessary. There is balance all in that."

Elizabeth: I suppose. The growl that I've heard now, twice now, is very scary but it's OK because I wanna take care of the person that it is in and I wanna get it out of them so . . .

Jesus: "Yes, yes, very good. Yes."

Elizabeth: Well, maybe that is enough for us today cause my brain is just mush I think. (Laughing)

Jesus: "That's very much information today and I want—that you ponder this until we meet again so that we can keep on going deeper with this. You'll see it will have a pattern that will all come together when we are complete."

Elizabeth: OK, alright. That sounds good. Thank you.

Jesus: "Alright, you are welcome. We will speak very soon again."

Elizabeth: Alright, cool. Bye Jesus.

Jesus: "Yes, goodbye."

CHAPTER 4

Understanding Free Will

May 16, 2013

Laurie was asking me to ask Him about Free Will before we started. To explain that. He had been talking to her about that that morning and He wanted to elaborate on that for us. And on a personal note, what information He could give her on her being plagued by noise.

Jesus: "Yes, hello, it is such a pleasure to be with you once again in this way. That there is this opportunity to interact with you and what you are doing is of such pleasure. It is a pleasurable experience to interact in this way that is both a teaching and learning experience and you will see that much will come out of this that will benefit all of you who are touched by this information. So, let us begin. Yes, I was nudging the Medium to bring up the topic of Free Will. Have you any particular questions or because that will help us to deepen our understanding of Free Will. So let me ask you this. How do you understand free will in relation to your experience here on Earth. What is it that you know so far?"

Elizabeth: Um, we have the ability to do whatever we want.

Jesus: "Exactly. Exactly. How does that-so, you have the ability to do whatever you want. But most do not feel that way, correct? They feel subject to external circumstances that determine their existence through one way or another, correct?"

Elizabeth: Yeah, they kinda let other people control what's going on in their lives when they don't realize that THEY have control of it.

Jesus: "OK, so say you are in a situation that-let's think of a situation-OK, you are unable to find work. You say you can do whatever you want. Someone has made every attempt to generate some form of income through creating a work experience and yet, does not find that. So, they would come to you and they would say, "But I've been looking for work for 5 years and have yet been able to find something that is appropriate or is satisfying or even work that would allow me to support myself and my family." How would you tell them, "Well, just go ahead, use your free will, you can have whatever you want." and walk away?"

Elizabeth: Um, well, sometimes we shouldn't be so picky though. I guess if you're going to be supporting a family you really need to have a job and not be so picky.

Jesus: "OK, but what if someone is not very picky. They are willing to work but, OK, because this gets into other areas because there are individuals who are not picky and continue yet they work at a wage that is insufficient for their needs, correct?"

Elizabeth: Yes.

Jesus: "So, they are, and you're telling them, "Well, use your free will.""

Elizabeth: I, if it was, OK, I'd have to put myself in the position then. For me-what I would do to find a job would be to follow the signs that I am being given.

Jesus: "Very good. So, in that case, would you say that that is your—you using Free Will?"

Elizabeth: Ah, to follow the signs, yes. But to ignore them, yes also. So you gotta choose which direction do you wanna go and you'll get help if you just follow whatever signs you are getting. Be it an actual visual sign that someone might see that might make them think, "OH! This is for me!" or reading something or someone saying something to you that's kinda connecting to what somebody else said . . . it's connecting the dots.

Jesus: "Yes, OK, So, that would be one way of saying how do you use free will. So let's give another example. What about someone unjustly imprisoned? Someone who is taken their situation and unjustly imprisoned and you tell them, "Well, you can have whatever you want just use your free will." And that person wants to be free and wants to be exonerated. What would you tell them? How could they use their free will in this case?"

Elizabeth: Um, I would just pray my little heart out. I don't know. You're kinda stuck in that situation there until someone decides to help you.

Jesus: "So, do you feel at that point, someone would believe that there is something such a thing as Free Will that allows you to have whatever you want?"

Elizabeth: No, someone in that position probably wouldn't think that.

Jesus: "Exactly. So, Free Will must mean something more. There must be more to this because it's not just knowing you can have whatever you want. Yes, free will gives you the opportunity to-to choose. Free will gives you the opportunity to make-put the-YOU are the one that is determining your existence at every moment. You are—your creative free will is the Tool that you Use to Create. So, individuals understanding that Free Will is what is the Ultimate Tool that they have available To Them for living an existence that is of the Highest Vibration that matches their needs and what they came here to accomplish at this time. You see, for you on your planet, to understand the workings of free will is very very important. To understand that you, at Every Moment, have the opportunity to choose. Not so much what direction to take in terms of connecting the dots because the individual unjustly imprisoned—what can that person do? BUT that person can Then have the free will to observe his or her experience through the eyes of free will. That's where it lies. It's in Choosing how you will Experience what life is handing you. So, first Accepting Responsibility that you have found yourself in the situation of unjustified imprisonment puts you in a place of Empowerment. And that is what is the result of knowing you have free will. Free will to believe that you are a victim or believe that there is a way out Through Faith and Trust and that you Then put yourself in a vibration of Reception and that is the connecting of the dots, as you say, of free will. So, one who is unjustly imprisoned will be able to possibly free themselves-that is their miracle to happen. Free will brings about miracles. One unjustly imprisoned having the Faith and the Trust that they will-that Love will win-meaning Good will Always Win-and having that Faith and knowing that this is-staying in that vibration of Faith and Trust. And Belief is a Choice which is what Free Will is. It goes much deeper than that. You are here at this time to understand TRULY what Free Will means for you and how you can use it to Create Heaven on Earth."

Elizabeth: OK, so a feeling of hopelessness isn't going to get you anywhere.

Jesus: "It will continue to give you experiences of hopelessness."

Elizabeth: Correct.

Jesus: "Again, we are going to go back to something that is very crucial for those-you and the others that are getting this information at this time—is Understanding what the Key Here Is. And that is Understanding Your Own Feelings and Your Own Thoughts. And then Trusting that you are here to have that experience and to Transcend that emotional body to the degree that you transform hopelessness into Trust and Faith and Belief. And that is why it is important to Learn to assist others In changing their own belief patterns, which is what we were talking about the last time that we came together. So, you see that you-because you are the one primarily asking the questions-but the Medium as well-and she and you will be delving into this so that you can assist yourselves and others into that Understanding of what you do to Transform one's underlying belief system and how-when you can say push-and when you need to back off. It is something that you will be learning in the coming times."

Elizabeth: OK, so if she wanted to use her reference of living by noisy places, um, how does that-what kind of resolution should-cause I suggested maybe writing a petition cause right now petitions are a big thing for things that concern people-using our free will to try to make positive changes.

Jesus: "Yes, how she does it, is in a sense irrelevant. Petition, yes, rallying others to her side, but if no one comes to her side she will then feel that she is battling this on her own. She must go into the Understanding of what are the Emotional Components of what she is feeling when she is disturbed by this noise. So, she continually creates this experience in the effort to transmute that energy because it's an energy OF helplessness and feeling defeated and it reflects for her, personally, in many areas of her life where she feels defeated that she has not put forth the effort-or she has put forth the effort-but all of her efforts have brought her very little gain. So, she has many ways in which to approach this but she is good example of Every One Of You has Something that is in your lives that is a constant irritation and it's there for you to look at in regards to what it's making you feel and Then going into that and as you say praying or however one then connects with the Oneness and Asking for assistance in That understanding and Then that is when Miracles occur. When you allow yourself to step Outside of it—of what it is that is your Emotional Trigger and observe it as someone from the outside but then look at it and try to see it-the best way is to try to see it through the eyes of love and the eyes of good. Try to see it in That way. Try to see whatever it is In That Way and THAT is the key to transforming any sort of underlying sub-conscious belief pattern within any individual. It is a process. It is an effort. And if you have something that is repetitive as an irritation in your life-something you have been carrying for a very long time, you can Guarantee that you have come here to work on that specific thing. And that you must move forward in-if you want transformation, you must move forward with that openness and willingness to try."

Elizabeth: Great advice.

Jesus: "Yes."

Elizabeth: K. That makes sense. Anything else?

Jesus: "So, just to continue on and it is not easy to fully understand and put into words these-what I am speaking of because it is a very experiential experience. One that you must go through and practice at. Too many will just mouth the words and know what to say but don't make the effort of going in really, and taking that time that it takes TO understand. TO reach that place of connectedness to Oneness to get their guidance. They'll get it in snippets but they won't go deep enough. And they don't put as much effort into it as they could possibly do."

Elizabeth: OK, I see what you're saying. When you say that, I think of people going to church and they pray but they're not putting the feeling and the meaning and what you're saying into it. You know?

Jesus: "Exactly. Exactly. And that is the difference between one who succeeds at that attaining that peace beyond all understanding-that I spoke of-and those that do not. It is-but some have a great block to this-and then each of you are unique in which you are doing here and what it is that you want to attain. So, each of you will have a different Method by which you will do this and you will meet with different struggles, depending on what it is that you are here to do, really."

Elizabeth: OK, so whenever we are in a situation that it feels that we can't do anything about, we really CAN do something about it.

Jesus: "Absolutely. Absolutely. It is being in a place of-we'll use the word Acceptance. And acceptance does not mean that you accept it as it is with the sense of hopelessness but you accept it that in this moment, this is the experience and when you are in a place of acceptance and allowance then you say, "I would like to know more about this." because when there is a dislike for something that you have in your experience, you are putting up resistance and the resistance is the opposite of being in a state of love and acceptance so you are not accepting this. So No Change can come about. For anything, for anyone, because you are in total resistance. You Aren't In A State Of Allowance. That is what is key also to receiving and bringing about change in your lives."

Elizabeth: OK, can we talk about miracles then too?

Jesus: "Yes."

Elizabeth: How do miracles happen? Is it just by Faith?

Jesus: "Essentially, yes, it is by Faith. And again that, Accepting, that this is what it is for the moment. That you are here In Service. That you are NOT alone. That everything serves a purpose of some sort and that you-by feeling victimized by circumstances that you are not in a state of allowing-that you are in a state of resistance—but when you accept and that means that you have Faith, that you Trust, that everything is serving a purpose that maybe you do not understand and may not ever know WHY. The why behind something—but that it's important to just Trust that everything is there-it's not there by coincidence or chance-it is There because it is meant for something

Greater than you. For some experience and you are involved in that experience because you will benefit from it. Everything is meant to lead you to Enlightenment. Everything. And that is why every experience should be looked at as an Opportunity to Reach Enlightenment along that path of enlightenment. That is really the best way of putting it, yes."

Elizabeth: So not to feel like you're being punished.

Jesus: "Exactly. But most people do. They feel as though they are being punished for something and that then they will continually be punished but instead if they can really feel and accept and say, "Yes, this is something in my experience that I am participating in that is bringing me closer to enlightenment." Which is why you're here, then you will find the opportunity for miracles to occur."

Elizabeth: That makes perfect sense to me.

Jesus: "Yes. And I believe that. Yes, good. Good. So what else?"

Elizabeth: Do we wanna touch on healing right now or do we wanna go on to something else?

Jesus: "You can ask me anything that is pertinent to your present experience. If you want to, the healing, is something that will take much talking about with us and you practicing so let us go there if that is something that you would like."

Elizabeth: OK, so I would like to practice on my 9 month old baby cause he's running a fever right now. So how do I go about healing him to break that fever. He's teething I think so. On one hand I'm thinking, well, it's your body's natural reaction. So, I don't know how to deal with that then.

Jesus: "Well, here is something that you-you said something-it's the body's natural reaction to-it's a normal thing. The fever I can see is not something that is life threatening, it is not going to harm the child. The child is running a slight fever because that is the way the body responds to what you call teething. To this experience. So, to heal him, you are a little bit going against the natural rhythm."

Elizabeth: OK, that's OK.

Jesus: "Yes. What you can do is, you, as in connect to your own divinity, your own eternal beingness and see that Within Him and that is how you will Support him in maybe alleviating some of the discomfort that he is feeling at this time."

Elizabeth: OK, good cause that is kinda the answer that I was looking for at this time cause yeah, for the whole body's natural stuff, I was just curious about letting it run its course.

Jesus: "Yes."

Elizabeth: What do I do for people that have been in car accidents and have actual-they've had to have metal put into their necks and stuff like that? Can I heal back pain and stuff like that that is caused from traffic accidents?

Jesus: "Anything can potentially be healed. Now remember that you are also living in a world that has moved along-100 years ago there were not the medical advances available for people to have the types of healings. You can look at those as being healings as well. When of course one can heal it's own form, it is always done the same way. When you, yourself as the healer, knowing that you, really really knowing that you are a Divine Being and that everyone that you are in contact with that is walking this Earth Is Also a Divine Being and therefore in that moment They Are Whole And Complete but you must really feel it and then really feel and connect with another and some will be healed and others will not. It So depends on where the other person is at."

Elizabeth: OK. OK. I guess I should ask—could I be performing miracles then in your name some day?

Jesus: "Yes."

Elizabeth: And that's a big thing cause after we got off the phone last time, I-usually I feel really awesome but I was very emotional, I think because of how big of a deal that would be to people and be the feelings for them, you know, having a miracle performed on them—I think I was feeling Gratitude to be able to give that to somebody.

Jesus: "Yes. So, yes, and again, there are many on your planet wanting to do that very thing and it is-too many are wanting to do it out of a desire-an evil desire. Not—that is not bad or that is not good but it is an evil desire so it runs contrary to the essence of you as an Eternal Being so that is too often what gets in the way of those who are looking to be-to heal as I have healed. They are-their own Ego desire is getting in the way. So, it is about being a Pure Vessel as well."

Elizabeth: OK. I understand.

Jesus: "Yes."

Elizabeth: I think I wanna just hop off the healing for now. Oh, I had a question. They talked about in the Bible that you were writing something in the sand when they were going to stone the woman that had committed adultery and I was curious to what were you writing in the sand?

Jesus: Looong pause (you can hear the birds singing)

Elizabeth: You don't wanna tell me?

Jesus: "No, that is not it. I am looking for, I cannot say, "I was writing blah, blah, blah, blah." like the sentence, the exact words, because it is, what I was attempting to do—at that time I was writing in the sand the essence of understanding about judgment. And by writing it in the sand, this was a match in vibration of energy so that this message would be taken into the Earth itself and therefore brought out into Humanity. You see, because of who I am and what I was doing when I was on your planet, I had many abilities that you are all looking to have and there was, at that time, the judgment surrounding the experience was quite pervasive. Many were, as you still are, in a place of judgment for anothers wrongs. So, they were symbols, if you will, that were Then Absorbed by the waters and the Earth itself and so that they could then be transformed by Mother Earth and then come up out through her own Etheric body to come into the bodies of the individuals, humans, walking the planet. Does that makes sense? And you can ask me more if you would like."

Elizabeth: So, what you were telling her (meaning Mother Earth), we absorbed it through her?

Jesus: "Yes."

Elizabeth: OK. I understand that.

Jesus: "Yes, it is bit of an engraving but it could not be permanent were it on an object it would have been permanent but it could have been done in the air, it could have been done anywhere but sand being a trans—flip tape—were meant to be permanent in the Etheric body of the Earth as well as Human Beings."

Elizabeth: That's amazing!

Jesus: "Yes."

Elizabeth: That like makes anything possible. Like, really I was saying the other day to my dad like anything is possible but for you even saying that, that's cool.

Jesus: "Yes, Yes. It is cool. It was fun."

Elizabeth: So can you tell me a little about when you said you left the planet? Can you tell me a little bit about that?

Jesus: "Yes. As you know and accept that you are not alone here. There are many other-beyond your possible understanding-Realms and Existences and many of them are far beyond your own ability to—for humans-and when I left, there were other planets that could offer me some schooling so to speak in what to do for Earth and but I was also needed in certain parts to do much of what I was doing On Earth-only in a different realm-so I essentially left. My physical form as you knew me, stayed here on Earth, but me as the Christ Consciousness left. So you could say someone came in, another soul came in to inhabit my form while I was gone and when I came back, we integrated together with everything that I knew. That I brought back from these other realms."

Elizabeth: OK, that makes sense. So is-when you speak about the Christ Consciousness, is that an actual soul?

Jesus: "Hmm, yes and no."

Elizabeth: Like a Being?

Jesus: "I'm sorry?"

Elizabeth: Is it like a Being? Is it an actual Being?

Jesus: "Yes, that would be a way of knowing it and understanding it. It is like a Being. It is . . . yes. The best that you could understand it—it is like a Being. It is like a Existence and a Being together."

Elizabeth: OK, so, it's kind of like, is it on the God level? Where you know, is God an actual Being or God Energy? You know what I mean? It's kind of hard to explain.

Jesus: "Yes, it is an aspect of what you understand as God. Now, everyone understands God differently but that is difficult to explain because there IS a supreme intelligence but it is not clothed in a robe and it is not with facial features and all of that. It is both a soul, it is a state of being, it is an existence, it is both a place-not time, but in a sense, an experience, an existence. It is where you-so the Christ Consciousness is an aspect of that existence. It is a LAYER of that existence. Everything-everything is God. OK? Everything in the Universe. EVERYTHING IS GOD. EVERY THING, OK? And Within That-there are many aspects. God created the Souls that are human and other as well that exist in other realms and it gets very complex. So within everything being God, so God is both within and without. God is everywhere at the same time. It is both energy and a state of being. So too is the Christ Consciousness. It is that aspect of the God Knowing that is of unconditional love and compassion and all those things that, all those good things that people want to know. It is the way TO God. Thru, that is why they say, "the way to God is through me, through Jesus." They mean the way To God is through the Christ Consciousness. Through Understanding what the Christ Consciousness is and as I have told you before, Humanity had not been touched by the Christ Consciousness until I brought it down during the Crucifixion."

Elizabeth: OK, Yeah. That all made sense to me. But it makes me think, so if there is a 2nd coming which I'm OK not knowing when that is, but so that makes me think that it's not going to be what everyone feels is, you're going to come down and be like, "You've done bad! You're in trouble now!" It doesn't seem like it's going to be that. Correct?

Jesus: "Correct. You could not possibly be that way. Remember, going back to what you have as your Tool Here, is Free Will. So in this state that you are in, you have Free Will to Do and Be Whatever. Depending on how you feel and think or think and feel as they go hand and hand. So when there is the 2nd coming and the end of everything, because it will not really end, but there will be an Ending because that is the natural process of things, Earth will eventually be a place that is not what it is now. I do not want to say it will be uninhabitable but it is not-it will be what it is not now. And at that time, that is what is being said, the 2nd coming. That there will be then those who through free will, chose to think and feel a certain way will be held in a certain vibration depending on where your belief system is. And that is why it is so important to understand yourselves and your own belief systems and have Faith and Trust in there being a Supreme Being who watches your every move."

Elizabeth: So, are people to look at this with fear at all?

Jesus: "No, No."

Elizabeth: Cause there are a lot of people that Don't believe in God so I don't really want to scare them into believing in You, so I don't wanna do that.

Jesus: "No, and they do not have to Believe in me to be in a certain vibration, that is of a higher vibration. There are many who do not believe in me but have a very high vibration. And again—you are sooo-because of being In Human Form—you unfortunately are so conditioned By the human experience and it's social conventions and what has been fed to you over many many thousands and thousands of years since your own personal recorded history on this planet."

Elizabeth: Yeah. So, I'm thinking, I'm just thinking here while you're talking. So, many people see when you come, the 2nd coming, as going to be Satan VS. You and they look at it as a war. So it's not going to be a war, right?

Jesus: "Well, in a sense, it could be observed as a war but it will be- Where are you going to place your Faith? And you do this on a daily basis anyway when—are you willing to believe that the External circumstances define who you are?? Or are you going to believe Who You Are in spite of the external circumstances?"

Elizabeth: I am totally going to believe who I am! Despite what ANYBODY says! (Laughing)

Jesus: "Exactly. Exactly. Because it's through that, that you stay connected to Oneness and that's where guidance comes."

Elizabeth: OK. Alright. So, I'm gonna, do you wanna go back to when you were saying when you left or should we leave it at that? People might question aliens. We call them aliens, right. So they are other people, other Beings on other planets, should anybody be scared that the aliens are gonna come and invade here? Because I know other people are kinda a little freaked out in thinking about that, so. Will they come peacefully?

Jesus: "And that could happen. That is not up to me to decide. That is so up to what is occurring. Which direction. But if you always know that you are safe, you can Never Be Harmed, then you will be OK. Because when you say that, in that aliens will come and destroy you, that's very possible. Depends on how things evolve and how there ARE existences beyond yours where they are more aggressive or they are conquerors more than they are peacemakers. So, it will depend on so many different things but they are-you are all children of God. You are ALL GOD."

Elizabeth: OK, that helps to hear that.

Jesus: "Yes."

Elizabeth: Let's see, I'm gonna ask about the safety of our food supply. Right now there is a lot of people going Organic, and I've started to do that too and there's a lot of talk about GMO's—genetically modifying things. Can you talk a little about . . . is that something we should be concerned about?

Jesus: "Well, again, yes and no. Yes, in that it is-here you have the, what you would call Satan, if you want to look at it-offering something that—pretending to be God. Satan is not God. Then you'll say, "But you said everything is God?" Yes, but Satan is there to be the balancing force, OK? So when I say that, God ultimately, that permeates everything, but there IS a Supreme Intelligence, is this is Designed to assist human beings once again, on their path of evolution. So, there will become a time when the physical form will be able to Adapt to what you call, Genetically Modified foods. Now, this is also a tricky area because at this time, it is a means of control. So, those, again, Love always Wins, Good always Wins. And you can, "What is the intention behind this?" is Really what you want to look at. And as it stands now, the intention behind it is one of control, manipulation and greed therefore, for the genetically modified. You have it on what you call the Organic side as well. So, it's not like one is good and the other is bad. Understand that what is motivating these things and then you'll understand whether or not it is Appropriate for you. This is something for Humanity At This Time, to Evaluate their Dependency on External Circumstances. You see, back to free will, perfect example, when you, it is a way of telling human beings-genetically modified foods—are a way of telling human beings, "You have no free will." "You must depend on "ME", what I will say in quotes is "SATAN"-that's how some people would observe this-"on ME for your survival". Instead of going within and knowing that, that can't possibly be, that there is only 1 God. So, really, it has a very strong spiritual connotation as well."

Elizabeth: I see that, now that you say that.

Jesus: "Yes, so if this were something, humanity may at one time, have the physical form that it will be able to have the same vibration of these genetically modified foods but they are too sanitary for the physical form, they are not LIVE Foods, therefore they—and as I said, they are motivated by greed and lust and all the other things, manipulation and control, therefore they are not-they are Meant to be Seen For What They Are. If they are-again, there is that resistance—in feeling that they can be more powerful, then you have lost. But if you can look at it and say, "No, I know where I'm going to put my Faith and Trust." And then you will have what you need."

Elizabeth: OK. So, I should be buying Organic? Cause that's kinda scary to me.

Jesus: "Well, ultimately, and this is personal for you, specific for you, is that by, for you, your physical form, cannot match the vibration of those foods that are genetically modified because they are not really foods. There's certain components taken out of them that leave them as being non-food. Therefore they do not nurture your body. So, in your case, yes, those foods that are most real and most wholesome will benefit you the most."

Elizabeth: OK, that's what I was thinking. Thank you for clarifying that for me.

Jesus: "Yes."

Elizabeth: K. Alright. Um, someone had a question, I think this comes from Africa actually. "Why do good Christians have money problems?"

Jesus: "Again, it goes back to. It does not . . . interesting. A "good Christian". What do they mean first of all by "good Christians"? Much to be understood from that. A "good Christian." Do you know what they mean by "good Christian"?"

Elizabeth: No, he didn't specifically say but I'm thinking probably someone that, you know, goes to church and prays a lot . . . I'm thinking, I don't know . . . I'm Assuming.

Jesus: "Yes. OK, so with that put aside. Anyone who has money problems has a belief that there is lack and does not have a belief in Eternal Abundance. Now, many of your churches have instilled that— indoctrinated that—into the belief system of your planet. Most people on your planet have that belief system—that there is a limited supply and there is NOT a limited supply—that is what I demonstrated when I came here. So, someone who considers themselves to be "good"-why do they suffer from money problems is because they believe that there is lack. Now, each individual is going to have specific ways in which they believe in Lack. And again it goes back to they Do Not Believe that they are a Divine Being. And then-because if they Truly Believe and Understand that they are a Divine Being-that they have free will to choose thoughts that are of the Highest Order—then they will begin to Change their own vibration. Because it is a vibration that they are emitting-Always

A Vibration Of Lack—and then each of you who has this, must look at how that is at a personal level. Some of you will feel victimized. Some of you will feel-most often it IS victimization-so you feel like you have no control and that you are-what we were talking about earlier. So, Lack—a belief that there is not enough and a belief that there-Somebody Else is the one to bring you your abundance Will Create Lack."

Elizabeth: I, I understand what you are saying. It's so very deep. It seems like it it's so—it could be so simple but it's very deep. Like for people really thinking that it's a simple thing of going to church-it's so much deeper than that.

Jesus: "Yes. Yes. So someone can have Faith and go to church and Believe and yet still have an incredible amount of poverty because they Believe that that is what I taught-to be a poverty consciousness. Instead, that was not what I taught—by ANY means. I taught about abundance with abundance and wealth COMING FROM Yourselves and NOT FROM some external source."

Elizabeth: Correct. OK. Great. Will you please tell us about your Mother? Because I really like her. (Giggling)

Jesus: "Yes. She's a nice lady. What would you like to know about her?"

Elizabeth: What's her personality like?

Jesus: "Well, again, once you are out of physical form, you have less of what you call personality than when you are in physical form. Personality serves you in physical form to do those things that you are wanting to do but she is Unlimited Abundance. She is Unlimited and Unending Compassion and Love. Unconditional Love. But more so the limitlessness of love/compassion. She IS THAT. She is That Which You Are As Well. She is the Example For Humanity of the Expression of the Feminine Energies of Nurturing and Love and Compassion. Not that the male energies are not-we are speaking of energies, not of the male and female as individuals."

Elizabeth: Right. So, my friend Denise wants to know, does she hear us when we pray the rosary then?

Jesus: "Yes. She hears when you speak to her in rosary's, in your own words, when you rely on her for comfort. She is the one to either come to you or send someone to you. Yes, she hears it all just as God and I do."

Elizabeth: That's soo comforting. And it's for everyone-it's not just one specific religion-she is.

Jesus: "Yes. She is-her embodiment-her energy, let's say, that Who She Is-has been symbolized by many religions in different ways. She is the great mother. Is the best way of understanding her."

Elizabeth: That's nice. All I can do is smile. I don't even know.

Jesus: "Yes, that is sweet."

Elizabeth: So, you said that she may send someone else that can help us more so whatever specific Angel might be able to help. So I'm thinking Archangel Raphael is the healing angel or whatever she'll send somebody that's specific that can help us.

Jesus: "Yes, or she'll send you a human that will be-that happens all the time. So someone who is praying to Mary and maybe not feeling it because they are so distraught, she will then send what you call Human Angels. A friend, someone who will say the right thing to you to bring you to Understanding to bring you that comfort that you are looking for."

Elizabeth: I love that you say that. My husband's gonna love that you say that too because people need to hear that it comes from all of us together-not just a specific angel.

Jesus: "Yes."

Elizabeth: My friend, Denise, wants to know-a personal question-if she will be doing angel readings?

Jesus: "If she will, I'm sorry would you please repeat that?"

Elizabeth: If she will be doing angel readings? Using the cards to give readings to people.

Jesus: "Does she WANT to do that?"

Elizabeth: Yep. Yes she does.

Jesus: "Then she will do it. Then she will do it."

Elizabeth: She wants to know a time frame, Jesus. (Laughing)

Jesus: "It will be up to her, because if she is waiting for everything to be exactly right before she begins, then she will be waiting a very very long time. But if she begins to just Trust and begin her process this moment—than she can begin in this moment. That's-so it is up to her. At what point She decides that she will Open Up and Be Confident in her ability to do what you call Angel readings."

Elizabeth: That is very good advice because my friend,Chris, had also had a question along those lines about his photography business. And I told him, it's just up to him whether or not how far he wants to take it.

Jesus: "Absolutely. Absolutely."

Elizabeth: A lot of people can do that.

Jesus: "Yes, and that goes back to what we have been talking about this whole time and that's how Free Will is connected to all of this. So, and what you will be assisting others in understanding and that is why you and the Medium and your other friend are seeking to understand this-because you want to help others. So we can step it up a notch on your planet."

Elizabeth: Right On!! OK, so she has a question now. Can she start her business without being able to see through her third eye? And I'm saying, "Yes, she can!"

Jesus: "Yes, so you got the answer. Yes you can."

Elizabeth: Laughing . . . you know what, the Indigo Bunting came back today and I am SO happy cause I was talking to him while I was running. Remember when we said in our conversation that when I run I feel close with the Oneness so I was talking to the Indigo

Bunting while I was running and I was saying, "If you're ready to come back, you can come back anytime because I'll welcome you and I just gotta go to Lowe's and get the right birdseed." And he showed up today!!!—Laughing

Jesus: (Laughing) "So, you SEE how you—you asked and you received. You and-this is what you understand so very well in that connectedness in at all times and being connected to that which you cannot see. So you were talking to the Vibration or the Energy of Indigo Bunting which has a certain purpose on your-EVERYTHING does-but animals all have more of a greater mass consciousness than humans do so they are not as individualistic as humans. Especially birds. So when they come, because you are Using the energy of Indigo Bunting at this time, for what it is you're doing, and they are Assisting you in that way and you understand that very well."

Elizabeth: Cool!! The Indigo Bunting is assisting me! That's awesome. When we were over visiting one of Denise's friends, well, she's my friend now too, I saw your lights falling down-it must—your energy-it was falling down like snow but it was like twinkling bright lights and then it-well, you were there and you know, but I guess I'm saying it on tape so I can have people know. I watched her reaction-the woman when she said Your name. I saw the lights coming from up on top of the ceiling and it was like falling snow upon her and her reaction-it was like Love but it was like, it was almost like she was comforted cause she was holding her shoulders like in a big hug. Like she was being loved!

Jesus: "Yes. So it was beautiful."

Elizabeth: It was! It was really very beautiful.

Jesus: "Yes."

Elizabeth: So thank You for allowing me to see Your energy. That's what I wanna say.

Jesus: "Yes. But we are—but I'm—you are ALWAYS able to see Me-the energy that I am—because I permeate the planet because it is in everything and everyone. It's that you were willing to Accept That and you opened your eyes to it and if you don't get it, you don't fret but if you do get it, you are very grateful. Remember Gratitude. That is another thing that we have touched on but I will bring it in again. Your Gratitude. It is a child-like Gratitude and being like children, I have said it many times, but it is a child-like Gratitude. Grateful for these things and that gives you more. Because it's not because you were good, you did it right, it's because you are matching the vibration of that which you are seeking. That's why it is coming into your experience."

Elizabeth: Good, that's good for other people to know because we all need to be more grateful I think.

Jesus: "Yes, absolutely."

Elizabeth: I think we all take things for granted as humans so.

Jesus: "Yes."

Elizabeth: I'm just looking through some of these questions to see the next one. Can we just touch on evil quick? I don't like to talk about . . . is there an evil force that we need to be concerned about?

Jesus: "Well, you can be as concerned as you want. Yes, there is an evil force because that is Necessary for Balance. You cannot have good without evil. But judging it as being bad is what keeps you in a place of concern for it. If you don't judge it as being bad and you just say, observe it, without becoming judgmental of it, you will Understand it's Function."

Elizabeth: So when someone does something bad and murders somebody, we're not going to judge them. I mean, I guess what I wanna say, is there an evil force that's driving that person? But I'm thinking it's choice that they did that themselves.

Jesus: "It's Choice, yes. And again, at any point, some individuals come to your planet with the expressed purpose of having the function of the evil aggressor because they're here to, in a sense, come in and take on that role to assist others in their Enlightenment. If you remember that you are here for Enlightenment-then it really will help-everyone is-it will help you to make sense of what you call evil or bad things that are going on. You've got to Feel it and stop judging it. Just Feel It for what it is. And remember good always wins."

Elizabeth: OK. Alright. Well, I think that could be it for today.

Jesus: "Very good."

Elizabeth: Yeah. I'm gonna collectively think about some other things till we talk next. So, yeah, this good for today I think.

Jesus: "I think we are doing very well as well, I am enjoying this. It is exciting to interact with you."

Elizabeth: It's extremely exciting for me too! And Denise! And the Medium!

Jesus: "Yes, Yes, I can see that you all three are very excited . . . end of tape."

CHAPTER 5

Your Own Personal Power

June 5, 2013

Jesus: "Yes, hello my friend. And you are doing well?"

Elizabeth: I am doing well. How are you?

Jesus: "I am doing well. This is a, as I have said to you many times, it is a pleasure-a delight to interact with you in this way. So, where are we now? Have you done your homework?"

Elizabeth: (Laughing) Have I done my homework. Yes, we were just discussing, the Medium and I, were just discussing the other day of how do we give Faith to someone that doesn't have any? And so, I've been trying to think about it and I guess trying to maybe lead by example, give examples, like the book that I wrote would be helpful to people because the Medium reads that and that helps her but then also to give people experiences that they can experience for themselves to give them Faith I guess.

Jesus: "Yes, so how would you give one an experience?"

Elizabeth: I guess if they came to me, I don't know, maybe to give them a reading, or if they needed healing that they could come to me and I could help them that way.

Jesus: "Yes, very good. So, you've given it thought. You've given it some true thoughts and that's what I wanted. If I give you the answers all the time, you will be less likely to go deeper with the topics that we are discussing here. And again, I can only give you so much and then the rest is done by you and remember, you are in a reality that is different than the reality in which I am residing. And I Have Been in your reality. But the difference lies in the fact that when you are in the reality-in the density of the human form—there are, let's say, Laws and Rules and Regulations but I do not mean societal ones but certain Conditions would be better I guess to say—that you are subject to and you are in a creative process that is much different than the creative process that you are in when you are not in human form. So, we here In Spirit can come through and can give you foundation for moving forward but remember, as you are doing things, you are also creating that which will become part of your experience or experience of many. Does that make sense to you?"

Elizabeth: Yeah, that makes sense to me that you can't give me all the answers because a lot of times that's what people, they wanna go to psychics and mediums to give them the answers but yeah, I understand cause really we have to figure it out for ourselves sometimes, so.

Jesus: "Yes, because the answer is not one that is just a what you would say a pat answer, a straight answer, depending on so many different circumstances. So there are many who try to Guide and Lead in this way, say in regards to finding Faith, but Every human being has their Own Journey that is Unique To Them and yes, there are some foundational aspects to your situations but how each of you perceives them, understands them, and then begins your own creative process, will give it all its unique tint so to speak. So, that is why I ask you many questions. That is why I ask you to think about certain things, so that you continually practice this, even though it is something you already do, but just so those who will be in the future, reading the information that is coming through or listening to it, they too will have the opportunity to create for themselves their own unique perspective on the world."

Elizabeth: OK. Alright.

Jesus: "So, what are we going to talk about today?"

Elizabeth: Well, we wanted to hear the story about when you walked on water actually.

Jesus: "So what would you like to know about that? I walked on water. HAHA"

Elizabeth: Laughing. You know, like who was in the boat with you and were you guys having a good time and you know, surrounding the situation, you know, what was it like?

Jesus: "Well, yes, it was another one of the teaching situations. Those that were in the boat with me were other followers, as you know, and we were discussing ones ability to Transcend the physical reality through Faith, essentially. Through Faith and Trust. And the walking on water was just to demonstrate that Everyone has this ability to override or not be Subject To the limitations of your physical reality. You can Use your physical reality for experience, but once you are Fully Understanding yourself as an Eternal Being with all of the same powers and abilities that-essentially that you are mini Gods—then when you will connect with that Eternal Divine Being so well, you are able to transcend these limitations and that is what the discussion was about and to Prove that, I demonstrated that by walking on water. And that is a factual thing that I was able to do that."

Elizabeth: That is so cool!

Jesus: "It was symbolic but also factual."

Elizabeth: Symbolic but also factual. And what was their reaction?

Jesus: "Well, by that point, they had been following me and had seen many of my healings so but their reaction of course was one of awe, which was something, again that I had to deal with-with many—was that then they revered me in ways in which I did not want them to because then they were giving Me the Power that was inside of Them and that was not the point. That was one of the difficulties was what, much that I did, was that others looked to me and gave me their power in a sense, unable to realize that they were able to do the same things as I."

Elizabeth: That's kinda what I wanna be, when people start coming to me, I don't want to be the center of everything. Do you know what I'm saying?

Jesus: "Yes, absolutely. And that is something that I do not foresee as being a problem for you. Maybe for a while but it is—won't be Your problem, it will be a problem for the person looking to-looking for something outside of themselves. So, they, you must be patient, and guide them Always back to their own center of Power. Their own center of Truth. When I say Power, I mean Truth. Also."

Elizabeth: OK. Can you tell us a bit about your rebel, you said you were viewed as a rebel. Can you tell us some things that we don't know about you?

Jesus: "Well, there probably would be many. I went against the—because my teachings went against what was at that time considered, you have the Old Testament and the New Testament just as a reference. There were many other holy books around but we will just use that because that is Your frame of reference at this time. That is all that your people at this time have access to-those bible studies. So, there were beliefs that were-in humans—of limiting beliefs and because I came to show them that they were Unlimited in their potential-Unlimited Beings with the potential to do whatever they wanted, that was what essentially created my image of being a rebel. Because I went and spoke out against these things that were-what I would say, falsehoods and misleadings. Again, without judgment. But those things that were-wherever I found others giving away their own personal power to something external, I was-I spoke out and became known as a rebel. And of course, there were many, many opportunities for me to do that. So, those who were in a position of authority, not all were bad, but there were many who were of course, misguided. Again, they served a purpose. But my purpose was to be that one to say to them, openly, without fear, so I was also, in my rebellion, was also demonstrating how to-because I was not afraid. I stood in my truth and I was not afraid and there were those who learned from that. Does that make sense?"

Elizabeth: That makes absolute sense because I have been feeling like if I am questioned about something or in a position where I need to say something, I feel like I am going to say it and not be scared at all of the repercussions.

Jesus: "Absolutely. Absolutely. And again, there are ways in which one can do things that are offensive, in putting-put people off—and then there are ways in which it is done to just state your own truth. And again, there is no right or wrong here. It is always that you Must Remember what you are not trying to convince another of YOUR Truth but you are only speaking your Truth at a moment to Demonstrate more Faith and Courage and Compassion and Love as opposed to trying to change a situation. Remember, that you will have No Influence of any duration or of any value in a situation where you are trying to manipulate the situation because you feel that what is going on is wrong. You do not know what the situation, what the individuals-what-you don't know. Only, so you must Always Stay In Your Own Center of Truth and from there, you speak your words Without trying to convince anyone else of your own Truth but just BE your Truth."

Elizabeth: OK. Will I have channeling ability? I have been watching Iyanla Vanzant speak a lot and she speaks like she's so connected and it almost seems like she is channeling but it's so easy, I don't know. Will I be having the correct words . . . I feel like I'm gonna be having the correct words for communication for people, that they'll easily understand what I'm trying to say . . .

Jesus: "This is something that anyone can actually do. It's not just for a few. All that has stopped you up till now is your lack of confidence in this and a bit of you feeling as though this was something that you would not be able to do. But remember, observing others is a wonderful way of learning. But Let It Come Through You in a Natural way. You are already doing it when you perform one of your readings as you say, you are channeling the information through your own Higher Self and through Guidance so you are already doing it. If you are seeking to do it as the Medium or this other that you have spoken of is doing, you will get there through practice."

Elizabeth: OK, yeah, cause I kinda would like to do a little bit of public speaking, I think cause just the way I watch certain people speak, and how it makes me feel. You know, it makes me feel really good, like WOW, like I wanna be able to bring that feeling to people. The same kind of feeling but in my own way.

Jesus: "Yes. Absolutely. So, you know the way to do it and set your intention and find a way. This would be a wonderful opportunity for you, for the Medium, to get yourselves out there in ways in which you can inspire others and lead them to find their Truth for themselves as well."

Elizabeth: OK, good. Oh, my daughter, Lexie, has a question for you and she wanted to know who she was. She wants a specific name and what she did from her previous past life, her most recent one.

Jesus: "Yes, her name was Rebecca. And I will not give you a last name because I do not have it. Her name was Rebecca and she was school teacher in a rural area of the country in which you reside now."

Elizabeth: OK! Oh, she's gonna love to hear that. And my son, Adam, he wanted to know the same thing cause he looks up to his sister so.

Jesus: "Yes. His name was Xavier and his was a lifetime that was a very brief lifetime and it was in the country of or the continent of Europe and that would have been during the-your last major war and he was one that died as a young boy in the war."

Elizabeth: Oh, like Vietnam?

Jesus: "No, your—in Europe."

Elizabeth: Oh, World War. World War II. WOW (That explained to me why Adam had been drawing pictures of tanks for weeks before that. The next morning he came up to me and told me that he remembered how he had died. He said he was in a tank with a friend and the bomb came and killed them but it didn't hurt.)

Jesus: "Yes."

Elizabeth: Wow. Thank you.

Jesus: "Yes."

Elizabeth: I have a question from a friend named, Evette, she wanted me to ask you, "What does Jesus say about this?" "This morning I woke up with a smile on my face and I started to ask myself about my ex husband and in my heart it said that I needed to let him go so he can learn about himself. Then I asked my heart about the guy I was seeing and I didn't get an answer. I just got a feeling of hurt and confusion."

Jesus: "So what is her question?"

Elizabeth: Well, she just is wanting to know what you think about that? I guess.

Jesus: "Well, it is interesting, she answered it for herself."

Elizabeth: I agree.

Jesus: "Yes. And she's just not, at the moment, wanting to accept that she's feeling hurt and confusion in some aspect of this and it is important for her to take it a little bit deeper. It does not mean she is destined for hurt and confusion but there is something that is triggering it within her."

Elizabeth: OK, I will tell her that.

Jesus: "But it is very good that she is talking to her heart and not to her head."

Elizabeth: Yes, that's great. That's what we learned at our retreat so yeah.

Jesus: "Yes, very good."

Elizabeth: And it's good that people can, I guess we all have our own answers, going back to what we saying at the beginning, we all have our own answers. So.

Jesus: "Absolutely. That is why, at this time, it is so important to be talking thru the Medium to you and that you are bringing forth these messages because we want, I and we, want so much that those on the planet understand Really How Much they are In Control of their destiny's and it may not seem that way but it is SO very very true and you asked about me walking on water and that relates exactly to this—your one's own personal power. Everyone has it. And everyone has the ability to create their own reality. It's just understanding How that is done."

Elizabeth: So, could you give them a 1st step of to understanding how that is done? Is it going back to Free Will?

Jesus: "Absolutely. Free Will is the first thing that you want to keep in mind in any situation. And every moment. Remember, every moment you are Choosing. You are choosing something. And if you do not understand what that means because it feels so elusive, "I'm choosing,

I'm choosing, I don't know, the government placed a higher tax on me, how is it that I'm choosing this higher tax and now I don't have the money to pay that." So that's a good example. People would argue with you. "How is it that I—it's the government that chose this." But YOU CHOSE the experience. If you take 100% responsibility for EVERYTHING in your life-that's the 1ˢᵗ step. Stop. Breathe. At any moment say, "I created this. I may not know how I have created this. In one way I know that I'm going to Trust that I will understand this but I have created Everything in my life. Those things I deem good. Those things I deem bad. EVERYTHING in my reality I have created and I have created it by Choice. Through my Free Will." So, starting there and allowing that to become your compass for everyday will then bring you to understanding MORE of it because all these answers can come to you but they will come to not so much through me and these lessons are important that they are brought out there but the Really True Enduring Lessons Are Those That You Find On Your Own. We give you information to plant the seed and then it is Your Job to then go and Understand it For Yourself."

Elizabeth: Wonderful!

Jesus: "Yes, and that is where humans have the most difficulty, understandably, I am not saying that it is something simple, but that is where we see you all struggling the most. Not getting past that point of being able to say yes. You read the books and you listen to the different things and you go to your workshops and all of that yet you cannot bring it to a deeper level and this is part of how you can do it."

Elizabeth: OK.

Jesus: "Takes practice."

Elizabeth: It does take practice. Yeah. Denise is saying, "Free Will and the laws of the universe."

Jesus: "Absolutely. Absolutely. If you understand the laws of the universe, which there are many, but if you understand some of the basic fundamental laws, Law of Attraction, Law of Cause and Effect, those are the ones that are coming to mind at the moment. Laws of

Compensation. All of these will bring you, if you understand that they ARE laws, just like gravity is a natural law, so are these universal laws, you will be in a much better position to execute things for yourself."

Elizabeth: You know, when you said that when you read the books and you do all the workshops and stuff. I have an aunt that she, periodically, she will send me kind of a snippy little message on my Facebook thing and I've figured out, I think, that whenever she is saying these mean things to me, it's like she's trying to-like she's going through something in her own life-so she's going to contact me to try and get MY energy but I'm not giving my energy out to her but if she would understand that energy is Unlimited-she doesn't have to go and be a stinker to people to try and gain that energy-you know what I mean?

Jesus: "Absolutely. But these are the people that are the most lost."

Elizabeth: Yes!

Jesus: "Again, they are looking Outside of themselves for solutions and every solution to any problem, every answer to any question-everything resides within yourself and within one's self. It is NEVER-you are NEVER without-you are Not Alone and you always have guidance. It is just that you have taken on the Belief that you are alone and that it is every man for himself."

Elizabeth: I, you, you know, sometimes when you're talkin Jesus, (laugh) you bring up things that I either do, like the day before, like when you say, "You are not alone" I just downloaded a song called, "You are Not Alone" and I mean, it's just, I don't know. (Laughing)

*It is really titled, "No One is Alone" by Bernadette Peters

Jesus: "It, it, the synchronicity is always so delightful, is it not? It just goes to prove that there is constant communication between us. How would this occur? How would I know other than I am communicating with you because you communicate with me. That is why. If you did not communicate with me I would not be communicating back with you. Not because I dislike you, but because you are not communicating with me either so there's no energy exchange."

Elizabeth: OH,yeah, so people need to start talking to you. It's not like you're probably just standing there just-I guess you're waiting for US to make the first move. Is that correct?

Jesus: "Yes. Free Will. We cannot intervene. We cannot intervene and if you do not choose-because many do not talk to us-or they-because they don't believe in us and that is fine. That is their Choice. There is not a problem of that. That is a journey that they have chosen to learn specific things. Not a problem. But there are many who feel lost and alone and continue to feel lost and alone when all they have to do is speak to one of us-pick the one that you like the most-and that communication will be-will flow-you will see it-why do you think you downloaded the song, I am not alone?"

Elizabeth: I downloaded it because it reminded me of a meditation that I did.

Jesus: "But it was a form of communication. I knew what we would be discussing."

Elizabeth: OOOOHH

Jesus: "And you heard me. So this is the way. We cannot always communicate-not everyone has the ability to Hear as the Medium does, as you do, correct? So we communicate also by sending symbols, by having you see something in a repeated form, you know that, by a bird or an animal, or a flower, something from nature, a title from a song, there was a reason you were directed to that so this topic would come up today. For 1. That you are not alone. And 2. That this is how we communicate."

*Cause I never thought about that! That meant that Jesus led me to picking out the movie, "The Jerk" so I would see Bernadette Peters and remember the song she sang! I also never liked that movie until I watched it that night! My husband even thought something was up when I suggested we watch it LOL

Elizabeth: (I'm laughing) So, I was really just hearing you?? (Laughing!!!)

Jesus: "Yes! You were asking, you talk to me continually. You talk a little too much by the way. Just kidding."

Elizabeth: (Laughing Harder!)

Jesus: "You take up too much of my time. I'm just kidding you. I have to tease you because it's so delightful. No, you've been asking, whether you were aware of it consciously or not, and I was answering the questions that you had. Because you direct most of your inquiries to either myself or Mother Mary. So."

Elizabeth: Oh, I love you so much!!

Jesus: "I know that you do, and it is the same for I."

Elizabeth: Oooh. Yeah. It makes me feel good. I'm actually blushing.

Jesus: "Because you think that I know all of your thoughts but that's not true. I only hear what you. Can I know all of your thoughts? Of course, but do they cause embarrassment? Only for you. There is so-no judgment here in the realm in which I am able to reside. So there is no judgment."

Elizabeth: It's funny. Cause I was sitting on the toilet the other day and I was thinking, "Hey, God, it's Elizabeth! I'm just checking in and I'm sitting on the toilet and I know you don't care." (Laughing)

Jesus: (He's laughing!) "Very good. Very good."

Elizabeth: No judgment, Jesus! (Laughing)

Jesus: "That's right! That's right. We don't care. It means nothing to us."

Elizabeth: Oh, here comes Adam. Do you wanna say something to Jesus? My son Adam would like to speak to you actually.

Jesus: "Yes, what would you like to say? Hello Son. Hello Adam."

Elizabeth: Adam, he's calling to you.

Jesus: "Adam?"

Elizabeth: Oh, he's being shy. (he walked to the other side of the living room.)

Jesus: "He is feeling shy?"

Phone lost signal.

Laurie: Powerful huh?

Elizabeth: Yeah, Adam cut our connection.

Laurie: OK, he'll be right back but I laughed because it was like, it went dead, that's never happened to us!

Elizabeth: I know!

Laurie: OK, let me go back cause he's. It took me a minute. I was still going, "Adam?" "Adam?"

Adam: (whisper) Jesus

Jesus: "Do not worry. If the child feels not comfortable we do not want to-by any means—make him feel uncomfortable but he is a blessed, blessed boy and he will do many wonderful things in his life. Right now he is just to enjoy his life. That is all."

Elizabeth: That's wonderful advice, Adam.

Adam: Hiii!!

Jesus: "Hii, Adam. And you are well?"

Adam: yes (soft and sweet)

Jesus: "Yes, I heard yes. Very good."

Elizabeth: He was asking me for a snack. Yes, you can go have a snack Adam. ("YAY") these kids eat all day long.

Jesus: "Yes."

Elizabeth: Let's see. My husband wanted to know, "What's the end result of our souls learning? So we reach enlightenment and we do our lifetimes and what's our goal looking like?

Jesus: "There is NEVER an end. So, you have an end result in terms of your obligation to journey through the Earth's cycles. As you know, there are boundless, endless, universes out there and dimensions and realities in which you can also reside beyond the Earth reality. Correct?"

Elizabeth: Yes.

Jesus: "So there is so much that you do not know about when you are on Earth, but so you, being who you are and having chosen this as a means—Earth, I'm saying—incarnation on Earth as a means of Enlightenment-when you reach enlightenment here, it is not the end of your journey. You then are no longer obligated-let's say you go to school and you get your PhD. There's not much you can do beyond a PhD accept maybe go get another PhD. So what souls will do then, is journey into other dimensions, other worlds, other universes depending on what it is that they choose to do. Some will rest. They will rest in a state of just Godliness which you would call Heaven, would be the best way of defining it. Some will just rest there for some time and not do much of anything in terms of Enlightenment. But all of you as souls-it is endless. It's like it's constantly moving forward and you are constantly creating-because you are creative beings and you understand your creative ability and that you are just naturally creative-all of you. When you are out of your physical forms, you understand this creative impulse that every soul has at it's core of it's being. So, creation means that you are constantly doing Something to expand and to grow. So, creating new worlds, entering new realms, it is ENDLESS. How much you can possibly imagine. It's THAT and EVEN MORE."

Elizabeth: Whoa!

Jesus: "It's endless. That's why it always has been and always will be. Words that are written. Always has been and always will be because it is Eternal."

Elizabeth: So, God creates even more worlds as time goes on? (flip tape)

Jesus: "God and You. You are not sitting there waiting for God to create another universe. You are creating other universes as well."

Elizabeth: WOW! OK. Lexie—my daughter just came in and she wanted to say hi to you too (laughing)

Jesus: "Yes. Hello."

Lexie: Hi Jesus!!

Jesus: "Hello Lexie. How are you?"

Lexie: Good.

Jesus: "Good. Are you going to have a snack as well?"

Lexie: Um, Adam brought me one down for me.

Jesus: "OK. You are a lovely child."

Lexie: Thank You.

Jesus: "Is there something that you want to ask me?"

Lexie: Um, no, mom asked it for me.

Jesus: "Yes. Yes. You are a very bright child and you will do great things also in your life. And you are a wonderful big sister."

Elizabeth: Can you maybe tell her to be a little bit kinder towards her brother? (Laughing)

Jesus: "Yes. But she is not to worry that she will be punished if she is not kind to her brother. I am sorry but I cannot do that." (Laughing)

Elizabeth: OK.

Jesus: "It's the nature of things. Is it not?"

Elizabeth: I get it, I get it. (Bye Lexie, see ya later) Yeah, we all gotta let them do what's the natural thing to do. Bickering, bickering. Yep. OK.

Jesus: "Yes, it drives the parents crazy."

Elizabeth: (Laughing) sometimes yes it does.

Jesus: "But it serves a function. A social function, really, in your society. Does it have to be that way? No, but is it bad? No. It serves a function. It really goes back to the primeval man where there were very few of you walking the planet. It is a manner of survival. So they are only reacting INSTINCTIVLY. Not intuitively. They are reacting Instinctively. As though they are still-it is in your cellular-in your DNA. It's Encoded in you and each generation comes forth and there is a Releasing of encodings in your DNA, depending on what you all do when we are IN the human form-that's what it is. So, as you go through the different stages of enlightenment and you are able to and with the assistance of the universe and God and energies that come forth-to Restructure that cellular memory. And that's what so much of what is coming forth in terms of self-help work and your planet is geared towards. It really is Reconstructing Cellular Memory. So, the bickering and the fighting that is so common among siblings, really dates back to primeval man."

Elizabeth: I-never thought about it that way.

Jesus: "Yes. So, it's again-nothing is good nothing is bad but it had served a purpose that is no longer really as necessary But it's still within the encoding and individuals like yourself that are coming through are in the process of taking on that responsibility of assisting humanity in the re-designing of that cellular memory. When you are able to transcend an experience that is maybe not something that is even yours so to speak but you carry the memory in your cellular system-within the cells-this memory-say of victimization we have spoken of quite a bit because that is what humanity is working on so greatly at this time-when you-an individual—is able to remove that cellular memory From Their Own Cells THEN you assist the Whole."

Elizabeth: OK.

Jesus: "And you do this removing of the cellular memories in many many many many ways. There are so many different techniques that have been made available for all of you and you are all using them. Every one. You just recently did a-an event-with many other individuals where that was a process of altering the cellular memory that you had of certain experiences."

Elizabeth: OK! That's what went on! (The Wonder Woman Weekend!)

Jesus: "Yes. So you, speaking of you, you were born into a specific family. You came in-you are more-you've had more experience on Earth-you specifically, right? So, you chose a family that has had less experience on Earth and you have greater understanding therefore you came in, you were less competitive. You have not in your cellular memory—as deeply encoded-this idea of this survival mechanism that your family members have had. Specifically your Mother and some of these others that are very accusing towards you. You were gentler, you were easier going and you were subject to ridicule or often-it was confusing for you as a child but you were not one to be the aggressor because you have transcended that and you did not carry it in yours. But you must remember that it is in the genes of those that birthed you so even though your soul no longer carries that-you've come in and it's in the genes of your parents and their parents-right? So you came in in an effort to influence-in what way you could-those family members-to bring them to a higher state. Because you are all working on this altering of the cellular memory and replacing it with something that would be likened to Compassion. That's why when we speak of Heaven on Earth-this is the process. When we speak of Enlightenment-this is the process."

Elizabeth: I-I'm listening to you. Keep going.

Jesus: "Yes. But you understand what I mean. So each of you that it may seem that things are-how can one individual have an impact—well this is how you have an impact. This is how you influence. And it's all done-there are things that the eye cannot see. It's just when you come here and you have situations that put you in a defensive mode or feel victimized, and you Choose through Free Will to Understand and Transform that energy or transmute that energy-you are working for the good of all. So you transmute it for yourself-you alter the cellular memory within Your Own Form and then when it's passed on down through Your offspring, then it's lessened and each one will do it more until there will come a time when there is no longer anyone walking your planet feeling victimized or feeling greedy or feeling unloved or any of these things because that is the whole point-when we speak of Heaven on Earth-that is the ultimate goal here. That everyone passing through here, reaches that state."

Elizabeth: WOW! That makes it so important for each person for each lifetime that they have, to make the better choices. WOW!

Jesus: "Yes. Yes. And so many people feel like, "Well I want to do more. I want to help other people." and they go out and they don't realize how working on themselves is helping other people."

Elizabeth: Yes, I understand that. For what you say about my family. Yeah, it was, it's nice to hear you say that. Cause it was ruff. Sometimes it's ruff. (Laughing)

Jesus: "It was ruff. Well, and you had to also deal with what was coming down through the generational lines as I said, so you had your own impulses that went contrary to who you remembered yourself as being this Eternal, Loving, Compassionate Being so that, for you—and most—many have that. They're in conflict with that. So it seems like it is baby steps but really it is quite massive when it is done and when there is an assistance of the Universe, which will happen periodically, that the energies will come through and they will assist you in erasing or removing the cellular encoding that you have and that is when you might feel drawn to do some type of self-help work or read a book or do something and then you get that, "Oh, OK." and it is a continual process. So no one should ever feel like they are not contributing in some way."

Elizabeth: OK. OK. Um, so that's why I probably feel-they gave me the name of Transformation at the Wonder Woman Weekend-and I do! I feel so much different now. That's . . . yeah.

Jesus: "Yes. And that will stick. That will stick. That isn't something that over time you will fall back into what you were before, no. What occurred there was Transformation. As you said. And it was necessary because of what you-you chose it. Again-you created that whole scenario because you have a certain role here and you're well aware of it and you want to move forward."

Elizabeth: OK. Yeah and I feel like now that I've done that, it kinda-I don't even know how to say what I was gonna say so.

Jesus: "It's alright. I understand."

Elizabeth: It makes me kinda like a better-I don't wanna say a counselor but better easily understanding of people. I don't know.

Jesus: "Yes. And because that is what you are wanting to do and what you are sending that intention out, that's the direction that you will be going."

Elizabeth:Yeah, I do. Denise says, "I'm a teacher on different levels." Yes, well, all of us are, right?

Jesus: "Yes, absolutely but don't take away from what your friend has just told you. That you are a teacher on many different levels and we all are-or you all are—but focus on yourself and where it is that you are teachings others and assisting others so that you can refine it. And again, it is something that isn't like you want reach a certain goal and Then you begin your work. Do your work now and do it as you Have been doing it and that is why more is coming to you because you're doing it without it being in a perfect state. You do not need to go to a school and get your degree, this is something, you just start doing it and you learn as you go on and that is what you are doing and that is the message, personally, that you are sending out to the Universe, "I AM ready." So, you just need to FEEL more confident and then more opportunities will come your way."

Denise: Just like when her and I healed Terry. She had back pain and Beth and I worked together to perform a healing on her.

Jesus: "Yes. And that's what you will be doing. It's what is placed before you and knowing that, "Yes, I will go forward with this. I don't have all of the answers but this is what I feel I must do." And when you feel you cannot do something, you will know that as well."

Elizabeth: I have the affirmation on my bathroom mirror. "I am ready. I am grateful for all that You are and all that You allow me to be and Please make me an instrument of thy endless abundance." (Words from Dr. Wayne Dyer-Thanks Dr. Wayne!!!) So, yeah, I just said last night when I was reading this Healers Manual book, I was just saying, "Please bring in people to work on."

Jesus: "And so, right? And you will. And you will. You Are Already and it will just be growing for you. Because you have-you will be demonstrating for others the Faith and how to find Faith and it is important that you do this. Like I said, you have other obligations at the moment that limit you but it doesn't stop you from doing what you CAN do."

Elizabeth: OK. This reading kinda turned into a reading about me (laughing)

Jesus: "But there are lessons within that. If you will look at it you will see that there are Universal Truths within these teachings today."

Elizabeth: Yes, I understand what you are saying. When I read when I go back and I write everything out, and I say that I'm understanding you when you're talking but really when I write it all out, I understand it SO MUCH Better.

Jesus: "Absolutely. That is why you have been given that task of doing that. Any-that is why-just to explain a little bit what is going on here, the Medium understands through the process of giving the information. Yes, she may get more by going back and reading it, but hers comes through in a more subconscious manner than it does for you. Yours comes through in this way. So you hear the information initially and then you have the opportunity to deepen your understanding of it through the listening to it again because what is happening is that your wheels are churning in your mind and you're deepening that understanding. So, that is the difference in the process and why it is less necessary that the Medium read everything to the same detail. Why you took it on. Why you said, "I will do this aspect of it." and why it is enjoyable for you. Because until it's not enjoyable, you are in the process of learning. And again, like I said, anyone who reads this information will be Inspired. This is meant to inspire. What we are giving here. Inspire. And help those with Find Faith and Trust in Themselves, in their Eternal Beingness and in the Oneness."

Elizabeth: Sigh. Adam just interrupted me. Can you repeat that please Jesus?

Adam: Sorry Jesus!

Jesus: "Yes. Your compilation of information that you are getting from me-through the Medium-and you are putting it together-is meant to: Inspire, it is meant to bring Faith to those who are seeking that Understanding. It is meant for those who are ready to connect to their Own Divine Being and Then to connect to Oneness so that none of you feel alone."

Elizabeth: I am going to quote that when I'm marketing it! (laughing)

Jesus: "Yes. Because that is our Hope here and our Desire. Because it is not-you are not the first to bring forth messages of Hope but you are different. You are new. You are fresh. It's a new voice. It's a new perspective and you are not better, you are not worse, it's just a new perspective. And who you will come in contact with through this-we hope-is a many many who will receive these messages and then continue on and do what they need to do as well. In their little worlds."

Elizabeth: Great! A chain reaction!

Jesus: "Absolutely."

Elizabeth: I'm really looking forward to it. I'm really excited. I feel like there's an excitement within this whole entire month-even July-I just feel like-oh yeah, my head is like tingling-the top of the back of my head is tingling right now-I'm so excited and I don't know what the excitement is about but I'm excited! (laughing)

Jesus: "Yes, because you are seeing things are moving in a direction that you know that you came here to do and they are moving in that direction. And you are Following Through On Your Guidance and I've said that to you many many times, you're following through on your guidance and does it always come to what you have expected? No. But you still follow through on it. You do not lose your Faith, EVER."

Elizabeth: Yes. (stillness) Awesome.

Jesus: "Yes."

Elizabeth: Well, you know, tomorrow Jesus, I'm going to the casino. It's our

Jesus: "Give it a shot."

Elizabeth: Yes! Exactly! It's our wedding anniversary and we're gonna see Huey Lewis and The News and I'm so excited about that cause I know all the words to his songs-pretty much-but yeah, I'm gonna try and win big.

Jesus: "Yes, and why not?"

Elizabeth: Exactly! Anything can happen.

Jesus: "Anything could happen. Exactly. And it's going with that spirit of Fun that makes it just . . . because you should do it with a spirit of Fun because where your abundance will come-you do not know-so do it and just have fun."

Elizabeth: Yep, yep. Even if I don't win, it will be a good time. So.

Jesus: "Yes, Absolutely."

Elizabeth: Um, what else do we want to talk about here? Adam and Eve. Were they really the first two people on Earth?

Jesus: "Yees. Yes, it is pretty much like that. There was, you know, your Earth goes through it's different evolutionary stages. So, they were the first to be here after-Earth went through Many different evolutions-prior to that-where there were inhabitants-you know, Earth was not destroyed, but the inhabitants were removed. So, Adam and Eve, yes, were the very first, what you would call Human inhabitants."

Elizabeth: So, when you're saying inhabitants before Adam and Eve, are you talking about dinosaurs?

Jesus: "Dinosaurs or what you would call extra terrestrials came here to see if this was a fitting place for them for their own evolution. It was decided that this was best for the souls that you are."

Elizabeth: Interesting. And so now I'm gonna ask a scientific question.- I've been trying to think of questions that scientists might have for you so well, two of them. So the Darwin Theory is that we evolved from apes so that wouldn't be correct then, right?

Jesus: "No, although, Although it's not entirely wrong in the sense that there have been some forms of evolution. Evolution is not incorrect. It does evolve but the evolving from an ape into a human-that did not occur. It does not mean that it could not occur but it did not occur."

Elizabeth: OK. And then what about the dinosaurs? How did they become extinct? Was it a meteor that came?

Jesus: "It was-that would be the best way of describing it. It was a massive meteor shower."

Elizabeth: Oh WOW! I betcha that was neat to see!

Jesus: "Yes. And it was time. It was time because Earth needed to be cleansed once again. And this has happened many times with Earth where it becomes out of balance and it needs to be cleansed and then there will be destruction of that kind."

Elizabeth: I feel like there's a cleansing right now that is going on. A lot of people do actually.

Jesus: "Yes. Yes, but when we talk about these kinds of cleansings, all inhabitants are destroyed."

Elizabeth: Right. Right.

Jesus: "And that is not occurring right now. You are having cleansings and things are changing. You know you had shifts in your-in the poles-in the axis of the Earth so that is why your weather has changes, you have earthquakes and such that have altered-but it's continual. You just feel because-you feel that it has been stationary but the Earth continues to evolve and change and change. It is Just the Way it Is."

Elizabeth: Yeah . . . the last two vacations we've went on, is this just coincidence that there was earthquakes and tsunamis while we went on our vacation? Is that just coincidence?

Jesus: "Why? What were your feelings about that? I'm trying to understand really why you are asking me this."

Elizabeth: I don't know. I wanna be able to go somewhere and not have to worry about people being in danger cause I'm leaving my house (laughing) It's not, it's not funny.

Jesus: "So you are worried about others but not yourself."

Elizabeth: No, I'm not worried about myself actually, but I don't wanna go to the Bahamas when we go and have to worry about someone else somewhere . . . it's not me!

Jesus: "And so I mean, in a sense, nothing is a coincidence. It is occurring for a reason. It's in your reality. It means there's something for you to look at. And again, one person may look at that and say, "Well, I find earthquakes exciting." Soo and they would find their line of truth there. For you it has some other meaning and I'm not going to give you the answer because this is something that you need to find on your own."

Elizabeth: OK. That's fine. I like to figure it out for myself anyways. (I DID find the answer later that week in John Edward's book, "Infinite Quest") :)

Jesus: "Yes, exactly and we can talk about it next time."

Elizabeth: Let's see. Was Mary Magdalene one of your disciples?

Jesus: "You could say that. You could say that. She was my closest friend."

Elizabeth: She WAS your closet friend. OK

Jesus: "Yes, she was . . . well, let me. Yes, she and Judas were my closest. And yes, and we were-but she knew quite a bit herself. I only had to awaken it within her."

Elizabeth: I see, OK. And you and Judas. Do you guys talk now or is he reincarnated somewhere else as well as Mary (Magdalene) and the other disciples? Or are they up in Heaven with you and they just stayed there?

Jesus: "Well, remember that you have a soul. And it will come forth-to understand reincarnation-OK.-You are many many many souls, correct? And many looking to come and reincarnate. You have-think of Earth as a stage where there are actors playing out roles. And each time-and then there is-you have time and space that you are working with, right? So, you can have . . . OK. I want to explain this as simply as possible. So when one reincarnates there is not just one soul who incarnates as Judas. There are many souls who try on that role as Judas. Because you would think of time as being Linear. And it is not."

Elizabeth: So, like is there another person-is there another part of me that is living somewhere else right now?

Jesus: "Yes. Very possible. In another time, space, reality."

Elizabeth: Oh Man! (Laughing) That's interesting.

Jesus: "Yes. It can really blow your mind as you say."

Elizabeth: Oh really!

Jesus: "So there will be souls that would want to have that experience and many will come back. That's why—you'll hear it. People will go to psychics and be told-many will be told that they are the same person-well, how can that possibly be? Well, it's true because they have come in as different-because these scenarios-think of time and past lives as not being in the past but being stacked up on top of each other, OK and it is like a line so you are in one line of existence right now. Although you-it doesn't mean it's the past-it could be a future time line. Think of them as time lines. Think of a spider web, how they intertwine with each other so I don't want to get too detailed on this but just to give you the overview because too much information, it will not make sense. So, you have a soul and it chooses to incarnate in different time lines and you can incarnate in different time lines at the same time. Usually you will not do too many because it is-there's no purpose to that but you can incarnate as Judas in one time line or you are incarnating as the person that you are right now-in this time."

Elizabeth: So, so, you're saying that I could choose to go back and live at that time period that Judas, that you were there-and I could experience that for myself?

Jesus: "Absolutely. And many Want To because of the experience. The role Judas played was such an Extraordinary experience, such an Extraordinary role and but you have to have a certain level of understanding of spiritual laws and truths and enlightened-you have to be enlightened to a certain degree because he was-as you know-a figure that when he was with me-he was my closest—besides John the Baptist. John the Baptist is the one who taught me much of what I knew or helped me to remember, I should say. John the Baptist was a very evolved Being. So, that being said, yes, if you think about it too much, it will confuse you. If you FEEL IT you will understand much better."

Elizabeth: Well, I get it. I just wanna say, "Holy shit!" That's amazing to be able to think that you could actually-that's cool!

Jesus: "Yes, cause if you think of yourself as energy, energy can go in many different directions and again, you are limited because you are in the human form and you're denser and again, all the limitations of the human mind."

Elizabeth: Yes. Wow. That's cool.

Jesus: "Yes. You are asking good questions."

Elizabeth: Yeah they are good questions aren't they? (laughing) Oh! Well, you talked about John the Baptist so he was your cousin then, correct?

Jesus: "Yes."

Elizabeth: And did you have brothers and sisters or were you an only child?

Jesus: "No, I had many brothers and sisters. Many relatives. Cousins."

Elizabeth: Oh, wow! That's great.

Jesus: "Yes."

Elizabeth: What else? I don't know what else to ask you today, Jesus. There's a lot of good stuff that we got today. Is the Shroud of Turin an actual-is that really the cloth that was used to cover you when they buried you?

Jesus: Sigh. "No. It does not matter."

Elizabeth: OK

Jesus: "It does not matter because there is a, in a sense, a miracle In That anyway."

Elizabeth: Yeah, there really is. It's very neat.

Jesus: "Yes. But it can be so-to say no because it could not have endured that time. But it is a type of miracle anyway because it is representative-represents what my experience was."

Elizabeth: OK.

Jesus: "But it came-it appeared maybe 300 hundred years after the Crucifixion."

Elizabeth: Oh, OK. OK.

Flip tape

Elizabeth: Is the Medium getting tired or does she still wanna keep going?

Jesus: "Yes, we can go another little bit."

Elizabeth: OK. Denise do you have anything that you wanna talk to him about?

Denise: I wanted to ask you Jesus if—I feel like I am going forward because my body has been feeling a little different. Am I right?

Jesus: "Oh I cannot answer that for you. You have to answer that. ARE you right?"

Denise: Well, I think I am because I think, well, since I met Beth, she has taught me how to be more Aware of things around me and things that happen so she did teach me that.

Jesus: "Let me ask you this. Why do you doubt?"

Denise: I—I don't know. Sometimes I guess I think that-well like Beth is so much farther ahead of me so then I feel like-you know-I doubt that way. When I know I shouldn't.

Jesus: "Well, again you are in judgment. And you are observing and comparing and you Limit Yourself and Hold Yourself Back when you are in a state of Comparison or Judgment. WHEN you take the time to understand—and you are listening to all of these things—and understand that you are-you are just at a different stage than your friend. For whatever reason. And you will find that you will-the doubt will be removed-and you will no longer be comparing yourself and you will be standing in Your Own Truth and moving forward in that way. That is all. Do not compare yourself to another if you want to move forward. When you observe another and say, "They are farther along than me and I cannot possibly catch up to them." You have no need to catch up to them. You only have to think about Yourself and where You want to go with what it is that you want to learn. Does that help you?"

Denise: Yes, because like, when I told you that Beth and I healed or we did a healing on Terry-I mean, I felt very powerful, you know, when I was doing that.

Jesus: "Yes."

Denise: Working on healing her-and I felt very strong.

Elizabeth: It was just as much me as it was you-Together.

Denise: Well, we did it together but I still—I did-I felt-it made me feel very good.

Jesus: "Yes, and remember, just to be observant. Did it make you feel good because you felt you accomplished something? Be-without judgment-observe yourself. Did it make you feel good because you feel—just look to understand Why you felt good for that. Was it the energy moving through you-pulsating through you that you connected with something? Did you understand a truth? Did you feel good because you finally did something-accomplished something? That is what you are working on right now. Is being Aware. Self-Aware. Who are you? Who are you as a human being in regards to you as a—an Eternal being. That is your job and everyone else's job on the planet-to understand yourselves as human beings-Eternal Beings-in a limited form."

Denise: Well, and it felt good that we helped her too.

Jesus: "Yes. Yes. Remember when you are-when you are dealing with helping others, that when you Feel Good helping another, that is a Very good time for you to observe Really What It Is that you're feeling good about. It's not bad. But it is Limiting. Feeling good by helping another. You cannot help another unless they are willing to help themselves, correct? You could give all the healing in the world to this person but if she was not open to receiving, it would have been all useless in a sense."

Denise: Right, right.

Jesus: "I am saying this because there is very easy to become attached to a certain feeling of, "it felt good to help another." and many of you on your planet will get too Consumed with helping others because it makes You feel good and instead of realizing that you are Only the means for-you are the vehicle by which you help another. So, it's not that it's bad but because what you are doing here-you specifically, my friend, you are here to understand yourself and you are at the beginning of your journey. So, I am going to keep repeating that. I want you to be

Observant of your Feelings and your Emotions and then understand the Motivations for them-Without Judgment-so that you can understand Who You Are."

Denise: OK. So, it's more working on myself than anything.

Jesus: "Yes. But it's not working on yourself-it's KNOWING yourself. You had a great man who said, "To thine own self be true." And that is what each of you should have engraved in your mind "To thine own self be true." And you can only be true to yourself when you Know Who You Are. And that is what you are doing right now. Finding out who you are."

Elizabeth: Isn't it awesome?! (laughing)

Jesus: "Absolutely. It is very good. And when-each one of you is at a different spot. Depending on experience, depending on so many different factors. So, by comparing yourself to each other you limit yourself. That is all. But it's neither good or bad but you have to ask yourself, "Do I want to limit myself or do I want to stay open to other possibilities?""

Denise: OK, that helps. That helps. Yeah.

Jesus: "Yes. Good."

Elizabeth: Well, I think the Medium's phone—there's something going on with it so maybe we should end for today. (it was beeping like a dead battery warning)

Jesus: "That sounds very good. I will then bid you farewell. It is a delight and we will be speaking very soon again."

Elizabeth: Alright! Thanks Jesus!

Denise: Thank you Jesus.

Jesus: "You are welcome. Yes, you are welcome and I love you very much."

Elizabeth: We love you too very much.

Denise: We love you too.

Jesus: "Yes."

Elizabeth: Alright, Bye!!

Jesus: "Bye."

It was a little over a month again before I talked to Jesus on the phone. I kept writing down questions and talking to Him throughout my days though. I had decided that after our last conversation I was going to ask him if Time Travel was possible. Many things happened in my personal life in the month that we didn't speak. So much so that I even asked Him beforehand—out loud—(before I made the phone call to Laurie) that He please direct the conversation because I had so much that I didn't know where to start.

The night of July 2 we attended my son's end of the year baseball party. There I spoke to one of the other parents. The man brought up the year 1977. I said I was born that year. It was also the year that John Denver made the movie, "Oh, God!" with George Burns. He told me that someone had just told him that John Denver had lived in Kasota, which is the town that my husband works-and that he attended Gustavis College in Saint Peter which is the next town over. John Denver has been mentioned to me many times now in the last few months, in talking with people and in books that have mentioned him. I said something like, "It's funny because he was talking to God in that movie and here I talk to Jesus." The Dad then told me that he talks to Jesus every Sunday because he is a Preacher. OH! So I asked him if he prays to Mother Mary at all and he said no because it is not written in the Bible so he doesn't do it. I replied that she is always there for him if he needs a good mother's love and we must remember that "No Mother-No Son"—something Mother Teresa said. Then I proceeded to tell him some of the things that Jesus and I have been talking about. He wasn't very receptive we'll say (some people are and some aren't). So when my husband interrupted I let it drop.

That night I had a dream. I was sleeping in my bed (in my dream) and this man had snuck into my house and awakened me by throwing copies of my book, "Love, God" onto me. I was naked and quickly tried to cover myself but I really didn't seem to care if my breasts were exposed. My husband continued sleeping next to me, not waking. The man told me that he didn't believe anything that does not come from the Bible. Then he knelt next to me at my bed and started to weep. He was "unloading" sadness from his heart. His emotional pain was too much to bear. I knew what the angels wanted me to tell him to comfort him but I afraid for my life and that of my husband's so I just kept telling him, "Everything will be OK." Then as quickly as he had come in, he left. I ran to my closet to get my robe. I looked out the window to see his wife fighting to get past him to get into the house to give me piece of her mind. She was yelling at him. Their children were in the car and then out and running around while they fought. He wanted Peace. I remember thinking, "it's the middle of the night-why is his family with him?" I then went downstairs after they had left and checked the lock. The key had been left in the lock-on accident by my husband when we had come home. But it really wasn't an accident because this man had NEEDED to come to me to pour out his heart. There had been such sadness that he needed to release.

My dream continued. I was on a sidewalk watching a TV show in a store window. Women had started to group together watching this show. I asked if we were all hooked on it now :) I looked at a girl and said, "You look like Juliette Lewis." and she said to me, "You look like Gorillas In the Mist." I said, "Sigourney Weaver!" (Which I don't but anyways) Then we were in a park setting. One of the ladies said Jesus' name. I said, "That is the 3rd time I have heard Jesus' name spoken today." Then I cleared my throat because it was feeling hoarse and spoke up so that everyone around us could hear me and pronounced boldly, "Jesus wants you all to know that He personally hears each of your prayers and knows exactly what you are doing at any given moment when you are speaking to Him." Then I looked around to the women sitting around me. One was laying her head in the lap of another to rest so I said, "Be it when you are laying your head in someone's lap or admiring the beauty of a horse, or getting your hair done, or laying in the grass or sitting with friends." And as I turned I saw what looked like a cloud over by the edge of the lovely green trees and shrubs. Then the cloud turned misty and started to take form. I gasped so loud that I started to wake myself up. There were 3 tall figures-I saw Jesus standing between His parents,

Mary and Joseph and Mary was holding the hand of a child-which I believe was my son, Jesse, but it was like the child could have been anyone's child-Mother Mary holds the hands of all our children. There were dogs running around and birds flying and they were all this soft mist with white light everywhere-they were all white and surrounded in the white light at the same time. There were other forms starting to take shape but since I had started to wake I said to the women I was with, "Can't you see them?! There they are!!" At that, they all started to back away and I waved my hand all crazy like a little kid saying good-bye. I woke with an excitement that I have never had before LOL I moved my arm to turn on the light once I was conscious enough to realize that I should write it all down. I knocked over my water glass spilling water all over my Rosary pamphlet and Rosary's. I woke my husband up doing all of this and I just couldn't contain all my excitement at seeing all of them! They were there-listening and watching-just like they do to ALL of us-whether we know it or not or Acknowledge it. I glimpsed Heaven and it was Happy and Loving and Wonderful. The dogs running around and birds flying said it all :) They send their love. Everyone does. Because the forms that were starting to take shape were all of my loved ones, which means that all of yours are there for YOU. Even if you are all alone here, you are never really alone because you have LOVE and SUPPORT from the Other Side.

My daughter came upstairs after I had awoken and told me all excitedly that she had seen a Bluebird in the tree. The Bluebird of Happiness :) Only the 2nd time we have seen one in our yard. The 1st time being when our son, Arron took his first steps last month.

Now for the reading with Jesus that followed.

CHAPTER 6

Compassion over Judgment

July 8, 2013

Jesus: "Hello, it is so easy to come here and I have missed our conversations but probably we have continued on in any case because I hear you talking to me all the time. As the Medium was saying, you all talk to me and that's what we—we keep the lines of communication open all the time. You really do not realize how much we actually hear, that there IS NO barrier-you just are so used to thinking that there isn't, but not you my friend, because you are continually talking and looking for guidance from us—you live in that realm-but this is something important for people to know that it is a continual-it doesn't have to "I will take time to satisfy to talk to us to pray" and that is fine too but all day long all the time-if you take the time just to remember that we are There With You because we can be in all places at the same time, we hear what you are saying, we are there to guide you, to assist you, to help you in any ways that we can, so that is where we want to maybe, I know you have many questions and I want to move to your questions but I want you to know that we KNOW that you are all seeking—you may talk to us but you don't hear what we say and hopefully we will also help all of those who struggle with hearing the answers to your inquiries-cause they're not always questions, sometimes you are just telling us how much you enjoy something that is part of your experience that we hear that and we will send you a response-always, always respond-and I use we here as the plural because you don't only talk to me but there are many who all of you talk to and we Hear it and we Respond-that's the important thing and you may not always recognize the response and-it's important to recognize the response-and hopefully today we'll get more clarity on that and also on the questions that you have for me. So, shall we begin with your questions or what would you like to do? It is up to you-I am here available to do for you what it is that you want to do."

Elizabeth: Well, let's see, I'm glad that you said that you hear all of our prayers because that has to do with a dream that I was gonna write

113

about when I get time, is that I announced to the people in my dream surrounding me, "Jesus wants you all to know that He hears your prayers, they personally hear your prayers." So then I saw you and your mom and your dad and you know, and it seemed like Heaven to me-in the dream when I announced that. So it's good that people hear that coming from you because I didn't even tell the Medium about that dream at all. So.

Jesus: "And I believe here would be important because I know what you've seen, that each time we have come together, you have had things on your mind or have thought of things or your questions or you've been talking to me and the Medium has had no idea of this-yet they come through her. So, right there, you know that you and I are communicating and now you are—she has no clue and yet she speaks of many of the things of which you have been thinking of. Well, at this point in your discussion when you are taking all of this information and putting it back into something that is more cohesive for others to appreciate, I would bring in your dream at this point so that others can understand the significance of what I said to you and Why your dream was so important-then it will have more meaning. You will find where to insert the dream but it would be valuable for you to put that in here as the beginning of this session so that others can understand."

Elizabeth: OH, OK.

Jesus: "So you describe your dream-as best that you can remember it at this point-and others that are, are Able to, will make the correlation between your dream and what we are discussing."

Elizabeth: OK, alright, alright. Good.

Jesus: "Yes."

Elizabeth: I think I kinda wanna go to um, do you want me to discuss the dream right now or I'll just put it in there when I . . .?

Jesus: "What you want to do. It is yours and you follow through because remember, I am Here for you to Access. This is Your Baby."

Elizabeth: I think I will just wait to describe the dream when I put it all together. So.

Jesus: "And you can speak with me at anytime, either through the Medium or in your usual ways."

Elizabeth: OK, Alright. I kinda wanna touch on, you said that you all hear us when we talk to you. I kinda wanna bridge the gap of the different religions like Islam and all this, like people have-they believe Mohammed was the prophet, I kinda wanna bridge the gap so this isn't just towards Christians, it can be towards everyone. Jews, Muslims, everyone like that so. If you could talk a little about that a bit.

Jesus: "Yes, again, this is-we Here In Spirit have no Attachment to those divisions and those categories and that kind of human NEED to categorize everything and put it into compartments and to exclude and include and define. We don't have that. We are ALL here. I was—I came forth in a certain manner and many of my teachings and my words were taken and misconstrued and put into a different context. The same with the other prophets that have come forth who are important and I will use prophets in this sense or others who have had a very open connection. And there are many who have come forth who have not been recorded in history, who have had that same ability to have that connection. So it does that You, As Humans, have the need to be selective and to categorize. We In Spirit do not. What is important is the message that comes through. And if you will Really Look at all of the teachings, if they Really ARE the True Words of ALL of us that are here from Spirit as what comes through the Medium and others like that, if it is of Truth it will be based in Love and Compassion and Tolerance. If it is not of Truth, if it is of human manipulation or of other realms manipulation, it will not be of that vibration. That is the simple way of understanding what is Truth and what is not Truth. Well, yes, the other is Truth as well because there are realms that exist and in your own Earthly realm where there is what you call evil or bad things again, that's your judgment. But what you are seeking for yourselves, as Truth, where you all originate from, those that I am reaching out to, you, the Medium, your friends that you are connecting with, this is the Truth for what you are here to bring to this world and move it forward

115

into that direction—that of a higher vibration—that 5th dimensional realm in which you are all moving into. Does this make sense for you?"

Elizabeth: Yes, it does make sense for me.

Jesus: "OK. Does that answer your question tho?"

Elizabeth: Yeah, it answers my question. It does, for you saying the Truth is Love and Compassion and if it was anything else that would be misdirected cause there's a lot of killing that's going on in the name of, do I say—God?—with the other religions and there's so much killing and war over THAT.

Jesus: "Yes."

Elizabeth: I just, I can't believe that any killing would be what God would want for us.

Jesus: "You ARE sons and daughters and children of God and you, in human form, have been given something that is your Ticket To Freedom and that is your Free Will. Choice. Free Will slash Choice. So, there is no right/wrong or good or bad there just IS. So God looks at any killing in His name without judgment. He sees that it has been a choice on the part of those individuals to choose those means to exercise their Free Will. You see it's a little bit different as I see it that way as many here see it and as you see it when you leave the human form. It is difficult when you are in the human form when someone like you who has come forth from a realm that does-you have been in many realms. You are experienced much. I am speaking to you directly, so you have had many experiences but your realm of-your origin-where you come from-there is the Truth, let's say there, or what is the existence is there is of very little conflict. It is-you understand that God, as you know Him/Her/It—however you want to understand is of Total Acceptance and Unconditional Love therefore even those that use His name to kill are loved like those that do not use His name to kill. This is something very important for all of you to understand as human beings. However, it is important that you have these values. They are necessary for your society. It is a tricky thing because you as human beings cannot just-not everyone has evolved to the place of being able to "live and let live" so

116

to speak and say, "Well, that one is killing but we cannot judge them." So, it's a-it's complex-it's simple but it is complex. So for you, a state of Compassion and Love is a vibration that You, specifically, and many who will hear these words find themselves to be most Comfortable With because it is your Natural State. You have worked through many of lifetimes of being the aggressor, being the perpetrator, being the killer, the murderer, the thief, the "bad guy", OK. You have experienced that and now are coming through all of that in a more evolved state. Those that are there using religion or God or whatever to harm another, it is not for us to judge them but it is difficult as a human being because you are in a state of having to have to Understand it. So, you, who do not live in a place where there is a need to protect yourself in that way, correct?"

Elizabeth: Right.

Jesus: "You are not living in a war zone."

Elizabeth: No.

Jesus: "You are living in relative safety. You have Chosen That because you do not Need those lessons."

Elizabeth: That makes sense.

Jesus: "You have done them. Yes, so all of you, you have chosen those-you have other lessons you are learning, but you are here to perform certain tasks that are of a very important nature and that is to help those who are still learning these things to find Their Way Through. Remember, God does Not Judge any of it as being right or wrong. He just sees it as being What Is. Because Humans—when you are in human form-when you inhabit your Earth suit, what happens is you become very serious and you forget that this is very temporary—and that you are just acting out a role. You have just put ON a costume and have stepped out onto the stage of life. You have forgotten that. It's all part of the whole experience. So you take yourselves far more seriously and you take everything far more seriously but it is part of—it is a necessity because it is part of the whole experience."

Elizabeth: OK

Jesus: "This all makes sense and leads you to better understanding those that use God's name to harm another."

Elizabeth: Yeah, cause I'm watching the news and I'm really not, like by talking to You and I'm hoping that by when people read this they will have a better sort of Compassion for these things cause I'm looking at the things-well, I don't really watch the news as much anymore but I don't really have that feeling of, you know, gosh, it's hard to describe, but it's like it has a purpose so I'm not gonna get really that, I just don't get upset about it.

Jesus: "And that is why these teachings now—they are not-they will— What we are doing here is not the first time someone has come forth with it, nor will it be the last time but there will be many who will criticize this or they will feel that it is callous and cold and inhumane to Speak in this way but all one has to do is to stop for one moment and FEEL within their Own Bodily System. Stop and say, "OK, if I stop judging another and I only allow myself to Accept and look at it with as much Compassion as I can-do I FEEL BETTER? Which makes me feel better? When I am in a state of Judgment or when I am in a state of Compassion?" For the most horrific crime. And believe me, I UNDERSTAND it is not that it is easy to do but if you can begin to FEEL it. Sometimes it is necessary to feel anger or You Don't Know What Another Has Chosen To Do Here. But if you can feel for yourself what it feels like and if it feels better so to speak or more relaxed or more open to be in a place of Compassion, than you have your answer, correct?"

Elizabeth: Yes. Um, Now I'm gonna say, some people get really angry about things like Immigration or something or politics and they just go on and on and on they bitch and complain about it, they just wind themselves up, why do they get so mad at that stuff instead of being in a state of you know, Compassion and just letting it be what it is?

Jesus: "Again, you do not know what one is here to learn."

Elizabeth: OK

Jesus: "So when you are looking at something like that and saying," Why are they getting all worked up about that?" You are then in a place of judgment."

Elizabeth: OK

Jesus: "I'm not saying that it's easy to drop that but the more you hear this, the more you begin to realize, and say, "You know, really, I cannot judge ANYONE. It's not my place to do that because I Do Not Know. I can Only look at my experience here and am I feeling that I am standing in my own Truth and being in Integrity with myself for what I can understand in this moment?" That's all you can do. And when you find yourself judging, than you are judging, and not to beat yourself up for it either."

Elizabeth: OK. Alright. Um, hmmm, I don't think I have anything else to ask about that. Is there anything else you want to add to that?

Jesus: "No, I think we have covered it and I think that it ties in with everything and where you are moving to now because you have just finished a cycle of time. You will go through these cycles periodically as you are evolving where you will "clean house" so to speak-emotionally and psychologically. The energies will come through-the universal cosmic energies come through and the planet is affected by it. So, basically all the inhabitants of Earth right now have just gone through another "spring cleaning" so to speak and it is now the energies of that are weening. So, individuals were Forced basically, or not forced cause no one is ever forced, but it got very uncomfortable for many and many felt like they were regressing, and things were not occurring as they had at one time. So, you are moving out of that and I bring this up here because you are moving into a more Optimistic faze but one-each of you must understand that you are never done with anything here. There IS NOT a destination to be reached. There is not a FINAL destination so to speak. You are-it is-because then you lose sight of why you are here. So, periodically these "cleansings" we will call them, this energy that comes through to kind of get you to kind of wake up, that makes you feel like you are stepping back into old patterns and old experiences and (flip tape) you can know that as you are here on Earth, you will continually, continually, be subject to these energy influences. You will, it is just the nature of Earthly existence."

Elizabeth: Oh, so, what you're saying is-Denise and I were kinda laughing because that's what we were talking about (Laughing) about

I don't know, a half hour ago. It was-we were talking about-I felt like maybe there was a lot of people with issues of self-worth. It feels like there's a lot of people-self-worth is a big thing right now so yeah, it's just emotionally and I kinda feel like um, like our bodies kinda pick up on that. I'm curious as to why I've been so tired lately and maybe it's not just me-it's a lotta Other people that are feeling that too.

(Denise and I had really been talking about that before the phone call. She had come over an hour early to chat and we had not been speaking to the Medium. We were sitting on my couch having a cup of coffee and what Jesus said sounded just almost word for word of what Denise had said. We were both hitting each other when He spoke about it and holding back laughing about it. It was really very cool to know that He was sitting in on our pre-conversation.)

Jesus: "Yes. Yes. And each of you will have certain things because you came here and prior to coming here you chose personality traits that you wanted to be part of your experience so you have ways in which you cope and function here on this planet that will stay with you forever. It is important for you not to identify so entirely with them that you are unaware of them. So when you have these experiences of these energy waves that come through to kind of trigger emotional responses that maybe are uncomfortable you want to wake, open your eyes and say, "Hmm, what is-out of all the deep Love and Respect that Oneness and Universe HAS for me, what are they trying to show me? Where are they trying to direct me?" And know that they are always trying to get you to take the HIGHEST path possible for you in your experience here for what you have Chosen to do and that-you then-you can get your answers. Then you can get guidance and that is what we were talking about at the beginning in communicating with us. ASK and we will answer. We are ALWAYS answering. So, it's up to you to know HOW the answers might come for you and each of you are individual and each of you have your own experiences. So they each-you will get it in different ways. And you will be clearing things in different ways and somethings will never be gone from your experience but you will live with them in ways in which they aren't influencing and affecting your experience to such a degree that they are monopolizing it and you are unaware of it. So, some of you may find that you are always-we'll use something simple-you will always have a tendency for certain addictions-say somebody who likes-what would be something-they like alcohol and they will always have that-it's the same thing but it does not control them-they control it. It becomes part of who they are. It becomes their experience with that. When they've Mastered it-because it's not about control it's about Mastering of certain experiences-emotional and personality traits that you have here within your environment. When you master them-you look at them and you say, "Oh this can be used in this way." and where it is beneficial for you. As opposed to it dictating to you how you will live. Does that make sense?"

Elizabeth: Yes, so people we'll say, just alcoholism, if they can't master it then in this lifetime, will that be part of their next lesson then in their next life? As to try and do it again?

Jesus: "It depends on what they want to experience. What they want to choose."

Elizabeth: OK

Jesus: "They will decide at that-when they re-enter. Maybe they do not need to have that experience again."

Elizabeth: OK, OK.

Jesus: "Or maybe someone comes in as an alcoholic but it wasn't meant for them to Master alcoholism. Maybe they came in as an alcoholic in order to teach another a Love for someone who was an alcoholic or maybe to-for another individual. We don't know. You will not never know until you leave your form-why that occurred."

Elizabeth: OK, so now I'm gonna jump into abortions because that's what we were talking about on Saturday, my friend, Tim and I. And he said that if somebody has an abortion that means they're saying to God, "Well, you made a mistake in making this soul, this baby." And I said to him, "Well you never know what the purpose would be of what that soul agreed to with the mother and maybe the mother had to learn you know, self-forgiveness or whatever. You just don't know."

Jesus: "Exactly."

Elizabeth: Oh good.

Jesus: "You answered-but that's what it is. But it would be-You Don't Know. You don't know. That's the thing that when another kills another because in essence that's how many view what you call abortion-that one would-it's a killing and in a sense, it IS but you don't know what they signed up for. So it becomes-from the eyes of society, you have your roles that you must live under that have been created but you, who are more evolved, can take these Understandings, these Teachings and find a way to find Balance. Because if you come from the place where there is no right and wrong and that God is all loving, no matter what, than it puts you in a place of greater peace. Does it not?"

Elizabeth: It really really does.

Jesus: "Yes. So, and others would say that they do not believe this and this is where the controversy comes in and it is all about not saying that another is wrong but Understanding that ALL is Possible and that life is a mystery. There is so many things that you will never fully understand. Even when you leave the physical form, there are many things that are not revealed to you because you have not gained that ability to understand yet."

Elizabeth: OK. So I'll jump into does that have something to do with the garments? My cousin wanted to know about the garments.

Jesus: "The what? I'm sorry."

Elizabeth: Garments? Is there such thing as garments in Heaven? Or the After-life?

Jesus: "Garment. You mean clothing."

Elizabeth: Yes, I guess there's maybe there's certain color of clothing for each different soul? I didn't think-I didn't really know about that.

Jesus: "Again, what is important to understand, it's very complex because it is so intricately woven. It is so complex beyond-look at just your physical reality on Earth and how complex and intricately woven everything is but yet there's Balance, correct?"

Elizabeth: Yes.

Jesus: "So it is Beyond the physical realm and what happens is that once you are-you are a creative Being In the human form as well as out of the human form. Thought creates your reality. So to it is when you are not in the human form. So, if another creates a reality that is where there are those who wears garments depending on their "Soul type", than that can possibly be. For those who do not feel that that's a necessity-that reality would never come into their experience."

Elizabeth: OK.

Jesus: "You see, and it's for everything so if someone dies believing there is NOTHING they will go into a state of Nothingness if they are REALLY convinced of that. Not too many people are. They may say that they are but not too many really are. But if there is someone who is completely convinced that there is a nothingness-there's absolutely nothing-they will go into a state of nothingness but they Will reincarnate. They Will come back and it's because of that State of the Soul Always Wanting To Move Forward-Always Wanting Experience, OK? So that's what is the impetus for what happens to you once you are outside the physical form."

Elizabeth: So when they are in a state of nothingness-what I thought was purgatory-

Jesus: "It is a—it is only a Perception of being in a state of nothingness. It is not Really a reality but it is a reality just to explain-they've created that state."

Elizabeth: OK. So but when I had the dream which I thought was Purgatory where they were just wandering around and they just didn't know that people were around them-they just didn't seem to know that ANYTHING was going on-they were wandering, um, and then I started to pray the Hail Mary and The Our Father and waved my hands so they could see me, so was that part of the nothingness then?

Jesus: "Yes, and when others assist-because the SOUL is, as I said, it's impetus is always to move forward-always to move forward. So there is a light in the soul. So, yes, you create your own reality but what is stronger really is that impetus for moving forward. That's the best way of describing it. It is the impetus of the soul-it's the heart of the soul-it's it's life. It's something that cannot be taken from the soul. So, when there are others-who as you said in that case, you were praying-that-the energy of that or that Vibration Can Reach the soul of those that are in the state of "nothingness" and possibly activate them that they can create a different reality once they are outside of the physical form."

Elizabeth: OK. That makes sense. So, and then, when we pray for someone like one of our friends or whatever and does our prayers work for them? I know it may sound like a silly question I guess but-

Jesus: "And it does."

Elizabeth: How powerful are our prayers for other people besides just ourselves?

Jesus: "Very powerful. And that's the thing, you have to always remember to pay attention to what you are FEELING. What is the vibration that you are FEELING at that time because if you are feeling one of desperation when you are in prayer you will be sending desperation to them-the one that you are praying for. If you are sending-are in a vibrational state of Faith and Trust and Love than that's what you are sending. And total acceptance of Whatever is the outcome because sometimes you don't know. You are praying that someone survives something and maybe it is their time to go. Maybe they have CHOSEN to go. So you pray that they are-you just-basically-we say prayer or you just give them the Love, and Unconditional Love and Compassion and Understanding that you would want given to you in any situation as well and that is how you assist another and you say this through prayer. It is important to understand what you are FEELING about the situation when you are praying."

Elizabeth: OK. Very good. I like that.

Jesus: "Yes."

Elizabeth: Boy there's so many questions that I had. It's been a long 2 weeks since we've talked. (Laughing)

Jesus: "Yes, yes but we will manage to do it all. Not to worry. Because this is something that is important for all of us and we will get it all done."

Elizabeth: OK, I wanna go to the dream that I had and I think I wanna say that I Time Traveled and I went back in time and I spoke to myself when I was in like 5th or 6th grade so did I really time travel or was I in a different dimension? How did that work?

Jesus: "Yes, I mean that's what is possible. When you do something like that, you actually-you did. You went back in time, in a sense, because you think of time as being linear but it really is not linear. Time you are using here in the Earthly realm, it is non-existent outside of the Earthly realm. There are realms that use something equivalent to time but think of Earth as using time and you think of it as being chronological and linear but Really once you are out of it, the best way of understanding the same experience would be that-again-you can be anywhere at any time-time:)—you can be in all places at the Same Moment basically. So what happened for you, you were shown what you are able to do. OK. Being in the physical form has-there's a reason for it. Why not everyone is allowed to come down here and to have this experience. So if you Are here, #1 it is a Privilege and a Honor and that is why it feels so horrific for someone to commit suicide even though there is no judgment with it. So, you are here and you are having your Earthly experience and ugh, I digressed a moment. So, you can accomplish things in the physical form with greater magnitude and significance than you can in the non-physical form. That is the purpose OF being in the physical form. So what you did in that experience, you thought that you were Only dreaming but you were Not. You were Accomplishing an experience yet you allowed yourself the conscience awareness of it—not just the benefits of it but you went back in time to understand something With the Perspective of the experience that you have gained-that your SOUL and the human you have gained over time—went back to understand something—from in this linear time frame but because you can be there if you are not (hmm,hmm) in the human form-so in a dream state-you are able to be there at any time. Cause it is co-existing with you at the present moment."

Elizabeth: My, all of my, everything is co-existing with us.

Jesus: "Yes."

Elizabeth: So, is it only possible to do that when I'm sleeping then-to be out of the physical form?

Jesus: "Well, for the moment, yes. But one of the things that you are attempting to do in this lifetime is to master that in a non sleep state—so in a more meditative state-that is something that you are hoping to accomplish. That is why you're working on that now in the way that you are working on it and that is why this came up. And there are individuals that will do this. They will come here to accomplish these things because THEY CAN." (I was totally kicking my feet in excitement when He was saying this!)

Elizabeth: That is so cool!!! (Laughing and totally excited!!!)

Jesus: "Yes. Because having that-going-being able to do that—and then being able to instruct others on how they might be able to do that is a form of healing as well. Another way To be a healer."

Elizabeth: So can a person go back in time-we won't say time-but can they go back into their own life and change something to change the future of the present day of where they came from?

Jesus: "They wouldn't want to do that."

Elizabeth: OK

Jesus: "That would be folly. It would be folly because then you would not-altering it all would then cause that future You to be altered and those that have tried to do it have gotten themselves-what we would say-stuck or lost because then they were not able to re-enter their future you because they did not recognize their future you."

Elizabeth: OK, that makes sense. I'm glad you put the disclaimer on there because I didn't have any interest of changing anything (Laughing) (Serious) I just wanted to make sure that people-if there was a possibility that they might not want to do that. So OK. Thank You.

Jesus: "Exactly."

Elizabeth: Wow, that's some neat stuff. I'm gonna have to think more about that. Yes! I'm gonna be able to do that!

Jesus: "Yes and we were hoping you'd bring that up. If not, we would have probably brought it up to let you know that's the direction you are going and others who will read this-or hear these words-will also go, "Ah HA! That's what I've been doing as well." And get that direction and keep on pursuing that."

Elizabeth: Oh, Great! Great! Is that something that you did then when you were on Earth?

Jesus: "Yes."

Elizabeth: OK, Alright. I wanna ask a question for the Medium because I know it's important to her. She always feels like she can never get what she wants and she feels like everybody else can except for her and when things get going really good, she gets thrown for a loop and has different problems and she's curious as to why that keeps happening to her. Is she punishing herself from a past life? Can you help her with some clarity on that?

Jesus: "Yes. We will try. It is the um-OK, it is a good example. She-OK-there are those who come forth-all of you have come forth to attain and obtain something from this experience here on Earth. Each of you. And each of you has chosen many things that you want to learn and many experiences and they're all UNIQUE to YOU as an individual. Because you are all unique each time you come forth you are unique in what it is that you are as a human being or who you are on this planet. There are Never any exact two of you. You never come back exactly alike. You gain experience each time. So all of you are here with different intents and purposes and that is for you to find out what it is. And that's where many of you struggle and beat your heads against the wall because you want to know, "What is my purpose here? What is my purpose?" When you have someone with things that-experiences, life experiences—that are of a extreme nature—you can BET that they are here to Master something and we mean Master and that is the Highest form of Achievement that you can have on this planet. That's why you come here. You live lifetime upon lifetime upon lifetime to

Reach lifetimes where you Gain the Permission to access Mastery of something. So one thinks, "I am going to have Mastery of something" as a human being they think, "Oh it's going to be easy." It is quite the contrary from a human perspective, but from a non human and a spirit perspective it is the Most Valuable Culmination of Events. The problem lies with you as humans when you begin to judge it. And you judge it and you begin to compare and judge and then you fall into a state of self reproach and disapproval. And again, that is part of what you may be here to experience. Again, it's not good or bad it just may put the brakes on things but I will tell you that anyone who comes forth to have-and you observe their lives-and you will say, "Boy, they've had an awful lot in their lives." OK? You know individuals like this. They have come here to obtain Mastery of many-of certain things that maybe they can not completely answer to but it is Mastery. And you can bet that they are Concluding lifetimes of experience. So, it is just the way that it is and the Medium can understand that when you give her this information if she does not remember it but it is because she has come here-she's paid her—she's spent many lifetimes here. Many many lifetimes and this lifetime she is here for herself—yes she is In Service and she has no problem with being In Service but she has neglected her Own Self Development so to speak. She has put herself-has always denied her own self for the better-for the good of all—as many have done—but this lifetime she is being-she set in writing-first and foremost-to gain Mastery here so that she can conclude her cycle of lifetimes that obligate her to the life experience on Earth, you see, so it is just that way."

Elizabeth: So, she's close to graduating then.

Jesus: "Yes. She is getting her PhD."

Elizabeth: YAY!! Good for her!! (Laughing)

Jesus: "That does not mean that somebody else who's life is-we don't know-we don't know-BUT an indicator of someone who has had many difficulties or so it seems-and this will help those who have struggled. Rather than to feel victimized but to feel EMPOWERED and find their-I guess Power-I wish there was another word-to find that Strength there-is that they are here to gain that Mastery and it cannot be any other way. It just is."

Elizabeth: OK. I think she's going to be appreciative of that.

Jesus: "Yes. So, the problem goes back to, again, and this pertains to ALL of you—is that you take your life here on Earth far too seriously. You CLING to it. And that is part of what is part of your cellular encoding and it is unfortunate in the sense that you HAVE to take this on and we have yet to clear out that cellular memory of grasping to life. Because at one time, it was Necessary for the development here of Humanity to—we Needed this and I say we because it was part of what I needed to experience as well-we Needed Earth to become habitable. It Needed to be a place for us to have this great experiment that we are having. So, there were certain very Primitive Emotions that were necessary that are NO longer necessary but are still part of your cellular memory. So part of that is clinging to life at all costs rather than Understanding and Feeling the flow of life and that life continues beyond the physical form."

Elizabeth: So the kicking and screaming that everybody does just to . . . just to relax and go with the flow maybe?

Jesus: "Yes. Because truly if you Remember-it's something that when they are nearing death they may feel a great-so those who maybe are dying of disease—will have—begin to move in between the worlds and they will come back and say experiences that they have had and they will find great peace. This is that they are forgetting that they are human and they are letting go of their physical form so that they are no longer so tied into that cellular memory of survival-survival of the human form."

Elizabeth: Is, I'm just gonna ask a personal question. Is that why my mom stayed alive for so long-not eating or anything for like a week or two-at the end of her life?

Jesus: "Yes."

Elizabeth: OK.

Jesus: "She-and there are many that they do this-they're Assisting In this Removing of the cellular memory. So when one goes through something like that-it's very likely that they are assisting Humanity in removing the cellular memory of that survival and the Forgetting. Because as you come here you forget that you are an Eternal Being. You forget that you are just stepping onto a stage and doing a performance for a period of time so you become very attached to life. And as those who die and move in and out, they are assisting the greater good or the masses in removing that cellular memory of survival. Because that is where you are headed. Yes."

Elizabeth: OH, OK. Well, that makes me feel good then.

Jesus: "Yes. You do not see because of your connection with your mother. You do not feel all the things that she was-because you do not know-you can not possibly know all that she was attempting to accomplish here. Because of who she was as a human you may think she was only about herself and she was in many ways but she was also assisting others In That Way and everybody does to some degree or another."

Elizabeth: Good. That makes me feel really good about her then too. I mean, I knew that there was good so . . .

Jesus: "Yes."

Elizabeth: Alright, boy what else do we wanna talk about? We got about 5 minutes till the Medium has to go.

Jesus: "You tell me."

Elizabeth: Oh, the reincarnation. We wanna know if a human-if we have to take form as humans when we come to Earth or can we also take form as animals?

Jesus: "Some choose that. However it's a bit of a—it's a Limiting Experience and that is why a soul that is a human or Earthbound or some other, very seldom, will take on the form of an animal because it is not beneficial to their own evolution. Animals and the nature world evolve in a different manner. Now on an occasion there will be necessity for a soul to take on a form-an animal form of some sort—but Very Rarely. What happens more though, when you see a personality trait of someone that was alive-say you have a cat that comes into your life and you say, "She-this cat-is just like my mother was." This, that or the other way, right? It is usually because that Cat has taken On That in order to assist you in something that you are experiencing here. Very very seldom it is usually a soul that is looking to understand shape shifting and has-but it is not a recommended means of evolution. It is very limiting for a soul that is a-you know, basically souls like you because it's part of collective and you are not part of that collective as animals so you are kind of Outside that realm when you incarnate as an animal."

Elizabeth: OK, we had a little kitten show up the other day and we were thinking that it was our little black cat, Bear Bear, that I wrote about in the book, ("Love, God") that he reincarnated into this little kitten. Can you tell me if that's really him?

Jesus: "Animals will-because if you think of the realm of animals and cats-we'll use the consciousness of cats—they are-within that consciousness are individuals but not like there are individuals for humans and such. So they are less defined. They are more united. They are more like One because as I said their evolution is a different process than yours. However, they are half individual (flip tape) . . . The best that could be said is that is a reincarnation of an animal that you had at another time."

Elizabeth: Haaaahaaa, that was a long answer! But it was what I wanted to hear!

Jesus: (Laughing)

My children in the background asking me, "Is it him???!!" I say, 'Yeah!" They run outside so excited! :)

Jesus: "That is a long answer because we want you to understand all the different realms and how things occur but because you need to understand that so that you can instruct others."

Elizabeth: Oh, I definitely will instruct others. So the animals are on their own evolution also?

Jesus: "Yes. As are plants, rocks, nature, the Earth itself. They all have consciousness and they are on their own evolutionary path as well."

131

Elizabeth: OK. My husband wanted to know if we should be cutting back on eating meat because of the animals I guess.

Jesus: "No, no, because animals-they are here In Service. And an animal is happy to give up his life for you to eat it and it is the way in which it is TREATED when it is Here but it is basically, not all animals need to be eaten, but they are here to BE eaten. Especially certain animals are here to be eaten."

Elizabeth: OK, so the treatment . . . it's the treatment. We need to treat animals better. I'm just sayin.

Jesus: "Yes."

Elizabeth: I don't like mistreatment of animals AT ALL.

Jesus: "No. And many don't. And you'll see that that is something that is becoming less of a problem on your planet because the more are becoming Aware of the mistreatment of animals. And that is something that will be Better for animals as time goes on but remember, they have their own evolution and they have to go through what they need to go through for their own consciousness to evolve."

Elizabeth: OK. Alright. I think we can stop there. That was good.

Jesus: "Yes, because we will be speaking soon, I can guarantee you that. There will not be a lot of time that will go by and we will be back on track again."

Elizabeth: OK, Good. Will you go with Laurie when she goes to get her stuff done tomorrow? If I ask nicely?

Jesus: "Yes. I am. I will be with her. If she feels me that is her decision, but yes, I will be with her."

Elizabeth: OK. Thank you.

Jesus: "You are welcome. So, it is always good, it is always a pleasure and we will speak-you'll see—we will see, we will be speaking very soon."

Elizabeth: Thank you Jesus! We love you!

Denise: Love you Jesus.

Jesus: "We love you as well. I love you as well."

Elizabeth: Goodbye!

Jesus: "Goodbye".

My Time Traveling Experience

I come from the generation of movies that made time travel popular. "Bill and Ted's Excellent Adventure" and "Back to the Future" are two such films. This school year I found myself telling my son, "Be Excellent" as he got out of the truck to get onto the school bus. I had meant that he would have an "Excellent" behavior checked from his teacher at the end of the week but what followed from my mouth was, "To Each Other". So all together I said, "Be Excellent To Each Other." To him and my daughter. I thought, "That is PERFECT!!" I laughed because it was a line from "Bill and Ted's Excellent Adventure". A line that Rufus, played by George Carlin, had spoken. My dad had always told my brother and I, "Get your A's and B's and HAAAAAAVE FUN!!" I hadn't had a saying yet and NOW I DID! :) I told my friends that this was my official saying now to my children every day before school. My friend Brandon, brought up how Bill and Ted would always play air guitar after they said it so I have added that heehee and my son is embarrassed but he has that look in his eyes of "my mom is cool" and gives me this great grin.

On the morning of July 4th I woke from my dream and stared at my ceiling. Then I began to cry.

This is what I remember:

I was at the gate of the tennis courts across the street from the house I grew up in in Green Bay, WI. I saw a group of children playing in the grass beside the baseball field. I thought to myself, "Don't tell her it's you. She won't understand." Then a girl came running up to me. It was ME! I was in about 5th or 6th grade. I had on my peach colored long shorts and a peach and white striped top and my peach colored headband. I had round chubby cheeks. I stood in front of myself. Little me stood in front of big me. I asked her what her name was. She said, "Beth". I said, "MY name is Beth. Elizabeth." Then I asked her what she had been up to lately and she told me that she was watching Twin Peaks. (Which was a popular show back then) and Yes, I really HAD watched that show. I replied, "Remember, Bob is scary!" And then I woke up.

What makes this dream so special is that I felt and still do now, with it being 10 days later, how it was to be a kid again. Innocence. I had no clue what my life would bring me through, what I would accomplish and what would make me cry. I hadn't given it any thought. The only things that mattered were my mom and dad and playing. I didn't care about anything else accept the present moment. I didn't have a clue and it was beautiful. Love. Love was such a strong vibration emitting from the girl. To myself and to those around her. News of bad things going on in the world hadn't affected her yet. I started crying at the Innocence that I was able to feel and Understand with this encounter and for the Love that I had for myself. Had you asked me before this dream what I thought about myself at that age, I probably would have said, "Those were my chubby years. I wasn't very pretty then." But by talking to myself and seeing for myself how cute I had been even WITH those chubby cheeks, I wasn't giving myself enough credit. I was pretty no matter what. No Matter What.

*And yes, I bought the Twin Peaks seasons on DVD because I knew it held a message for me. Many, it turned out! My husband and I watched them together every night. Good news! Bob doesn't scare me anymore but he scares my husband hahahaha! It was great fun to watch them!! We actually miss our Twin Peaks nights now.

* Note—A few months after I had time traveled I had the opportunity to share the story with my brother. He is 2 years younger than me. When I described the outfit I had been wearing he remembered it. He told me that the only way that he would believe it was if I could show him proof and find our family picture from that year. There was a specific one that we remembered that I had been wearing that outfit in and we had taken our family picture at my grandparents farm. I told him that when I find it, he will have some explaining to do. ;)

Many months passed without looking for the picture. Then one day as I passed the closet that holds all of our old family photo albums, I decided to look for it. I went through all of the albums and all of the loose photos and could not find it. I was starting to get bummed out. Where could it be? Then I found something Even Better! It was a photo that was taken at my Great-Grandmother's 100th birthday party over in Michigan that we had gone to celebrate with her. My mom and dad and brother and great-grandma and I were in the photo. I had on my outfit and my mom was wearing the same dress from the photo I had been looking for. And this is the really neat part! The date can be proven by my great-grandmother's birth certificate! The year had been 1990 and that was the exact year that Twin Peaks had come out. Crazy Evidence, right?! I could not have asked for anything better! :)

Before this next session with Jesus, I told Denise that I wanted to do this privately. Something was telling me to be by myself. I thought we might be speaking about my mom and if that happened, I didn't want to cry in front of her so I asked her not to come over and not to take it personal. She understood.

One of the questions that I had been wondering since Jesus and I's last conversation was, "Who am I?"

Before we began, Laurie was excited to tell me how she had begun to heal herself. I asked her to repeat it all so that I could include it because it will be very helpful to people to understand how this was done and how they might be able to use it in their lives.

CHAPTER 7

Listening and Paying Attention

July 17, 2013

Laurie: That was the difference between-from the times that I have done it before and I just realized it now talking to you. Other times I've done this, to try to heal myself or whatever, I did it because I wanted to heal, I wanted to be a whole again, I wanted, you know, the pain to go away or whatever. Instead, this time I didn't expect it to go away because I feel like I can't do that. I was just Curious about What the Pain Wanted. What it wanted to tell me and could I do anything to help the pain? Like, energetically. And that was all just very natural how that happened. You know, going in and asking the pain what it wanted. Are you recording this? Cause then I'll repeat it.

Elizabeth: Yeah, now I'm recording but you can say what your answer was when you asked it.

Laurie: Right, so I went in, asked the pain what it wanted, the pain said—sent me the energy of feeling unloved. And I said, "oh, the pain feels unloved, right?" And then the fairies that look like, they were so tiny, they were so cute, they look like they had little hats on their head and I kept going, "This is Beth, this is Beth." It was just like-I was so excited to tell you-so it was fairies that look like dragonflies came and started kissing the pain in this like oval shape (the pain was in a big black oval shape), and the pain started to feel-like the sadness and stuff—so I started to go, "Oh, this is **My** pain and **I** feel unloved. That's right, I don't have anyone that loves me." and then I remembered my kids that love me. And I tapped into that love that I feel from them and I directed it to the pain so the pain could feel it and then I did all of this without trying to get rid of the pain but just out of curiosity about what the pain wanted. OK, that was the Readers Digest version.

Elizabeth: Laughing!

Laurie: Laughing. And the pain has subsided and the pain has subsided.

Elizabeth: That's Amazing!! Remember when I sent you that text a couple weeks ago? I said I have something to read you when you get time. Well, that was from my angel book and it was Heal Insecurities and it was specifically saying, "You feel unworthy and unloved and that is not true."

Laurie: How interesting, right?!

Elizabeth: AND get this! Today, this is for you, I'm gonna send it after we get off the phone. I saw a cloud formation that was-it looked like someone Surrendering to God. It was arms up, like a head, arms up towards the sky and the feet, it was like kneeling. It was like someone kneeling with their arms raised.

Laurie: Wow, Wow.

Elizabeth: It was amazing, so.

Laurie: OK, and that is kinda what I've been doing. Cause I was getting so frustrated and I was like, "You know I gotta stay away from the doctors, every time I go I leave there and I'm in worse shape and blah, blah, blah." And I'm like, "No." I got set up with feeling victimized by all this, right? And I just said, "Laurie, you know you can try to do some of this stuff. It hasn't worked in the past for you but maybe you'll feel a little bit better." That's all you know, psychologically. I just wanted to psychologically feel a little bit better. Feel like I had some control or SAY over what is going on here with my body, right? Cause that's what I'm feeling and I'm going wait a minute, I'll talk to my body and I'll ask my body what it wants. I believe our bodies have consciousness.

Elizabeth: Yes.

Laurie: And you know, outside of what we have as our consciousness so it told me exactly what it wanted. (Chuckle) and I've been doing that lately, like with food. I've always kinda done it but I've been doing it very consciously with a mindfulness like ask my body, "What do you want to eat right now?" And if it tells me something, I go get it.

Elizabeth: That's perfect!! I'm so glad that you've been doing that cause I've been doing it too, my friend, Barbara, said that she just started doing that. She said she walked the other-last night-because her body decided that she wanted to walk to relieve some stress instead of going to eating or doing anything else. Her body chose to walk.

Laurie: Yeah! My body told me the other day it wanted a hamburger. Really badly. Like a Good hamburger so I found this place, it ended up a friend came to town and said, "Hey, let's get together. You wanna go grab a bite to eat?" I said, "Sure!" ended up in this place where they have really good hamburgers and it was the cheapest thing on the menu, there was all these good steaks and she was buying and I was like, "I want the hamburger." (Chuckle) and it was like they directed me right to where I could get-and it satisfied me. It was like, that's Exactly what I wanted. Ya know?

Elizabeth: That is Awesome!

Laurie: Yeah, yeah. So, you're doing it. It's funny, you know, maybe Jesus has got some info on this.

Elizabeth: Yes, definitely!

Laurie: There must because we are talking about it but ah, yeah, before I go in to start channeling, anything else that's going on? Isn't that interesting, Beth? And I really, I know I asked you a question and then I start talking but I really am grateful to you and these other friends of mine that are like, Reminding me that I Have the ability to heal myself and that I can, that there ARE you know, like the fairies and the different spirit realms that can help me.

Elizabeth: Yeah! That's cool!

Laurie: Yeah, yeah, I think it's really cool and maybe I'm this way and this is why we are doing all this and this is going to help people who are LIKE ME in the fact that, I don't Believe. You know a huge part of me doesn't Believe, but as we're doing this process and I'm connecting with people like you and a couple of other people. You guys just really Believe and I see it works for you and so it's helping me to start to Believe and to Trust. You know?

Elizabeth: You're gonna to be a walking proof that it works.

Laurie: Yeah! That's what I'm thinking. I'm thinking that this is what's really going to help people that are, you know, don't Believe in this stuff, and you know, yeah, that's probably why I'm bringing so much of this stuff on in my life.

Elizabeth: Yeah.

Laurie: Yeah, yeah and it's interesting so, but ah, yeah, anything else going on that we need to chat about before I start?

Elizabeth: No, I was just gonna, I was supposed to come next week and visit but I canceled the trip because I have a feeling like, "Don't go now." Like I just have a feeling, "Don't go now. Just wait." So, I'm waiting.

Laurie: OK. A friend of mine stopped by and I was talking to him about you cause we were going to do this and I was telling him how you're the person, and I always tell you this about your child-like faith, right?

Elizabeth: Yep.

Laurie: That you Trust and I said she's really helped me to develop that more and to tap into that in myself as well and so I was saying, "She's coming soon and I'd like for you to meet her." But you're not coming soon so it will be when you DO come and it's good that you're listening to what it is so for some reason you need to stay home.

Elizabeth: Yeah, and I don't know what it is (laughing)

Laurie: Yeah, and you may not know, you may not know ever, you know, it may be one of those things that, you-who knows.

Elizabeth: Yeah, and I wanted to come. I wanted to do work on you, I just, it's just something is saying, "Don't go right now." So.

Laurie: Beth, you're doing it at a distance and that was the thing that I got when I saw my friend because I wanted to go to her but she lives in Shawano so I'm like, it's not that much of a drive and I love going out to her house, she has a beautiful home with all these gardens and I really trust Jean, and I don't trust a lot of people to work on me because some of them could really be a mess, right? So I really trust Jean and I really trust you. So, when I told her that, I started to laugh. I said, "Oh, I suppose I'm gonna have to pay you for that too now?" She doesn't charge me—but um, "Now I owe you 60 bucks, right?" What I'm getting at is she said, "Laurie, I wish I had a conscience memory of that." I said, "I know you don't but I do and I think and I think I got that experience." and also with the fairies that came from you, I really believe that they came from you, Beth. So I think that if you, I know you wanna work on me but if for some reason that you're not supposed to be here, for some reason I couldn't get out to my friend, you can still work on me. I think that we're at that point. And I think that you can do whatever it is that you need to do at a distance and it will be just as effective. I mean, as soon as I saw the fairies, all I did was say to the pain, "What do you need? What is it that you want?" very gently, and out come all these fairies and immediately I felt YOU and that's what Beth has been trying to get me to open up to, these fairies. That's all I got was like Beth has been trying to and they've been there-you've been trying to do stuff, but I didn't open up to it until today or yesterday when this happened.

Elizabeth: When you're ready you will do it. Yeah.

Laurie: Right, right, so that's why I think it's OK. I mean, yeah, it's always better, it's always Nicer when somebody works on you directly because you get that connection but I think that we are in a place that you and I, and this other friend of mine, and others like us, we can do it at a distance. You know, I don't know even have to be aware of the fact that you're doing it, I'll just probably get it, like I said with the little fairies. I still do my part.

Elizabeth: Yeah, just ah, you know, I've been telling people to write those letters, you know those "no send" letters? Where you just write it to whomever, whatever is bothering you and then you burn it and then they, somehow the person doesn't read it but they still get the information so that's what we can be doing.

Laurie: Yeah, yes. Yes.

Elizabeth: Energetic-so it's just sending you the energy and sending you the feelings and that's what's workin.

Laurie: It has to be. And like I said, I was not open. I get so in these funks. I must be dealing with understanding what these funks, this like depression, unrespondancy, it's all connected to the pain and the cancer and all of that so I think I'm really trying to learn this stuff so I can also help other people. So I gotta be a little bit more serious about it in the sense of I've Got To Trust Here and that's what I got in all of this is that feeling of I'm Trusting more and I'm Believing more. I'm Believing, yeah this stuff IS for real. And I know it is but that part of me that doesn't Believe. It would be too cool for it to be real. You know?

Elizabeth: Yep. Yep. You're feeling natural feelings that so many other people feel when they're in that position where they have sickness and disease and all that other stuff. You're just going through it. So.

Laurie: Yep. So, it's pretty cool. OK, well, I'm gonna go under.

Elizabeth: Good for you! Good for you, Reiki Master! Finally working on yourself and all that too! (Laughing)

Laurie: That's exactly what I'm doing. I'm realizing that. Like talking to you and a few other people, you know, it's like, I do this for everyone else but I don't do it for myself out of Sheer Laziness. Bottom line. And it's like, "Why? Why am I not doing this for myself? I have all this information." And I'm starting to feel more powerful, you know not like powerful like, uugghhhh domineering but I'm starting to feel more confident with myself. I can handle all of this.

Elizabeth: You're Empowered. Yes!

Laurie: Empowered. That's it. I'm Empowered. Alright, I feel Jesus pushing me here. And uh, it's funny cause He's showing up to me, I'm seeing His face and His body with a white robe on and very very dark dark skin and hair. He's very dark. He's not shown up for me That Way in a long time, really. So, I just thought I'd tell you that because He's got this, you know, kinda the classic white robe from that time. But He's really really dark—the dark eyes-very penetrating dark eyes and like the facial hair is dark and His actual hair on His head is dark so and His skin is very—like this olive colored skin so He's very-and intense. Today I feel like he's got a real intensity. So, we'll see what ends up happening.

Elizabeth: Thank you for describing Him-Great!

Laurie: Yeah, and that's the first time and that's how He showed up when I was talking to Him about my pain and talking to Him, you know, just talking. So I found that interesting because and I don't know if He's ever really shown up looking that intense for me. It's usually that I just feel His energy. So, I'm gonna go so, let Him come through.

Elizabeth: OK.

Jesus: "Hello my friend. How are you today?"

Elizabeth: I'm good and yourself?

Jesus: "Quite well, quite well. Very Excited to be here. To talk with you. There is a lot of promise in what is happening on your planet. That is why I am excited. That's why I have come here. That is why the Medium she felt me with such intensity. There has been such a dramatic change or shift in these energies. You had some very-because it's all part of the process-we've talked about this-these energies that were cleaning out-you know, spring cleaning energies that came through and humans were—all of you-were feeling this quite intensely. Now what has happened is there is this wave of Freshness coming in but with— what happened is all of that cleaning of those emotions-that's energy, right? And everybody-so many were doing the work that needed to be done for themselves that to not get rid of, not to let go, but to Transform those energies. Those emotional energies and to Understand them. So what happened is the Power of That Transformation is what all of you will now begin to be able to benefit from. So it's like you're all the-say all the sadness that one had, rather than avoiding it or continuing to feel it they said, "Let me understand this." and went in and Cleaned it out one more time and understood even more so that energy of sadness became an energy of Knowing, of Understanding of the opposite-an energy of Belonging, an energy of being part of One. So that is what's there and so much easier at this time for ALL of you to tap into because you continually do what is necessary. You get the guidance. Which is very important when you speak with us, when we come through-whether it be me or another. And many like you, and the Medium, and those that you share these messages with-take them seriously and do what we give as guidance. You Follow Through and then that is why this is such a powerful time for everyone because you are all Actually Paying Attention And Believing. Not all of course because you will never have all-that's impossible-but you have many. That is why I am excited because of the possibilities that are now available for all of you. So yes, yes, it is an exciting time. What do you feel about all of this?"

Elizabeth: I have been having my heart racing for the last probably like 3 hours and I can't seem to calm it down. Is that why? (Laughing)

Jesus: "Yes, yes. Because I have been-obviously you are part of this experience and you are in your human form which you view as being very limited-although you are experimenting-we are Happy to say-with yourself as an Unlimited Being. You are practicing it-you're going beyond your physical form-so practicing, understanding your unlimitedness, in a limited form. So you knew I was coming through and I am full of excitement so your heart racing, you already knew what was going to occur here, as it is with the Medium, as it is with those who are listening in and are connected to you and the Medium-anyone that you will be connected with today whether they hear this directly or not. So, yes, and you know our connection goes very deep. And you know, you know, that you opened yourself up to this at the right time so that you and I could communicate through the Medium and could get some work done here-I will say it that way to put it into your terms but actually to put together something that will be of great value for those who have the opportunity to read these words or hear these words and this guidance and take it as a little journey for themselves as well."

Elizabeth: Excellent.

Jesus: "Yes. So that is why. You know because we are so connected, your heart was racing so things are calming down a little bit, it was just so exciting to come together again here because part of the excel oration of it is I'm waiting to come through the Medium and you are sending out your energy-cause you help bring me in you understand. When you are-I want that you understand that you are part of this process more than what you are fully aware of. You think that it's the Medium who brings me in and yes she does, she opens herself up in such a way so that she can use her physical form to communicate with you but you are calling me in as well. Your racing heart was just a consequence of the energy you were sending out as though you were giving me a phone call. Or calling me out on the street, "Hey Jesus! Jesus! Come out and play! Can you come out and play?"

Elizabeth: (Laughing)

Jesus: "That was the—and plus you get excited. You enjoy speaking with me. So that added the excel oration in your heart rate."

Elizabeth: Well, I'm glad that was having to do with you cause I was trying to pinpoint when did this start today? And I was thinking, well I was back at the library so I didn't know if it belonged to somebody else or what was going on so."

Jesus: "Yes. When you see that it belongs to someone else you want to get rid of it but no, this one's yours. But it's a good one. Yes. Don't go trying to give it to someone else because it's not theirs."

Elizabeth: Alright, Awesome! So, is this, the racing heart, is this kind of equivalent to when my cheeks turn on fire with you? (Laughing)

Jesus: "Yes, yes, yes. You see, you're also-one thing that I am going to tell you now and I think we can do this with confidence without you being too uncomfortable because we have shared many things. When you were-you and I walked the planet together here-when I was Here on the Planet and you were with me, you had-you and I had a very special relationship-as I had with many-and this relationship went beyond just a friendship or a teacher relationship-there was a you would call it a sexual relationship between the two of us and a very deep love. That's why your cheeks also turn red because your body—your cellular memory-is bringing back those memories of when you would get excited at seeing me and the sharing of the love that we had for each other."

Elizabeth: WOW. (Laughing) Whaa . . . WOW! That's . . . . um . . . . I . . . I'm flattered? (I mean what do you say to that??!)

Jesus: "You should not be. I could say the same. I am flattered. I will tell you. You were quite a bit younger than me and there was, this was, what you and I shared was before I, when we were very young we lived in the same village. And you were the daughter of a friends of my parents. So when we were young we would spend much time together but I did not really, because you were part of this whole close family and friends, but you were close to 10 years younger than me. It was a very brief time and your parents and my—did not want you to be with me because when things started to get-you see I was known as a rebel-I was considered a rebel and I was considered by many to be trouble and they did not want you with me and therefore there is this sense of unrequited love on your part that you could not be with me so you still become very like a young girl with an infatuation when you are-there is a part of you that feels that when you contact me and that is part of that cellular memory within you. I find it very-it helps here-and I would suggest to you that you explore that because remember everything is energy. All emotion. Everything is energy and just because that is something that belongs to—it's origins are in a time that you are no longer consciously aware of right? Does not mean that the energy does not still exist-it still exists and it's very much a part of who you are and it can give you great insight into many things. If you, when you feel your cheeks on fire or that excitement with your heart going and start to recognize these things are being connected To Me and our relationship and allowing yourself to explore that so that you can get more information. And this is something here personal between you and I, but again, many will read this or hear these words-everyone can do this. It is about becoming aware and mindful of your emotions. Whether they pertain to now or another time. Let me ask you this. Have you ever had a Feeling that you were not able to identify and came from nowhere and it was something that you could not-had no association-it wasn't like anger or sadness but you still had a Feeling. Has that ever happened to you?"

Elizabeth: Yeah, I had a feeling when Dale Earnhardt passed away. I had felt him, I felt his death. Yeah. Along that lines? Or just lots of other feelings? Yeah I get those too.

Jesus: "When those things happen, for you to really become the Master of what you came here to Master, you would want to stop and allow-because that energy is moving through you and it's messing with something on some level in your own system that understands it and recognizes it. So because of that, you want to stop and Feel it moving through and see what information that it can be giving you, OK?"

Elizabeth: OK

Jesus: "That's for everyone. Maybe it is another Being who is trying to communicate with you and has information so, that you, like you said, when someone died, you were able to feel-experience the dying through this person. Now, Everyone has this ability. And it will be part of the way say, I don't know maybe 50 to 100 years from now-I cannot say exactly cause again, who knows, but this is the direction that the humans are going. In that, which you call your ascension or 5th dimensional reality, you will be communicating so much with just that sending of energy. OK. And you'll call it feeling or emotion but you want to know, "Is this mine or does this belong to someone else?" Cause it's going on already, it's just that humans don't recognize it or understand it. They're too much in their heads, right? But to be in this 5th dimensional reality there will be communication that it will be very telepathic. Now, I was listening to what you were saying with the Medium and her experiences with the pain and the energy and all of that. Now isn't that interesting she's been in pain many times, but has she now just chosen to become aware and serious about how to use energy, it's because the time is right. She couldn't—it's always been there-for-and others have used energy to heal and to do a number of things, right? And many have understood energy but in the case of the Medium, we'll use her as an example, just so others know that this is their-this could possibly be their journey as well-similar, OK? Not exactly the same. So she was not ready because of various factors in her own life experience so she had much of the information but put it on a back shelf or on the back burner and as she progressed through her different experiences And the energies that are prevalent in the planet, she had to clean house, she had certain things that were still there that without cleaning house, getting rid, when I say that, you know I'm meaning taking care of emotional-emotions that are in your system that you'll no longer serve-are no longer serving you-so she had to go through that in order to be able to use the energy in the ways in which she will fully be benefiting from them at a conscious level because she wanted to be able to do this consciously even if she was doing it unconsciously up until this point. I know this may seem all a little muddled but does this sort of make sense to you?"

Elizabeth: It all makes sense to me. I was hoping that she would. I knew that I had suggested her working, doing the Reiki on herself at one point, but she thought it might be too hard to do. I just figured she would probably do it on her own when she was ready, so.

Jesus: "Exactly. And there are others. So, let's go back to use that as an example. What she did had-she has the opportunity now to be aware consciously of what is going on. Two individuals, you and another friend of hers, were working on her, have suggested many of the same things, both of you, and she heard them, stored them in her memory bank, and when she was ready to use them, because she got to the right place where she would be Able to, it's like learning to drive a car, you can't—or learning to use something, you need—a car's a good example. You can't just jump in, somebody gives you a key and you know nothing about it, right? So, she had to prepare herself. But she became consciously aware of what goes on in that-it is the astral plane—what's going on that often, that most individuals do not see or are aware of. That is what is changing. To have that awareness. Of someone, say in the case, she understood that you had sent the fairies. But you sent those fairies a long time ago so she was not able to open up to them until today-even though they were still there working on her, she was able to open up even more to them but to see it in a conscious way. To have the memory of it to be able to share that with others. Now she is ready. And so are you. This is why I'm bringing this up. So are you. So you must continue to do these things for each other so that you can Understand Really how energy works cause it's very beautiful and it's a very interesting experience so it all ties in with everything we have been talking about in terms of self-healing the physical form, the emotional body and such."

Elizabeth: OK, I will continue to work on that then. We had been talking about, a lot of people have been suggesting and I suggest it too, like if you are having issues with somebody you write the person a letter but you don't give it to them, you just burn it because they WILL get that information. So that's basically the same thing, correct?

Jesus: "Yes, yes, absolutely. Because it's energy. And they'll get what they are Capable of getting. OK? The rest will be stored consciously. OK. This is to explain. Back-this is what happened with the Medium. They are not aware of—so you write a letter. We'll use that example. You write a letter to someone that you feel you need to clear something out of YOUR OWN system. It's not about doing it to get the other person to hear what you have to say, it's about you being aware of something that's in your Own Body System that Needs Addressing. That Needs To Be Acknowledged. So you write this, and the individual that you are writing this to, maybe you feel they are responsible for something and you wanna get it out but the whole time, really as we have talked about-and you know this-they are only playing out a role that you have given them, OK? So they are just the catalyst for you to take care of something in your emotional system. So you write this letter and if you write it with the intention of getting that other person to "get it" and understand, well, it could happen or not, you don't know where that other person is at. But if you write it with the intention of wanting to be curious about what these Emotions are for you and what do YOU need to know here? What is it about all of this that you need understanding and awareness of, right? When you do it with that intention and then burn it, what then happens—all of that is energy and different forms of energy because as you are writing it the anger may come through, sadness may come through and maybe even things of a fondness for somebody that may come through-all sorts of emotion come through which is energy. So you burn this and as you burn it with ritual and you give it to whomever in the Spirit world and ask that this be cared for, one other thing that is important-that if you do not want that to be part of your experience anymore than you say, "Never to return to me." or "To return to me in a different form." Right? So this is what's been going on. So the other person will then receive because you've had the measured focus, right? They will then, in their bodily system, basically, just to make it very academic let's say-there is a pocket or an area in the bodily system, where this information-this energy-because that's what it is-these emotional experiences-you've written the letter so fondness, love, anger, hate, revenge-all of these emotions go into this individuals energy field. OK? So things that that individual is Capable of Understanding and Connecting With will then be something that this person will become aware of, OK? So, they will, if they are somebody who has worked on himself, will feel it and say and do something about. If he is Not capable of understanding because there is not an awareness, it gets pocketed in these areas within his bodily system. That's WHY when you HATE someone you CAN harm them in that way. So when you send True Hate to someone, it Can reach that place."

Elizabeth: Wow. Yeah, I believe that.

Jesus: "Yes, so it's all very intricate. So it's important that you—when you do this-to make yourself responsible for the emotions that are coming From You towards this other person. Because really if you must-it's about you taking 100% responsibility for everything, OK? And as I said, if love can heal-think about the power of hate. If you are sending hate to someone, how you can harm that individual as well as yourself."

Elizabeth: If the individual knows that someone is sending them hate, should—I would think asking for protection would be a good idea then?

Jesus: "Yes, BUT to truly be in a state of Empowerment-because that's what you-when you-and there's nothing wrong with that-BUT what I would Suggest, rather than turning your back on the hate, I would turn and accept—take the hate IN with Compassion and Love. And when you do that"

Elizabeth: OH that's what I! OK. (I interrupted, oops)

Jesus: "Yes?"

Elizabeth: I was gonna say, that's what I did with my aunt. When she sent me something negative, I did that.

Jesus: "Perfect. Cause then you send it and you take it, you receive it with Compassion and Love, and you are part of that process—because you're always part of the process-but you're even-but your part then becomes an elevated process of Compassion and Love that you can—because it's Energy-that's all that it is-and on the opposite side of that spectrum of hate, there is Love."

Elizabeth: OK

Jesus: "So when you take it in with Compassion and Love, you are then able to make it BE that. And then you assist the other person too in finding that within themselves."

Elizabeth: So I'm gonna ask, why then, when I was pregnant with Arron, did I have, I felt the protection of Archangel Michael because I thought that I needed protection I guess from my mom's side of the family, so.

Jesus: "Yes, so. Why you needed protection? That's your question?"

Elizabeth: Yeah, was I just unable to . . . do I wanna say, "Fight it" and Michael protected me then?

Jesus: "Yes, think about it. Back then, in your time that you are living within this "time frame" here, you have learned a lot more. Your confidence and your abilities to do things have advanced. At that time, you were not as advanced as you are right now. Plus you were in a weakened state. You were going through an emotional journey that was weakening you cause that can happen. So, that's where you went, "OK, you know what? I can't do this right now because I'm not Feeling it but I Can ask for protection and I will do that. I will ask for protection and then that is the 2nd best thing that I can do for myself and for them.""

Elizabeth: OK, alright.

Jesus: "Because if you were to allow it just to come in and create havoc within your own system, well, then, then that's what most people do-they just let it-the energies come in-and create havoc within them."

Elizabeth: OK. Yeah, I'm just-I'm thinking back that yeah, I was, I'm much more empowered now. I feel WAY different than I did then and that was only almost a year-it was a year ago-so, (laughing) OOOH, imagine 5 years from now!! (laughter)

Jesus: "Exactly, exactly. But that's just it. You, there was much that you make-and everyone is like this and you each have your own journeys-but you specifically, you went through a particular journey at that time that needed your attention. That brought—you know—you were with child. You were also dealing with the Assisting in your mother leaving her physical form-you knew where that was Headed and you-there was much that you were trying to accomplish with her and there was much that you were trying to accomplish for yourself at that time. So that is why you have spirit guides and there ARE the angels, like Archangel Michael, he is There for that reason. To say OK, right now you have your focus and your attention needs to be Here and anything coming from outside would just be too much of a weight. So lets put some protection around you so you can continue to do what you need to do and then once you are through this process then come back out and you can go back to taking it in with Love and Compassion."

Elizabeth: That makes sense.

Jesus: "Yes."

Elizabeth: Let's talk about our body and how our body will talk to us. I'm curious as to the care for our physical bodies.

Jesus: "Soo, yes. Remember that your body, even though you, there are different—let's say awarenesses of consciousness, OK? You're body is a very intricate-not complex-well, it is complex but very-it's the connections and the energies are all very precise yet your body is able to function without so much that you're-it's really an amazing apparatus—it's an amazing vehicle that you have at your disposition for your journey here on the planet. Now, your body, as you said, has it's own awareness, it's own consciousness. That you are inhabiting it, you want to respect it, OK? So when you are-as you were discussing prior to me coming in-how asking your body what it Needs and what it Wants and it will tell you but what is important is to listen to it. Because maybe your body IS telling you to eat a pint of ice cream and then, saying that, maybe there's something in that that needs to be done but you need to be Sure that that's what it is and it's not telling you that because it's something more debilitating. Again, how do you tell the difference? When you ask your body, "What do I want?" Say your body says, "A pint of chocolate ice cream." Right? Or a whole chocolate cake or something very much you think, "Oh that can't possibly be but my body's telling me to do it, so let me do it." How do you tell if that's REALLY what it is that you want? You Have To get quiet and Listen. Does it make you feel lighter or does it make you feel heavier? If it makes you feel lighter, it is YOUR

TRUTH. So, ask your body, "What do you want?" and it says, "A pint of ice cream." Then you pause and if you feel lighter, than that's what your body needs. If you feel heavier, you know it is from—it is generated by one of your human addictions or emotions. Does that make sense?"

Elizabeth: Perfect sense.

Jesus: "So, again, practicing that, being aware, and like I said, there will be times when you think, "Well, why would I want that? I don't like that." or "That doesn't seem to fit." You MUST pay attention. It's what Truth is for you and your body. What it needs at that moment. And you will THEN be able to strengthen your body and USE that body as a Tool for your Own Expansion. Because that's how you do it, you can Advance Through to the next stage-for all of you who are in human form—you do it through this physical form and through your journey on planet Earth. That's how it's done."

Elizabeth: So by taking care and eating the right foods and stuff it would be more helpful then?

Jesus: "Yes. Absolutely. So, again, you need to ask your body that, "What do you need?" Maybe your body needs a fat. Maybe your body Needs that pint of ice cream. It's not bad. It's only-again, you Must Understand, is this truly—"Does it make me feel lighter or heavier?" And if it's lighter than it's Truth for you and in that moment you need it."

Elizabeth: I would think, "If I ate this pint of ice cream, how will I feel After I've eaten it?" And if my answer is, "I'm gonna feel really bad." Then I probably won't eat it. (Laughing)

Jesus: "Exactly. Because then you know it's been generated by some sort of NEED at the very Human Level. That it's not something that is Truth for you but there could be a time that there was a pint of ice cream, and I use that just as an example, because you want to be Aware and not use your-what you have given Consideration To and Value To and Already Judged as being good or bad, right or wrong. You've already judged that pint of ice cream as being something that is not good for you. (flip tape)

Elizabeth: I gotta repeat that for a second cause my tape had to flip. So your body and your soul knows that you need that at that moment. OK.

Jesus: "Yes, yes. OK? And I use something like a pint of ice cream because most humans do not look at that as being something that's a good thing to do. That's why I brought it up. More than likely, your body is not going to need a pint of ice cream but it could happen. It could really happen. Maybe there is something in it that your body at that moment needs to Experience. Maybe the coldness, maybe the experience of eating it and feeling that disgusted feeling that one might get when they've eaten too much of something too sweet. Or maybe they need the sweetness. You don't know. But that's where it's up to you to become very Mindful of yourselves, you're eating, and talk to your bodies and they will give you the information that you need. Always. Yes."

Elizabeth: Alright. OK. Where do we want to go from here?

Jesus: "Do you have questions for me?"

Elizabeth: I DO have questions for you. I kinda wanted today, I didn't have Denise come over today because I DID want it to be sort of personal. Just to kinda find out who I was and you've—clearly you've done-telling me that we had a relationship back when you were Christ- holy cow that's huge!

Jesus: "Yes."

Elizabeth: Sigh. I think that'll be good enough for now. I wanna ask you, are you aware of what I'm putting out on Facebook because I had to put, I kinda made a comment about a legal case, the Trayvon Martin and George Zimmerman thing today and I was thinking that you guys wanted me to put that on there so . . . are you aware of what I'm doing on there?

Jesus: "Yes. Remember that you communicate with us So Much. So the ones that you are communicating with, of course we are there Responding to your communication and communicating with you as well. So we don't so much get the words as get the Intention from the

Vibration of what you are putting there. So you could be putting, as an example, you could be putting, "Love, Love, Love, Love, Love, Love, Love, Love, Love, Oh I Love You, I Love You." but really you're feeling, "You annoy me." and what We get is the vibration of: You annoy me, and Dishonesty and Frustration will be the energy that we get, OK? So, what you wrote there, we did get. A feeling of Injustice-which is OK-and a NEED—so I do not know the words-I'm telling you what we-I'm trying to put into words what we got from your communication cause there were several of us who watch over you-and the other was a Need to Find Compassion for this situation. So you were striving for Compassion with those words. So that was what came to us in what you wrote. It was not Anger, but there was Frustration and this NEED For Others-and That is something that you may want to look at-because you cannot make another think or do anything. Again, you are going outside of-you need to FULLY stay within yourself. Not go outside of yourself and try to get another to change."

Elizabeth: OK. I just wanted to put it out there so they could look at it a different way. I don't know.

Jesus: "Absolutely, absolutely."

Elizabeth: Was I sticking my nose in other people's business when I shouldn't of?

Jesus: "OK, We, Again, we don't have those kind of judgments. What we see is that some have become irritated, others have ignited-you've been part of igniting this Passion about Injustice here-because there was a great Injustice done here. This is why it all happened. This is why these two individuals Volunteered-one volunteered to be assassinated so to speak-because he was assassinated. And the other volunteered to do that so that all those who are involved in this-and that means you and anyone who knows anything about it-feels anything about it-is to Explore what Humanity is in regards to Injustice and such. Because that is a common theme in your existence. It is something that you are all working on understanding. Once again, you know, Injustice. How Humanity-Humans are cruel and unfair to each other for the sake of Many things like greed or such."

Elizabeth: OK. Thank you for saying that. That clears up a lot of stuff.

Jesus: "Yes. So whatever you Did in regards to this was part of what you felt compelled to do. There is no right or wrong. It is what you felt at that moment that you needed to do."

Elizabeth: OK. You answered a question of that they volunteered to do that. So, do we have a plan then when we come down here? You mentioned the other day that Laurie had "put in writing" so do we have a specific plan then as far as things-as to what's going to happen to us then?

Jesus: "Yes. It's-you could call it a blueprint. You know, so there are things that you—say you sign up for. So, this young man, he signed up for playing out this role so that he had things at a intimate level with his own mother is demonstrating great-how is-here is a perfect example-she is showing she has lost her son in a very unjust way, there is much here that can be said about that yet her words-not just her words-the Energy that she is emitting is one of Compassion and Love and Understanding even though she is feeling great sadness. So she is also an example. They are examples to teach humans about turning the other cheek essentially."

Elizabeth: That kinda was a question that my husband had. He wanted to know, where is the line between judgment and holding people accountable. Is it safety?

Jesus: "It's a difficult one. Because again, you must—as humans you have your laws, your rules, your standards. And then you are all Divine Beings. All of you. So you are in this where each Moment of your lives you are having to have to be connected to that Inner Guidance that will Always give you the answer that is Truth for you in that moment and for you and you alone. Again, you cannot find it for another. Well, you can see it for another—or sense it for another-but your responsibility is to yourself and not to another. In that regards. So your husband, the line between, you said the line between judgment and what was the other?"

Elizabeth: Holding people accountable.

Jesus: "Holding people accountable is—again, it's a gray area. It's a blurry area. Where is it? That's why those who get into fields where they must enforce these human laws are usually very cut and dry people. This is what it is and this is what you do. Because if they allow themselves for a moment to question individual cases, they would become connected with the individuals on an emotional level and it would not allow them their-in the way it is designed in the moment-not allow them the opportunity to maintain a certain amount of control. This is about control. You will be moving beyond this. These are all control mechanisms and this is why you will be seeing Much More of these experiences of Injustice. So, holding someone accountable, ultimately, that is the responsibility of society. You are living in a world that has these laws so you must just always go back to Trusting that everything is in Divine Order. And I know that sometimes you want to slap us and say, "This is crazy!" When we say these things but really, it's just-so your husband who asks this question-if he can just-when he's pondering these things-take a deep breath and connect. Because he has this ability. We Know him. That he can connect and say, "OK, I Trust that there is something here I may not fully understand but that it is ALL serving a purpose. It's ALL being taken care of." And when he can Connect to That Energy-because that is Faith and Trust, right? He will calm down and he will stop feeling that there needs to be anything changed or anything different. And this is the direction you are moving into. This is that 5th dimensional realm where you will be existing where these kind of realities are-where you will be existing in that way-but right now you are not existing in that way. You are existing with strong rules and trying to fit human emotions and humans into certain boxes and that will be changing where the boxes will have to be carved out to fit the human in the 5th dimensional reality."

Elizabeth: When you came through with the excitement, was there anything specific that happened or is it just as individuals that we're all working on it together that made you so excited today?

Jesus: "Because I have been Observing the Progress that has been going on on your planet. The entire planet and yes, there are many areas that could be different some may say, "Well there are wars here and there is injustice over there." but it's all moving, as I said at the beginning, So Many Of You have worked at Understanding and Becoming Aware of your emotional state. What serves you and what no longer serves you. Releasing that which no longer serves you to be transformed into the energy that is it's opposite so to speak and so what occurred is the energy that's coming in-it's a Wave of energy of freshness. It's the best way I can describe it. It's new. It's the sewing of the future. It is your carte blanche, it's blank right? But it's full of energy of creation. That's the best way that you have as a group of people have-because of what you have done-this wave of energy is even Greater Than it would have been Because of everything that you've done. So that's why I am excited. I am excited to bring that information to you and I really, you see, I see everything but I see things-when I come through in this way-I see things More with the perspective of a human because I am bringing myself back into that perspective of humanity. Even though I am always watching out over you and observing, when I come through in this way, through the Medium or someone else, or communicate with you, I'm having a human moment as well. So, I was able to see the possibility in this wave that is coming in of creation. So that's why I was so excited. And that's what you were feeling because you are aware of this as well. Does that make sense?"

Elizabeth: Yeah, that makes sense.

Jesus: "So when you brought it up again, I got all excited again because the wave is much Bigger than was anticipated months ago because we did not know how many were going to actually do what was necessary to be done for this to come in. You know, when you clean something out, they say the Universe does not like a void, right? So, when you clean something out you make room for something else and that's what ended up happening. So the possibilities here have increased At Least 50 fold."

Elizabeth: Wow! That's huge.

Jesus: "Yes, because many are getting the information that they did not get before. Through computers and such. So the technology is assisting in getting out this information, more people are connecting with each other. More like-minded. So more individuals are getting the guidance that they So desperately need to move forward and to make the changes and the advancements that are possible now."

Elizabeth: Wow, that's great!

Jesus: "Yes. So that is why I am so excited. And then I am excited always to speak with you."

Elizabeth: Oh thanks :)

Jesus: "Because we are so-as you are with me-because we are so close."

Elizabeth: Is . . . uh, what do I wanna say . . . . It's just that for what you said to me is going to be something that I'm going to be thinking about a lot. So did, when you went through the Crucifixion was I aware of that?

Jesus: "Yes. Yes. You were not-you really were not present-you were present in a way because of who you are you were able to essentially teleport yourself but your parents did not allow you to go and witness any of it. Even though they agreed with the Crucifixion because they saw me as being-let's not say they agreed with the Crucifixion, they felt that that was wrong, they knew me, they felt that it was a very Cruel thing to do but they felt that I needed to be stopped because I was preaching things that for them-and doing things-that were very Radical and I was misunderstood by your parents. Your father was a very wonderful man but was—misunderstood many things-was misguided in his life."

Elizabeth: OK.

Jesus: "So, he prevented you from being present, but you having the abilities that you have of transporting yourself, you Were There in Spirit so to speak."

Elizabeth: So, where do I-I don't wanna say, what's my origin. Someone referred to me as an Earth Angel the other day and she said she saw my wings so . . . where?

Jesus: "Yes, you come from a realm that is equated to the Angelic Realm. The thing is, is that you're not an Angel because that would Limit you too much. If you-Angels are here and yes they can incarnate into human form and such and someone using the term Earth Angel fits you because of what you are able to do but you are from a realm that is much Older-let's say that the Angel Realm was Born From this realm that you are originated from and this realm has-there are many that are on your planet at this time that originate from this realm, and you are one of them, and you have a very strong connection with this section-yes, I guess section-of Angels-who were created specifically to assist humanity. Because there are many different levels of Angels. There are the Archangels, there are the Seraphim, there are the Cherubim, there are many different realms let's say of Angels. So these were essentially created to assist humanity. And that's why you know them so well and why you're so drawn to them."

Elizabeth: Now, the Fairies, when I suggested to Laurie working with the Fairies, like, Fairies have only really been brought to my attention in the last couple of months so I was surprised that Fairies really do exist. (Laughing) Honestly.

Jesus: "Yes. And they were a good one you suggested them for her because she has a fascination and an appreciation and also the desire to know that they exist as well. Another would want Gnomes or another might want something else but she loves the Fairies as you do, so yes. Now you know that they Do exist."

Elizabeth: WOW! So do Unicorns exist on a different level than too?

Jesus: "Yes."

Elizabeth: So basically it seems like all of our "Fairy Tale" creatures all exist.

Jesus: "Yes. Anything that you can imagine exists. Yes."

Elizabeth: That is cool (Laughing)

Jesus: "Yes it is, isn't it? It's quite beautiful really."

Elizabeth: Yeah it's neat. Oooh! I wanted to ask you, are you aware of when, say the cartoons like The Simpsons and South Park, they do animation of you, and are you aware of that and do you find it funny? (Giggles)

Jesus: "Let's say it's not that we are aware when these things are done in the case of me. Yes, I do find it funny because I don't take offense so they are trying to use irony and my-the symbolism of who I am-because that's not really who I am, but they use that to send a message forth and that's OK. So, I don't get too upset by too much really."

Elizabeth: I find it really funny.

Jesus: "Yes."

Elizabeth: Cause they had you with a pair of binoculars and it said, "Jesus is watching." and I thought that was funny. (Laughing)

Jesus: "Yes, yes. So you see? They are,you know, making-because it's important that you do not be so serious. Mankind gets too serious so it's important that you are not so serious and that's why it's delightful that these things are done. And if somebody takes some image of me and draws a mustache on it and glasses, that's OK too. And gives me missing teeth-that's OK too. I do not care. Cause it's not-it-you have to remember everything is energy. With what intention was it done? And I cannot be harmed by anything-nor can you. Only if you allow it."

Elizabeth: OK, now I'm gonna ask, so when I was transcribing the rest of the stuff the other night, everything was fine. Until I got to the question about the garments. And then I smelled this really nasty like dirty sock odor and I smelled it and it wasn't until I realized, "Oh, this could be something bad." Like, I don't wanna say evil or whatever but it didn't smell right. So then I said a protection prayer and then the smell went away. So, was that a legitimate presence of something bad there?

Jesus: "Well, again, we really want to direct you and get you to stop-to redirect you let's say-in your usage of good and bad. Something that you want to just be aware of. There was something there that did not serve a purpose and presented itself as a smelly sock so that you would know to not let it come into your presence. So it wasn't bad. Somebody may need that bad energy for an experience. And I'm bringing this up with you because that is what you are working on right now. So that you Really let go of ALL judgment and you see everything as just being that which it is. It's very important that you do that. It's part of what you are learning right now. And for many-is what they are learning right now. To let go of the judgment of Everything so that you can really Rise Up and become-moving into that 5th dimensional reality-that's what I'll keep stressing here."

Elizabeth: OK. Because I caught myself at the dentist office today. The lady was-we were talking about discipline and I was saying I was disciplining my almost 1 year old so then she said there was a lot of parents that don't discipline, they just let their kids do whatever they want-and I caught myself. I was so happy I caught myself! Because I thought, "OK, like obviously this child Chose this parent because they knew that they would lack in the discipline because they could learn something from that." So I was pretty happy with myself.

Jesus: "Yes, there you go. See? Instead of saying something to this person. Is that what you are saying?

Elizabeth: Yes, instead of adding to the "oh, they're being a bad parent" you know, this and that.

Jesus: "Right. Right."

Elizabeth: I stopped myself, so.

Jesus: "Yes, good, good and so you have an example and that is what we are talking about with you."

Elizabeth: Yeah. Anything else that we wanna talk about today? I've been watching that show, that Twin Peaks show because that was from my dream and I've been getting a WHOLE lotta stuff from that and I'm taking notes. And they were talking about schizophrenia and what's the purpose of schizophrenia? What do you learn from that? (now that I'm thinking about it-maybe they didn't use that word . . . Anyhow)

Jesus: "Well, that is a very intricate-that has many aspects to it. Someone Choosing schizophrenia is looking for-some may have it as a means of-not redemption-of-so schizophrenia in someone may be the result of something that came through the family lines. OK? A family lineage. Someone may have murdered someone-cause it's usually connected to that-so or the soul of the one who is a schizophrenic may have been the same one who did the murder back there in this family line but let's say it is passed down through generations and when it reaches the 7th

generation is when it manifests as schizophrenia. That is One of the reasons that someone has schizophrenia. So what they are trying to do in that is to-because when they committed the murder they judged what they did and then that judgment came through and resulted in schizophrenia several years later and that's what many different diseases and such are connected to. Something done in your family line. What else it's trying to is-when someone chooses schizophrenia is about control. Understanding control and not having control and the false sense of control is another aspect of it. So it is, it's a very complex one but those are some of the general guidelines for it, yes."

Elizabeth: OK. Now I'm gonna ask a question for Denise even though she's not here. Is it possible for someone that has passed away to come back into the body of someone else?

Jesus: Big Sigh "This is more frequent at another time. I think what you are wanting to know is they are called walk ins. So, what will happen is that someone who is having a journey here may find it too difficult. The soul-or the spirit is actually what it is—finds it's journey too difficult so the spirit of someone else who has died will come in and take over for the spirit of that individual so that they can finish the journey so that the soul can still benefit from the experience. This is becoming less and less common but they are called walk ins. But that is all done with permission from all involved. Someone just taking over, no. Not possible."

Elizabeth: OK. I told her only with permission. OK. Alright. Um, let's see. Boy is there anything else that you wanna talk about?

Jesus: "No."

Elizabeth: Oh, the ways that people listen to your answers can be in many different ways so I was talking to girl, she got her answers from license plates but she did admit that she did need to listen more so um.

Jesus: "That's what is going on when I spoke of when we talked about my excitement coming in. This chapter here in this will be to let people know that Listening, Paying Attention, that's where you're in this wave of now. Those who have cleaned house now they're in this wave of being able to pay more attention to the messages that are coming with more clarity and more depth."

Elizabeth: OK. In many different ways so OK.

Jesus: "Yes, absolutely."

Elizabeth: Cause a lot of times I do get feelings and then I go, "I don't know where this is coming from but I'm just gonna wait and I'll ask, so."

Jesus: "Exactly, exactly. And that's what's going on right now. It's always been there. But this is the focus of the time period that you are in-you will be in this for many many years. This is where you are evolving. You're letting go of certain things and moving into others. And this will be a state of Being for humanity. This is, as I said before, where you will be able to communicate with each other without being in each others presence and Being Aware that you are communicating with each other. Like in the case of you sending the Fairies to your friend and she was aware of this gift that you sent her."

Elizabeth: OK. I'm trying to clear out my feelings-like I've really been thinking about my mom so much and if it's part of a plan and then she acted that way towards me. That I feel good about myself after this-I'm just-does she feel like she's sorry-even though she's playing a role for me?

Jesus: "No. She doesn't feel sorry because she sees the bigger picture. So to feel sorry for you-it's just not part of the vocabulary that she has where she is at. It's just not part of it."

Elizabeth: OK. Alright. I don't know if that even makes sense to you.

Jesus: "No, absolute sense and it's something that-see you experienced that so that you can Fully Understand it and bring that type of healing to individuals who have suffered with that kind of parenting or parental or Lack of parental guidance and love and nurturing so they-cause this is something that is very fundamental—mostly in your country— that your country is always so-the example. So, you were, the lack of nurturing, you could have been victimized by it or you can understand it in this greater way. And when you understand it—when you have the big picture-there Is No feeling sorry for you because really, why would she want to feel sorry for you? You Gained incredible abilities and skills through this process. By what she did."

Elizabeth: Does she . . . would she feel sorry for the things that she said that were lies about me? Or is that part of the bigger picture then too?

Jesus: "No. EVERYTHING was part of the bigger picture. Everything."

Elizabeth: OK. Alright. I'm just I'm sad about it. I don't know why I should be but.

Jesus: "That's OK. You want to go through and experience that sadness. What that means for you. OK? Because that's part of that cleaning-you're always cleaning house, OK?—you always have something. There's just bigger times when it's greater house cleaning than others. But what you want to do here is go into that sadness. Remember that it was something that you came here to learn and experience so that is what you were doing so take it and use it so that you can understand and experience it and fully benefit from it."

Elizabeth: OK. Alright.

Jesus: "Don't just try to say, "Oh, I shouldn't be feeling sad and sorry for myself blah, blah, blah." No, No, you are feeling sad and sorry for yourself so go and find out what that has to tell you. What do you need to know there? Go and find that out."

Elizabeth: OK. I think we'll do one more question and then we can get off. Someone wanted to know, "According to the Bible, children are God's gift. Why is it that marriages in God's (church), sometimes it's difficult to have a child and why?" I mean, I could answer this but I figured it would probably be better coming from you.

Jesus: "So why is someone who . . . I'm a little confused."

Elizabeth: Fertility problems. Why would someone have fertility problems if they got married in, well, it doesn't even matter if they got married in a church,why do people have fertility problems?

Jesus: "Again, what are they here to learn?"

Elizabeth: Exactly.

Jesus: "What are they here to learn. Again, I would advise anyone that has something like that, I felt your question had the energy of someone who feels very much a victim and that is where I would go with this and say, "OK, this energy of feeling like a victim, what do I need to know about it?" But I feel like this person yet isn't—not that they are not capable-but that they haven't got the tools yet so I would suggest that she sit quietly and talk to us, again, and just ask and just be curious and want to know, What does the fertility, the lack of it, or however she wants to phrase it, what does it want to tell her? What does it want her to know? Just like the Medium. She sat down and asked the pain, "What is it that you need from me?" "What do you need to tell me?" She got Curious about it. She didn't try to change anything. She looked at pain as yes, it was part of her, but a little bit outside of her, and very lovingly and compassionately said, "What do you need to tell me?" "What is it that you need me to know?" That's what the woman with the fertility problems needs to say. In her best way can she get curious about this and not try to change anything but just try to know and get curious."

Elizabeth: OK. That's good. Thank you.

Jesus: "You're welcome. See she is still thinking in very human terms and that is OK This is what she has known. So she's looking, "I've done everything right, I've followed the rules, I've done what, you know, the church has told me to do." That is her mindset. So she feels that she has been a good person so why would she not get a child as a reward? And that isn't the way things work."

Elizabeth: Thank you for saying that.

Jesus: "God does not reward in that way. She has more control over this than she realizes but she wants to-it would benefit her for her to get curious about this lack of fertility. What does she need to know? And just be very gentle with it because what she uncovers could very well lead her to becoming an entirely different person. Or give her great Understanding or bring her to a place of Compassion and Love and it won't matter for her anymore. That will be up to her. I'm just saying that it has great potential there. Things that are very intense, any sort of physical or emotional pain has so much intensity-Has So Much Information For You-it has something to Tell You that will be-once you know what it is will be your ticket to Freedom from whatever bonds that emotion or experience is holding. And again, it all is done in time. So to not beat yourselves up if it doesn't-you do it and you don't get the answers right away keep at it. Have Faith and Trust. You should read about Job in the Bible to remind yourselves of what that means to have continual problems but to maintain Faith."

Elizabeth: OK. Good advice.

Jesus: "Yes. Yes."

Elizabeth: Alright, well, I guess we can end for today. Is a publisher on the way for publishing this book like I'm asking? (Laughing)

Jesus: "Yes, you keep on doing that because again, in that area, because the Medium, unfortunately, has had setbacks she says, but they are not setbacks, they are actually things that are moving her forward but her focus has been on her health so it has been up to you to bring in energetically the individuals in this case, like the publisher, so keep at it and once the Medium gets both feet back on the ground, she will assist you with this as well. You will not be alone again. You will see. That is your responsibility in all of this. Each of you have taken on different things and that is something that you have taken on. You said that you would draw in that. Not in the human way, it was something you said in BEFORE this was all started."

Elizabeth: OK! Alright, good.

Jesus: "So we are good for today, are we not?"

Elizabeth: Yeah, I would love to keep talking for 2 more hours but in case the Medium has something she needs to do then I guess we could stop.

Jesus: "Yes, yes. We do not want to tire the Medium out too much cause it does require a certain amount-more it's the talking for her it's not holding this energy, it's the talking she tires. As anyone would. So I am going to leave you and give you, as Always, my love and my blessings and we talk all the time, so I will be talking to you very soon."

Elizabeth: Definitely. Thank you. I love you too Jesus. Talk to you later.

Jesus: "Yes, Yes. And we will talk soon."

Elizabeth: OK. Thank you.

Jesus: "Bye-bye. You are welcome. Bye."

CHAPTER 8

Action Steps

July 30, 2013

I was telling Laurie that Jesus guided me to buying a ring that was from Him. She was saying that He was wanting to come in when I stated that. (We had been talking, she and I, for about 20 minutes before that about our personal lives-especially about exercising.)

Laurie: You must be right.

Elizabeth: Oh really?

Laurie: Yeah, yeah, you're right. OK. Let's go. I'll talk to you when we're done.

Elizabeth: OK, cool.

Jesus: "Hello my friend."

Elizabeth: Hi Jesus :)

Jesus: "Hello. How are you?"

Elizabeth: I'm very well. How are you?

Jesus: "I am very well also and I know that you are very well as usual. Well, you're not always very well, but you have been—of late—so what have you got to share with me this time?"

Elizabeth: I, I, um, what do we wanna talk about first? (excited) I feel like I jumped a hurdle with the girl that you knew, that we had the relationship. I feel like I healed her sadness. Is that a correct assumption there?

Jesus: "Yes, yes. So, tell me, tell me what you did. Tell me how You remember what you did. OK? What occurred. What were-you don't have to give every minute detail if you don't want but there's a reason for this because this is being recorded and Documented and I also want that you understand the process. If there is something that you do not include than I will give that to you as well because it would be of importance to you."

Elizabeth: OK. Alright. So, when you told me that, the next morning when I woke up I was crying so I knew, the emotion of sadness was so much, that I knew that it must have belonged to her cause I cried for like a week-well you know that! So I thought to myself, I thought back to the slave girl that I had been, that my children were taken away from me, and I thought, "How did I heal her?" (This past life had been the source of my postpartum depression) and by healing her, I went out and did things that she couldn't do, since she wasn't allowed to do things and be creative, I went out and I did things. I gave myself the freedom to do whatever I want-anyways, so I thought, "How am I going to heal this girl?" So, I talked to you. I tried to meditate but I wasn't getting anything. I just seemed to be in this sadness. It was a lot of sadness. So then, eventually a song by Byonce started to play in my head and it was, "Love on Top" so I thought of my Wonder Woman sisters for the weekend that I had been and I listened to that song and I put myself in the moment of when we were in the room and we were all dancing and enjoying the weight of everything off of our shoulders and so I went out and I ran. And as I was running I was thinking to myself, "I need them to be there for me." and I was calling out to them in my head and I was asking them to hold my hand and just let me talk to them and having no judgment of what I was telling them about you and I and how I was feeling about that and then I was sobbing, like choking sobs but I kept running and then on like lap 10 or whatever I thought of you and I and I thought of a circle. I saw a circle in my third eye and then I wanted to put like Moments that we had together, like pin point moments around this circle but there was an edge of it that was missing. That was incomplete. So I thought to myself, I had been thinking that we wouldn't have been able to be together anyways because they killed you so and this also shows that you were human because you couldn't be with somebody that you wanted to be with-even though you were Jesus-and by me doing this book and connecting with you now, it was Completing that circle. So it was like, all of a sudden the circle was completed and then when I looked into the sky after I had those thoughts, I saw a cloud that had the cut out and you could see the blue sky and it was a circle and so then I just knew it was gone! Like I had worked THROUGH the sadness. Like, I went into it, I let it run it's course I guess I'd have to say.

Jesus: "Perfect. Perfect. So, IN THIS. Something that you-Because you are a teacher and a healer. Both. And you are meant to work with others and that will be happening as soon as you feel the confidence to allow the people into your experience but much of what we are doing here is in preparation For That Time. So, you are learning A LOT and then what will be documented here and those that will read it will then have an opportunity to Also practice these things and use these things-this is why I bring them up and why we speak of them so much-so each of you-what we point out here-is that each of you does your healing in your own unique way. Each of you knows there is—in your case—there's nothing missing here because it wasn't the actual action steps that you took-yes, they were important-you took the Time to focus in on yourself. That is the number 1 thing. We are talking here, now you will want to pay attention to this process but it will be documented by your recording devices. So, #1. You Focus in and take regards for yourself and say, "I'm important enough right now to do this for myself." So you tried meditation, it did not work. You found that "thing" that worked. You removed external distractions. And they were removed for you because you were asking for that. You did not have your children in need of you at that time or someone else took over and you #1 said, "I'm so important Here that I will focus in on myself." First and Foremost. OK? Things you'll want to tell others. Second thing, you opened the channel of communication between yourself in the physical form, your Higher Self and Guidance, whatever guidance is out there in whatever form-much of it comes from your Higher Self but much of it comes also from those Guides that are there to assist you and redirect you back to paying attention to your Higher Self because ultimately that is where YOUR Truth lies. To thine own self be true. That is why you've been seeing that of late, OK?"

Elizabeth: OK.

Jesus: "So you are to know that to thine own self be true means to be paying attention to respecting that which comes through to you from the Higher Self. OK. So, #1. You took the time for yourself. #2. You Opened the channels of communication by just letting go of resistance, OK? A process. You were ready as we have said. OK. Third thing—very important—and this is something that cannot be taught, it can only be acquired is the Belief and Trust that this IS a form of communication. That there does exist something beyond here. That Guidance Does Come. That you are CAPABLE #1 of healing yourself. The Belief and Trust In Yourself. Three important factors in this process and that is why I wanted you to explain it because others do not know and they follow someone else's way of healing. They read the books, they see the television programs, they go to workshops, they do this and all of these things have tools, but they are just tools. What is important is the Feeling. And you MUST HAVE THAT. And those are the 3 Most Important Elements Required For A Healing On Oneself. As I said, the one that most people, what they do not, why they are not able to heal, is they Do Not Take The Time to do what is necessary. They do not respect themselves enough to focus attention ON themselves. So, step number 1 is not done. Therefore anything else that they do, they're doing it maybe, "Oh, let me take 2 minutes here or let me take a minute there." You continued on until you found that the process was moving forward. And had you not found the process moving forward, you would have continued on-let it sit-but gone back to it. Sometimes you need to stop. If you find that you're not moving forward-you're very stuck-with this type of healing. Stop. Set it aside. Sleep on it as we say, as you say, I would be more appropriate, and Then begin the process again. But starting with you, knowing that You are important enough To Do something like this for yourself. Questions."

Elizabeth: Um, no I don't have any questions because what you are saying is all making sense to me. There's a lot of people that do want to heal themselves but like you're saying, it's the Belief that they can DO IT! They have to believe that they can do it! I knew that you told me that stuff because you knew that I COULD do it, so I didn't give up. I was bound and determined to make it happen that I was going to heal whatever needed to be healed.

Jesus: "Yes."

Elizabeth: And I didn't know HOW to do it but I tried just opening myself up to know to, you know, get the guidance to do what needed to be done.

Jesus: "Yes. So. And it worked. Cause you, the sadness is now something sweeter or less intense. It's taken on a different tone, has it not?"

Elizabeth: Yeah! I went out-we celebrated and went out to dinner. (Laughing) That night.

Jesus: "There you go, there you go. You see because it's not that it will be GONE. It's that it takes on a different tone. It's the transformation of that energy because that energy is something—it's energy. So, this would be something else you may want to pay attention to. Would you be able to identify how that energy transformed and what type of energy you may now be holding instead of sadness?"

Elizabeth: Um, it's kinda like Understanding.

Jesus: "There you go! Perfect. That's absolutely what it is. It would be something like Understanding."

Elizabeth: OK.

Jesus: "So, these are very abstract concepts. Are they not difficult to give someone in a book, in a-in speaking or any of that. It has to be done experientially. So, that is what-this is for you and for the Medium. Very much for you. The Medium is-will be using this as well—but you are very much to begin thinking in terms of how you will draw to you those people that you need to work with. OK? To Heal in that way. And you will have some tough cookies but it will be something that you want to be prepared to help them in their healing so that they know that THEY are the ones healing and that you are not the healer. We call you a healer because you carry the messages. You carry the information. You're bringing it forth. But you aren't doing anything nor did I when I walked the planet. I mean they said that I did but I didn't. I SHOWED how it was done. In the same way. And that's what you and our time together when you were walking the planet-that's what was missing for you was in that time, that we were just approaching those teachings and you did not receive them when I was no longer in your world. So, that is why it was important to get that now. But you got it through your own-your own practice-as being true to yourself. And giving, I cannot reiterate and express how important it is to say to yourself, "I am important enough that I will take the time to do this and do it NOW." However it is. You sit down and you focus ON yourself and exclude and remove the distractions-whatever they are-the excuses Why you cannot do these things. "Oh, I cannot meditate!" or "I don't have the time." or this and that and the other things. And it's not to scold. It is just to say it CAN Be Done."

Elizabeth: I think that they need to know that there is Hope. Cause there's a lot of people that are saying they're in Stage 4 cancer and they're dying. They're saying, "I'm dying."

Jesus: "Yes."

Elizabeth: Like they've given up and yeah.

Jesus: "Yes, yes. So, each of you has-again-the Opportunity to Choose whether or not you want to pursue this but again, I know, and those that are assisting on my end of things-others In Spirit-that are assisting because of course, the many guides that are the guides of those that will be Accessing the information here are present here. Making sure that it is another means for them to get this information which, of course, that is what is going on here. So, Mr. Joe Smith, who lives in some remote part of your world who has no idea who you or the Medium are-his guide is here, Present, knowing that he might potentially access this information and therefore he is present here to assist at this time so that should all things come together As We Hope—that this individual will then find the information that he needs for his-Mr. Joe Smith I am saying—will find it in this book we will call it and if not here then maybe from another source but his guidance is in here with me as well as many others."

Elizabeth: That's really cool. That's what I've always thought! We've got our guides up there and they're getting all excited for us so they can bring back the information if we're ready to get it so (laughing)

Jesus: "Yes. Yes. And you should. And we are excited. We want that you're excited as well because being excited about all of this is what brings on even more greater and deeper discussions than have been before. Each time they become a little bit more-with more information."

Elizabeth: Yes. So, who's with you right now Jesus? Who's listening?

Jesus: "There are many. And I would say they are not so much listening as assisting or contributing. There are many names I have here, in-spite of what people as humans may understand that, when you are outside of your physical form, you can be in many places at the same time because space does not really exist as you know it. So, if someone says, "Well on that day I was talking to that Guide and I know that he was over here with me." Well, understand that they can be at many places at many times. So, there are all of the Archangels that you are familiar with and there is specifically Archangel Michael who is in here. We have some guides by the names of Isaiah, he is of primary importance right now because he is a guide for Many, Many on your planet. He is part of the, what you call, The White Brotherhood and that many of your people on your planet are part of this White Brotherhood. And no it is not the Ku Klux Klan and I am joking with you. It is a White Brotherhood of a different nature, of course. I had to just clarify that because I felt a strange energy move through-not from you-but probably from someone who may have access to this and would want to dispute some of these things. Anyway! So, Isaiah, and he is important because he is overseeing, as I said, he is the Head Master of those who are on the planet who are part of this White Brotherhood and he has been and will be for many of Earth years, overseeing things and guidance for you. For there is also, Mary, my, the woman, or the Being that was known as my Mother, there is Miriam here. There is also many many many—Miriam and . . ."

Elizabeth: Now who is Miriam, Jesus?

Jesus: "Miriam was-in Earthly existence?"

Elizabeth: Yeah.

Jesus: "The last lifetime too for her was, well, an important lifetime, it was not her last, she is reminding me, but she was also around at the time that I walked the Earth and at the time of my Crucifixion. So she was a part of this unit. But she was an older woman at that time and was part of the religious group that were called, The Essenes and she was one of their spiritual Leaders in the Essenes and I was part-we were very close-she was like a grandmother figure for me. So she carries much wisdom also and has been guiding Many of you over the years as you have walked the planet because she has finished her cycle. Not that lifetime but 2 or 3 subsequent lifetimes After that lifetime she finished her cycle of evolution on Earth and has Chosen to participate in with those who are acting as Guides for those on the planet here at this time."

Elizabeth: OK

Jesus: "So, and there are many many others. Was there someone in particular because there are hundreds here maybe closer to thousands here that are participating because there are that many out there that are in need of this information. So, was there someone in particular that you were hoping to know if they were here?"

Elizabeth: No, probably Archangel Michael and Mary. That's so neat that everybody is there! Hiiiiii! (Laughing)

Jesus: (Laughing) Yes, they say hello back. They give their greetings back to you. And they say yes everything, they hear you all the time. So yes."

Elizabeth: That's cool.

Jesus: "Yes. Yes. So."

Elizabeth: When you speak of the White Brotherhood, um, was that the group of men that I met in my dream with the caribou?

Jesus: "Yes. Yes. The caribou you said."

Elizabeth: Yeah. Caribou. They were standing next to the caribou and they came and talked to me. Yeah.

Jesus: "Yes, absolutely."

Elizabeth: I figured they were something important. I thought it was a council of something.

Jesus: "Yes, they are The White Brotherhood. And it is from where you originate. You, the Medium, and Many Many others. The White Brotherhood is a Very Large-you could say organization of souls that we have been part of this Evolution here on Earth but we were also part of evolutions in other realms in other Universes and Planets so we have been around for some time helping with the Evolution of the Universe, basically."

Elizabeth: That's neat. So when Earth completes it's evolution then we go on and we-with God together-we create-will we create another like, Earth, and have to start all over again?

Jesus: "Nnnno. Let's just say it's a continual moving forward. Earth will-not at least-it-Earth will always kind of exist. Again, it's a density of energy, right? So energy never really can never be destroyed, it can just transform. So, Earth is always changing. And it looks different than it did 200 hundred years ago, 2,000 years ago, 200,000 years ago. It looks different. So Earth will never stop Evolving. It may not be what it is now and it may not be habitable as it is now by the Beings who are now inhabiting it so what is-what will happen for Souls that are inhabiting Earth-there will be-what is already in existence-there are other realms that are similar to Earth and will be the areas that are possibilities of the same type of evolution for souls to be moving forward. Cause you always need something like that. So, time will tell what is actually created by all of us and by God, Himself, but there will always be a place for souls to evolve. So when they speak of the end of the world and the end of things with those threatening things being destroyed, it's Really Not Possible."

Elizabeth: Well that's gonna ease a lot of minds.

Jesus: "Yes. It's just there will be, maybe Earth will no longer exist, but there will be some other realms where things can continue to move forward because why would . . . OK. Humans have such lofty ideas of themselves and that is something that is interesting because they consider themselves superior to so many other Beings such as, if we use just your own planet-they feel-Human Beings feel superior to everything else that coexists on the planet and really, they're not. Where did this come from? Where was this instilled in Humanity or Humans, this little piece of-this Idea that they are superior? Where did that come from? What purpose has it served? Well, it was in the very first humans that came along. Back when, whether you believe that there was a Adam and Eve or not, THERE WAS, and that came to—when Adam and Eve were placed on this planet. And it was a little bit different of a story than what your Bible or you know, less . . . much of that was symbolic let's say. But at that time there was planted this seed let's say of Arrogance. Superiority. It was meant to be Used by man-again—in their Finding Balance with Free Will. So, man, when they are born, it is in their cellular memory almost, "I am better than so many other Beings that inhabit the planet. Or the Universe." Think of it. So many of you feel afraid of lifeforms that come from other planets-threatened by them or feel superior to them in some way, correct?"

Elizabeth: Yeah definitely.

Jesus: "So, it's something that was put in Man to see what—because Man needed some anchoring. Emotions let's say—to keep him anchored to Earth and that was one of them. This sense of superiority and the fact that he is so Godlike. The more the memory of being Godlike than the animals say or plants don't have the memory of being Godlike As Man Does. Because they were created-MAN-those that are inhabiting the planet Earth-who are going through this cycle here-those Souls that have been created-they have been created By GOD for this specific purpose. It's called that Experiment. So that's also the other thing going on here-which makes you special to—let's say God-are a little bit more special than the other Beings in a way. If that makes sense, even though you aren't but there's a special purpose here that if it all goes well then other areas, other realms, will be created for the same purpose as Earth has served."

Elizabeth: OK, so whatever Earth accomplishes then (flip tape) (I asked if Ego was) . . . part of that superiority complex then that we have?

Jesus: "Yes, absolutely. Yes. It serves that purpose. It's necessary. It is How Man Evolves. It Assists man in his evolution-mankind. So it is important to have it. At least for now. At least for now. So, trying to overcome Ego is let's say impossible in a way. Understanding Ego is really what should be your approach. Understanding It. And Recognizing It for what it is. And that it's limiting and that you are an Unlimited Being. Remember Ego will always keep you in some limited state where as anything that is Not Ego will be very expansive and unlimited."

Elizabeth: OK . . .

Jesus: "OK? It makes sense?"

Elizabeth: Yeah, I'm just thinking that anything that isn't Ego, so, my mind is going in a couple of different places, so um, so, remember when we talked last time about going into the sadness about my mom? And so I wrote her a letter and in the letter I had the Understanding like a Clarity of that whoever hurts you, no matter how much somebody hurts you, it's always based in Love because God created us, God created everything, and God is Love.

Jesus: "Yes."

Elizabeth: So, I don't know how that fit into the whole Ego thing, but . . . (laughing)

Jesus: "Maybe because it's in a sense that, what you might be thinking is that Ego is not to be—like, someone might say to you, "Well, sadness is Ego." and therefore you-it belongs in that category so to speak, well, it may be or it may be not but the important thing to remember is that it's all Love and it's there to serve a purpose and it's up to you to find why you are using that human ego. Because it IS part of Ego. So sadness IS part of Ego. As is happiness. The way you understand happiness. It's part of Ego because it just is and therefore you use it as a tool. It's when you are Not Aware of What It Is and you're letting it control You that it becomes dysfunctional."

Elizabeth: Yeah, I know a lot of people that-Ooh, I won't judge! Nevermind! (laughing)

Jesus: "Exactly. Exactly. Cause they are where they're at for the reasons that they're there."

Elizabeth: Right, right, right. Yep. Sigh. Well, can you explain God a little bit to us to help us understand more about God?

Jesus: "OK. In what way? Because yes, it's all very simple yet very complex. Because God, He is EVERYTHING. And God is not hmmmm, separate from YOU. Soooo, and you are Part Of GOD yet God can Function without you being part of Him. OK? So, it's an energy, of course, that you've understood. A Massive energy that is Creation. It's a creative mind (clearing His throat) would be one way of explaining it. It is the epitome of creation and creative mind."

Elizabeth: How did God come to be?

Jesus: "Very good. Well, prior to God there was something prior to God. Was there not?"

Elizabeth: Well I would think so but I don't know. It's God.

Jesus: "Because that's the way that it has been taught to you. That there's God and that's where the end of the line is or the beginning. But Really, because there's no beginning and no end, it's a continuum. So prior to God there was another impulse. Towards life. And that's what is the best way of understanding all of this. There is an intelligence that you call God. It is an intelligence but prior to that there was another impulse and prior to that impulse was another impulse and it goes back-it just keeps going back forever. Just as you continue to move forward forever and ever, so does this impulse too for God. OK? So, the impulse prior to God is considered God and then the impulse prior to the impulse that is God, you know what I'm saying? Does it make sense? So it's all God."

Elizabeth: Um, it kinda makes sense but then I think, well, if God is an energy then it's not a Being than God would have a mother and a father but maybe I'm totally off on that I don't know.

Jesus: "But no, no, you're in the right direction. It is-so it IS an energy. It is a—and yes, the thing about a mother and a father but you must think of it more of a coming together of energies of 2 different kinds coming together from 2 separate sources, coming together to Create. And that is the impulse that I was speaking of. So you have God, right?

And prior to God there were 2 like—an impulse. A creative impulse and energies coming forth that DID create this Pre-God let's say for terminology. Cause this is hard to explain without having the words to explain it, correct?"

Elizabeth: Yeah. (laughing) Well, where did God come from then? How did it come to be that God just "the Original" we'll say started just making things. Like how did that come to be?

Jesus: "That's always been there."

Elizabeth: OK

Jesus: "And always will be there."

Elizabeth: It's kind of like the chicken and the egg, right? I don't know.

Jesus: "Yes."

Elizabeth: What came 1st? (laughing)

Jesus: "Yes, the same frustration that you get from trying to figure that out is the same frustration you get trying to figure out where this starts. But if you think in terms-because your mind right now is encapsulated in a human form, which has it's limitations and is coming from "Well I live in a time and a space reality." When you are outside of that, you are in a—there Is No Space as you know it and there of course, is not time. So things exist Differently. So therefore there does not need to Be a beginning place."

Elizabeth: OK. I can accept that.

Jesus: "You can accept that?"

Elizabeth: Yeah. I can accept that.

Jesus: "OK. Then let's hope the rest of them do."

Elizabeth: Yeah. (laughing)

Jesus: (He's laughing)

Elizabeth: It Sounds confusing if you don't just be like, "OK!" You know?

Jesus: "Yes. There are things that cannot be explained in completeness."

Elizabeth: OK.

Jesus: "For the reasons that Your Minds are not capable of comprehending. Not because you are stupid or incapable in regards to having an intelligence, but your minds are not developed to that Degree because you Use your mind-you're understanding. But if you try to understand through that other place—that place of Just Knowing. That makes sense, right? And that's what you are doing."

Elizabeth: Totally.

Jesus: "And that's what we would ask those who are reading this, that they just ask to understand from that place. And anybody who is reading this that doesn't understand what that place is, then, well, we cannot explain it because . . . some of you call it The Zone-being in the The Zone. It's THAT PLACE-where all understanding is."

Elizabeth: Is there a place that you can get-can you get to that through meditation?

Jesus: "Yes, absolutely."

Elizabeth: Can you give us some meditation tips on how to-what can help us better to-like I've been trying to mediate and I've got a couple stones here but I-all I've been doing is just closing my eyes and you know, feeling my breath I guess. Trying to breathe. Is there anything else that I should be doing that could be helpful?

Jesus: "Well, no. No. Because it is practice. That is all. It is practice. It's about focusing on your breath and just continuing to do that. You can focus on different things in regards to that-music in the background or some words or words that are repeated or a mantra or that kinda thing—that helps a lot of people but Ultimately, to be successful at it really is about practicing. You can focus in on the pause between your in-breath and your out-breath. All of that will-are means of working to a meditative state. It's about Letting Go and Trusting. Many do not know what that FEELS like. Here it's a feeling state it's not a mental state. It is a feeling state. It's an emotional state. That's why it's difficult for many."

Elizabeth: Interesting.

Jesus: "Yes. Because it's about being in that place and allowing yourself to Not Think your way there but to BE there, FEEL your way there and just be there."

Elizabeth: Cause I wanna GO places! (laughing)

Jesus: "And that's fine too but that is a different type of-that I would not say is necessarily meditation. It's a different type of experience. Meditation is about stillness and a letting go and Allowing things to Come to You. When you journey-that is a more active form of-it's a dream basically. It's active."

Elizabeth: It's a Dream! OK! Good that I got the difference now because I thought I was doing something wrong! Cause at first I saw a little hole and I saw someone's backyard so I thought, "Well, maybe this is the way I can time travel." But if I'm time traveling in my dreams then I'm not gonna-I'm still gonna take the Stillness meditative route but OK.

Jesus: "OK. So you understand."

Elizabeth: Yeah I understand.

Jesus: "OK. Good."

Elizabeth: Um.

Jesus: "Yes, go on please."

Elizabeth: Um. I wanted to ask how my husband Kevin fits into you and I.

Jesus: "In this lifetime?"

Elizabeth: In the lifetime that we were together. I wanna ask about him.

Jesus: "OK, well there's much to give you about him. So . . ."

Elizabeth: You said you know him so.

Jesus: "I'm sorry?"

Elizabeth: You said that you know him.

Jesus: "Yes. Yes. Because he has been with me when Here, when I was on your planet-walking your planet-he was there. He was a follower also. He was a-an inquisitive follower. He was much more skeptical than many so his questions and inquiries were much Deeper which was good because it gave him a means of Understanding and following through and going deeper into that Understanding so that he has developed that over time so he has more Confidence with what he knows. As opposed to 2,000 years ago."

Elizabeth: That's spot on about him that's for sure. (laughing)

Jesus: "Yes. Yes." (laughing)

Jesus: "So what else, I mean, did you want to know about him? What else could I?"

Elizabeth: Well I think he was kinda feeling a little left out. I'm not really sure what. I don't know. Because he doesn't feel like he needs to listen to what we talk about. He'll listen to it if I ask him to but he really doesn't seem like he needs to hear it cause he feels like he KNOWS it. I don't know.

Jesus: "Yes. Well, it would fit with what I just said wouldn't it?"

Elizabeth: Exactly!

Jesus: "So, yes, he knows. He has a lot of Wisdom that is lying beneath the surface that comes out in different occasions, on different occasions."

Elizabeth: He feels like he is here to protect me. Is that correct?

Jesus: "Yes, he's also here as one of your teachers."

Elizabeth: OK, Alright. (laughing)

Jesus: "Yes, yes. That's always good to know, correct?"

Elizabeth: It is! It is!

Jesus: (chuckling)

Jesus: "As you are for him of course."

Elizabeth: Well I feel like I try to teach him sometimes (but he is right a lot of the time.) said quietly :) (laughing)

Jesus: "Yes." (laughing about that)

Elizabeth: He likes to hear that (giggles)

Jesus: "Yes, you'll make him feel good by telling me when he hears that."

Elizabeth: Yes. I wanna say Thank You to you for this ring that you led me to.

Jesus: "Yes. You are welcome. You are welcome. Soo."

Elizabeth: I'm gonna write about it in the book I think.

Jesus: "OK"

Elizabeth: The whole thing about how I healed myself and the ring and stuff because I feel like I'm on about the ring so.

Jesus: "Yes, absolutely. You understand it and it is a good example that others will benefit from knowing it. That's the thing with ALL of this. You Will Be inserting these kinds of information into your-this book that we are creating here-this personal experience as a result of listening, or for in the case of the Medium, having it come through her personal experience of utilizing the information and what might have occurred for you in that case."

Elizabeth: Oh really?

Jesus: "Yes. Why not?"

Elizabeth: I don't know. That's interesting.

Jesus: "Yes. And if you choose not to, that's fine too but it's an Option."

Elizabeth: OK

Jesus: "That's what I was seeing you were planning on doing."

Elizabeth: As putting it in the book?

Jesus: "Yes."

Elizabeth: Yeah. (laughing)

Jesus: (chuckle)

Elizabeth: UGH, I'm getting embarrassed now. (laughing)

Jesus: "Of course. Of course. Once again!"

Elizabeth: Um, so. I just wanted to ask. So we weren't secretive about our relationship, were we?

Jesus: "No, no. There was no need to be."

Elizabeth: OK. And did it come to the time that-did you Want to marry me and then my father said no? Like it was OK we were together up until then?

Jesus: "Uum, yes. It was prior to that however. Marriage was like a solution to a problem. It was a what you might call a last ditch effort in a way for us to stay together and yes, your father was opposed to it Prior to that and therefore nothing I did would have changed his mind plus it would have been-I would not have been able to move forward and do what I did Had I married you and that was all-had to be that way."

Elizabeth: That's understandable. I thought about that. So.

Jesus: "Yes. So it was never in the cards."

Elizabeth: Right. And is it because we're doing this book now here too? Does that have something to do with it?

Jesus: "Yes."

Elizabeth: So it makes me think that things are planned-are laid out Waaaaay long ago. (laughing)

Jesus: "Yes. In regards to Human Time, yes. But it is really, not-we do not have time Outside of the earthly existence. It's only here on Earth and maybe some other existences where they use some form of something similar Like Time but you need it for your own expansion here. The way it's all been designed."

Elizabeth: Right.

Jesus: "That's why it's all very Unique. And that is another thing why humans feel that little bit of superiority is because they are in a "one of a kind" environment that is a-an experiment that is being looked at closely. So they know that they are special to be here on Earth or to be there on Earth—when I speak with you I feel like I am with you so-although I am not on Earth as you would know me to be on Earth. That is why I say, "Here". But. So, does that make sense?"

Elizabeth: Yeah that makes sense cause I was reading that when I was typing it all up the other night-that made sense to me so.

Jesus: "OK. Good. Good."

Elizabeth: So did we have a daughter?

Jesus: (pause) "Yes."

Elizabeth: HA! I GOT IT RIGHT! Ah Ha! Really!! OK. Wow! I got it right! I just got that today when I was laying down and being quiet. I just heard, "Our Daughter" so.

Jesus: "And you knew. So Yes."

Elizabeth: OK. Alright. So. WoW! (Excited laughing)

Jesus: (Laughing too)

Elizabeth: (Sweetly) That's really neat, Jesus!!

Jesus: "Yes. Yes."

Elizabeth: So. OK. Um, (sigh) let's see, let's ask some questions here um . . .

Jesus: (chuckle) "Yes. Let's ask some questions here like oh, let's get down to business I would just like to sit and chit chat with you." (Laughing)

Elizabeth: (Laughing) Well I Would too Actually.

Jesus: "Yes."

Elizabeth: Now it seems like I don't have enough questions here that would be you know, helpful to people.

Jesus: "Well what have you got there? What might be something—let's see if we could . . . see if we could expound on it."

Elizabeth: Um, I was gonna ask, how close is the nearest life on another planet or galaxy?

Jesus: "Oh, it's hard for me to put, but-it is hundreds of thousands or Billions really of miles. It's some distance. I'm trying to get something that's a little bit more Precise in when we start using measurements it feels too Awkward. So it is like the distance from your planet to just outside what you know as your little Universe here or cosmos you know with the Sun and Mercury and the Earth and Jupiter etc, etc. OK. So it's just beyond that. What encompasses that."

Elizabeth: So we have nothing that would be able to get to that.

Jesus: "Not yet. No. But it will be created, yes."

Elizabeth: Well that's interesting. A lot of people wanna go to the Moon right now (I was meaning taking a trip there-paying to go) they wanna go farther than that.

Jesus: "And it Will Happen because that's where you are-as humans-that's what you are developing. You're heading in that direction always. Cause it's meant to be."

Elizabeth: OK. I'm gonna ask you. After the Crucifixion was it 3 days after you rose? Is that an accurate um.

Jesus: "Yes."

Elizabeth: And did you continue-some people think-and I pondered this-if you actually went-if you continued to Live after that happened and lived to be an old man. Did you?

Jesus: "Yes. Yes. Old, old man? No. But another 20 some years beyond that time."

Elizabeth: REALLY??? So explain this to me cause I wanna hear, like, tell me exactly what happened. (So excited!)

Jesus: "Well, there was of course the Resurrection and at that time basically, there—there was a Choice on my part-again Free Will-did I want to then dis form that I had and move on or did I want to stay in the physical form and have a lifetime here on the planet to it's completion. Now, I chose to stay here because it was going to be important for the continual evolution of Mankind. It would be in a different capacity. The thing is, is that many were not able to "See me" again because of their Perception of things-their Understanding kept them at a vibration that they were Only able to understand the Crucifixion and my death and not anything beyond that."

Elizabeth: So when you came to the disciples and they say "doubting Thomas" how you had him put his hand into your wounds, then you were an actual-were you in the same form as you were prior-like at the Crucifixion or did you change-was your features changed at all?

Jesus: "No. It was the same. There were some modifications because I-there was-of course on my part-as a SOUL Ultimately-there were-what

I had done had advanced My Soul where I was of a higher vibration also. Correct?"

Elizabeth: Yep.

Jesus: "So I looked different. Especially over time. That is why I'm saying that some, because of their Perception—were limited in what they were able to Perceive so I-to them I was dead. Or and if they DID see me, they could not actually SEE who I was."

Elizabeth: So. A different vibration. Is that kind of like when a Medium sees Spirit-that it's just on a different frequency?

Jesus: "Yes. Yes. A good example. Yes."

Elizabeth: OK, so where did you go then after wards?

Jesus: "What do you mean? Yes, I left the immediate area. I went to—of course stayed in the middle eastern-you call it—area. I-there was much traveling that was done but I moved on to a part of the world that you—would be like considered part now that is in the South of India."

Elizabeth: OH! OK.

Jesus: "Yes. Because it was necessary or it was Accommodating because they are Open to much AND it is where I spent time for a while, while I was-those years that no one knows anything-were spent There in learning many things from Masters in the East Indian world."

Elizabeth: So you just went back to where-and you just showed up and they were just like, "Hey, Jesus, good to see you again!"? (starting to laugh)

Jesus: "Yes, yes. Good to see you again. You left your shoes here the last time. You left some stuff behind. Yes." (he's joking) :)

Elizabeth: Did your your Mother then go with you too?

Jesus: "No. She stayed behind. Continued her journey and when she was-what is known about her is true-she did Ascend—a few years after the whole experience and hers actually was an Ascension and she did not come back here."

Elizabeth: OK. So, she Ascended-like her whole entire body.

Jesus: "Yes."

Elizabeth: OK. Alright. That's, that's cool, Jesus.

Jesus: "Yes." (chuckling)

Elizabeth: That's some good stuff! What else can you tell me that we don't know?

Jesus: (Laughing)

Jesus: "Yes."

Elizabeth: So when you-when you went to the place in India or whatever then did you get remarried or were you just a bachelor for the rest of your days?

Jesus: "Well I was with others that were followers also. And we, we. Yes. I did marry. And was Content there and had—we did not stay there forever. We stayed there for sometime and then we moved to what would be what you know as Europe and that's where I spent my final days with my children. Because I had children."

Elizabeth: Oooh, that's so nice :)

Jesus: "Yes."

Elizabeth: Are you buried somewhere that anybody could find your grave?

Jesus: "No." (flip tape)

Elizabeth: OK so you were saying that there would probably be only bones left, OK. Well, we'd have no way of identifying you, right? No DNA-nothing like that?

Jesus: "Exactly. So."

Elizabeth: Well that's good news. I think we can end on that for today. (Laughing)

Jesus: (Laughing)

Jesus: "So you are satisfied for today."

Elizabeth: Yeah! I'm really happy for you!

Jesus: "Yes. So that is good. What we will do is, we will speak very soon so that we can continue on and I am very happy that you are happy for me. Yes. And that you take to heart everything that you hear from me."

Elizabeth: Thank you. You did so much for all of us and it just-it's a happy ending. And we all want a happy ending and you, you know.

Jesus: "Yes. And it Was a happy ending. Although to have departed here would not have been an unhappy ending. It's not-it's what all of you have to do anyway because leaving is something that does bring Great Joy once you are on the Other Side. You'll see. When your time comes."

Elizabeth: Right, right. Good to point out!

Jesus: "Yes. So. Alright. We are done and we will speak very soon. I love you very much and you have a wonderful time and continue doing the great work that you are doing."

Elizabeth: OK! Thanks Jesus!!!

Jesus: "You are welcome."

Elizabeth: "I love you too!"

Jesus: "OK. Very good."

Elizabeth: Alright, bye!

Jesus: "Bye."

The detailed story of how I healed myself.

After almost a week of what I would call a low laying cloud of sadness and confusion, it finally lifted. The initial shock of what Jesus told me about us having a relationship left me virtually a puddle of tears and in my own world of thoughts. When Jesus told me about our relationship I immediately thought about the boy named Luke, that I had had a most heart-breaking crush on from 5th grade when we met (he was on of my brother's close friends) until I was 21. So I know how unrequited love feels. I believe that was the whole point of my crush on Luke. So that I would have a reference point of feelings.

That night as my husband and I sat in the living room listening to the tape I began to cry. It was hard to put into words what Jesus' words had sparked in me but my heart knew it was true. I would now have to wait a week or two to speak with Him again, at least hear Him talking back. I was already missing Him. I had so many questions but yet I told myself that I would keep talking to Him in my thoughts and somehow He would answer and I would "just know" His response like always. "I can do this." Is what I kept telling myself. Kevin, my husband, reminded me of this also. He said I don't have to wait a week to speak to Him because I can anytime.

As I got ready for bed that night, I noticed the little box on my nightstand that held the pure white moth that I had found the week before-I knew it was from Jesus when I found it because I had just been speaking to my cousin about Him. So when I found it I told my daughter I needed to find a box for it (it was dead and in mint condition.) She handed me a blue box with a cross on it that a rosary of hers had come in. Inside were the words, "Jesus Loves Me". It was perfect! As I opened this box now, those words took on new meaning. Beside the box was a new ring I had just bought the weekend before-staring at me from in IT'S ring box, waiting to be taken in to be sized. It is a large blue sapphire with diamonds on the sides (this is the ring that is from Jesus that I thanked Him for). When I saw it on my nightstand I began to think that Jesus had me buy that ring as a sign of His love for me.

That night I wanted to cry myself to sleep and yet I didn't know why. In my heart that is what I felt. I held back my tears so that my husband wouldn't think I was being over dramatic about it. I couldn't sleep the whole night. I tossed and turned and was throwing out thoughts and questions to Jesus all night long. At 5a.m. I woke and said to Him, "I am waiting for a response." I fell asleep and when I awoke I had Prince, the singer-songwriter, in my head. A picture of him. I thought, "Prince is Jesus?" This was to get my attention. And then I heard the song by Prince, "Purple Rain" in my head and in my mind's eye I saw my Wonder Woman Weekend bag with the thought of, 'I Am Wonder Woman". I grabbed my phone and immediately searched the internet for the words to "Purple Rain". I was already crying because I love that movie and already know most of the words by heart. I sat on my couch and when I began to read them, I began to sob. Deep deep pouring out of the soul sobs. My emotions were running very high. He had sent me this and must have been with me because as I moved to the kitchen to feed my baby and other 2 kids (still sobbing) Laurie sent me a text message-perfect timing—saying, "Another reason you are in awe of Jesus is that He healed you in that lifetime. I think you had leprosy. He and I were just talking and He wants you to know these things now. You're to talk with Him today as soon as you have a quiet moment. He has a message for you and for Kevin. He and Kevin know each other from that time also. I think that's it." I told her that if He would like to speak with me through her to call me because my daughter would watch the baby for me. She wrote back, "I don't have a problem doing that but I know He wants you to try first. Let's do this if you really can't get anything we will talk. This is about you and your unique relationship with Him. You are healing something from that time. I feel Kevin fits in cuz he was there also. He may have been your father. But not sure." I forwarded the text to Kevin and he wrote back, "Cool see, it didn't take a week to hear from Him :)" This made me smile also.

I agreed with her about me having to heal something there. With the emotions that I was feeling I knew that I had unfinished "stuff". Just like I healed the girl that I had been-a nursemaid slave—when I had postpartum depression-that was where the depression stemmed from. Some part of me needed to be healed. So, after I layed the baby down for his nap I went outside and sat on my rock overlooking the fields and sky. I began to cry more and more and talk to Jesus. The breeze picked up and I felt a presence on the left side of the middle of my back. It was His hand.

At first I didn't want anyone to know what Jesus had told me. I thought I would leave it out of the book. I wasn't even comfortable with Denise knowing so I sent her a text message saying that He had told me something very personal and that I was processing it and I needed to be by myself. That is what I did for almost a week. Yes, I went through the motions of playing with my kids and making dinner and taking them fun places and whatnot but my mind was elsewhere. It's not every day you hear something like that. I took every opportunity to be by myself when the baby would take his naps and I trusted the other two to behave themselves and read books and play (they are 11 and 8 years old) while I either went outside to sit by myself or went to my room.

For many days I was in my own world with Jesus in my thoughts. I tried to meditate and connect but wasn't "getting anything". I was just too confused. Too sad. I felt pulled between 2 men. My husband and Jesus. I needed to separate the two but somehow join them at the same time to be able to heal my heart and move on. The final night, before the healing occurred the next day, the moon was out and shining bright upon our bed. I layed there admiring it and I gave it all the things that were bothering me.

The next day was my "rest, walk, or be active" day on my workout routine of Hip Hop Abs (which I am really enjoying). I took the baby for a walk in the stroller. It wasn't hot out yet and the wind felt so good on my body. I decided that I would run when we got home and I layed him down for a nap. (Running is when I feel most connected and I hadn't done it for 2 weeks because of doing the Hip Hop Abs and because of the heat-too hot for me out there!) On Arron and I's way home, the song, "Love on Top" by Byonce played in my head. That is one of the songs from my Wonder Woman Weekend. I turned on the computer to listen to it before I went outside. I danced and cried. I closed my eyes and felt what it was like to be in the room with all of my sisters from that weekend when all of us were dancing and smiling and enjoying all of the weight from our shoulders lifted. After it was done I went for my run. Back up my driveway on the 1st lap of 10 I sent out a "call for help" to my Wonder Woman sisters. I needed them to listen, not judge, and hold my hand like they had done that weekend. I kept running through the chokes of sobbing. They may have been aware of what was going on or they may have not but on another level of energy and consciousness, they were there right with me holding my hands and giving me the strength to bring up the sadness and let it out. Then I remembered to breathe-just like like Iyanla had told us to do, so many times.

As I ran I had my conversation going with Jesus. I went through the events of our life together the best I could with the understanding of what I know now—we would not have been able to be together very much longer anyways. The thought occurred to me also that He was human. He-even being Jesus-was not allowed to be with the one who He wanted to be with. I then saw a circle in my mind's eye. The circle between He and I. There was a hole at the bottom of it that needed to be filled in to complete it. All this-the book, etc—was part of how to complete it. I wanted to draw a picture of it with points of moments we had together and was happy that I was now making it whole. I looked up into the sky and here was a hole in the clouds showing me the blue sky. Just like the day when we first talked on the phone when the flying bird was the cut out of the cloud. I put my hands together and out in front of my face to match the hole in the clouds and waved my finger from my head and out to it showing that we are in sync. I got it :)

That night for dinner we went out to the lake to celebrate. I held my husband's hand and wanted kisses. He looked so handsome and I was happy to be with him, enjoying that moment, enjoying our life together. :)

The Ring From Jesus.

My Saturday had started out with a vision of seeing my toenails painted a light shade of pink with glitter on them. Not a color I would choose, so it stuck out to me. The plan for the day had been that we would go as a family to Mankato, drop off the car to get the brakes fixed, and then all go shopping and out to eat. As the time approached to leave, baby Arron got tired. I suggested that we just lay him down for his nap and that I go by myself to Mankato. Kevin was OK with that. On my way there it was raining so hard my wipers could barely keep up and lightning was flashing all around me. When I got to Tires Plus I had to stay in the waiting area until the storm passed. My plan of walking across the street to get a pedicure was delayed. I ended up having a delightful conversation with a college student whose car was taking extra long to fix-nothing is by accident-we were meant to be there, on that very day, at that time, discussing things at that very moment. She believed that too. It's amazing how friendly people are if you just start a conversation! Our talk lasted an hour and then her car was done, the rain had stopped, and I was off to get my pedicure. It is not very often that I treat myself to one of those. As I sat in the chair with my feet in the warm water, I was left alone to relax-through 2 full stages of the massage chair! I had picked out a dark pink color-not being able to find the color I had seen in my vision among the many colors on the racks but I still found some glitter. As I sat there I noticed the exact color that I had seen in my vision across from me on the table they paint nails at!! I asked the lady if I could switch mine to that and she had no problem doing that so she went and got it for me. After she was finished, I looked at my feet and they were EXACTLY how I had seen them in my vision! Again I knew that I was right where I was supposed to be. After my polish was done drying I walked next door and sat by myself and enjoyed a sub sandwich from my favorite sub place. The time to myself was so very nice. I decided to "check in" on Facebook with the title of "ME Day". After I was done eating, I walked across the street to the pawn shop just for fun to see what they had for emerald rings and there was the blue Sapphire ring!! As I admired it on my finger, the gentleman said, "It matches your fingernails!" Yes! It did! I told him that I would have to go home and sleep on it and if it was meant to be, than if I came back for it, it would still be there. Then I walked around the corner to the thrift shop. I found myself over by the VHS tapes. On the shelf was a tape of The Rock, Dwayne Johnson, a wrestler that I used to watch and once I saw that on this video were his old interviews, I started to laugh and knew that this would be the best .25 cents I had ever spent! I continued laughing about it as I left the store and began my walk back to pick up my car. (That's how I know things are good-if they make me laugh-and when I watched the video I laughed so damn hard that I had tears in my eyes!! I felt Great!!) As I drove out of town to begin my way home, I had to stop at a light and noticed a truck in the other lane next to me that had a license plate of UUU-*   *   * and I KNEW that I had to turn around and go get that ring! It was for me! Remember, it was my "ME day" I parked outside the pawn shop and Googled what the powers of Sapphire were. The first site I opened was the title, "Jewels for ME!" I am so serious!! It was just like that so I went inside even more confident about purchasing it. As I waited for the guy to help me, I noticed a WWF wrestling belt above the register in front of me that I hadn't noticed before-The Rock has been the WWF Champion and here I had the video I just purchased in my purse! Again I laughed at the synchronicity of it all.

About a week later, still before I talked to Jesus on the phone about it, I picked up that blue Sapphire ring from the jewelers. It now fits perfectly on my finger. The lady gave it to me and I looked down to admire it. All of a sudden, my cheeks turned on fire. I thought, "Yes, this ring IS from Jesus!" :) Before I went back home I had to stop at the grocery store. When I came back out to the parking lot, I was talking to Jesus and thanking Him. I opened up the trunk to put the groceries in and there was a binder my daughter had left and at the top it said, "True Love". Then I looked at the van that I had parked next to. It was still there. I now noticed that someone had written in the dirt all over the sides of it, "I (heart sign) U". I smiled and went to put the grocery cart away. A little dragonfly followed me the whole way flying about 2 inches off the ground. This made me happy too. It reminded me of the Fairies I had sent Laurie to help heal her. Hey! They must have helped me too! Thank you, Fairies!!! Feeling very special, I got in my car and turned the key. The song on the radio got my attention immediately.

"And between now and then, til I see you again, I'll be loving you, Love, ME."

My dream about The White Brotherhood.

In my dream I was out in the middle of nowhere. I was at a crossroads. I started to go one way and then decided to turn around and go another. I saw their Caribou first. They were lined up-spaced evenly-maybe 7 of them or more in a mist. They were along the edge of a ravine of sorts. As I got closer I noticed the men standing beside each of their caribou. Then 2 of the men were in front of me. They wore very long animal hide coats that had white fluffy collars that seemed to be wool-or maybe it wasn't wool-it was longer threads of some animal hair that looked very soft-puffy. And the collars were not short-these were very thick and wide at the top and then tapered down towards their middles. They all had very VERY long beards. One of the men approached me and said something like, "Make your request." Which meant that whatever I wanted, like a wish, would come true. I said, "I want to change the world." and I was confident in this answer. Then a man dressed as Batman approached me and my son, Adam, came from behind me dressed as Wolverine from X-Men. And then I woke up with the knowing that I had met some sort of very special council.

CHAPTER 9

Patterns

August 15, 2013

Before talking to Jesus, Laurie and I were talking about some personal matters and how to pose the question of how to resolve patterns in our lives. We didn't know exactly how to phrase it so she just let Jesus come through to take charge, basically :)

Jesus: "Hello. Yes, we've already begun, so to speak, prior to beginning, we've already begun and here we are once again, communicating from the different realms. Your lovely, and sometimes confusing, physical Earthly realm and our much more Insightful, so you think, Spiritual realm. But. So where do you want to begin today? Because as I have observed from your interactions of late and what is going on in your world right now, you would—the information I give you today may be pertinent for the moment in some regards but will never be completely disregarded. So, do you want me to tell you a little about what is going on for you now or do you want to go straight to your questions?"

Elizabeth: Well, let's talk about what's going on with us now. Please.

Jesus: "OK. Yes, so this is a part that is pertinent for this moment right here at this time in the Earthly experience but the Earthly experience is tied into the Universal experience so it's all tied in together. As you know. So what happens on Earth has-is either influencing or being influenced by universal forces as well. It's not that the universe is coming and saying, "Oh, let's spray this energy on Earth!" It's that, if you think of this as being-it's endless-the universe, the cosmos, all of it, everything that Exists, EVERYTHING THAT EXISTS-is Possible. So those things that are thoughts-everything-all energy-that's the best way-is expansive. It's all-you can't possibly fathom How Much there is because you are living in a limited form. So all of that, and inside of all of that, you have Earth, and you have humans. The inhabitants of Earth. Correct?"

Elizabeth: Yes.

Jesus: "And you are really very much like dust. A speck of dust or a drop of water in the ocean of Existence. You really really are. Yet, without your input, it would alter things and what is going on universally affects what goes on on planet Earth. So it's important that you understand that maybe at the moment, the energies are such and they will not be exactly the same again Ever, But the concept of the fact that you, as Humans, are Emitting energy, you are Absorbing energy, you are part of something very very big and very very important Is the purpose of what we want to discuss here. Presently, in this evolution that you are in, where you are going, you are all Moving Towards the expansion of your consciousness. That is the best way of explaining it. You are expanding, you are growing, you are raising your vibration, and in that process, you call this Enlightenment, you call this the Ascension, you have many different names for it, but you are moving along with the rest of everything that IS. ALLLL that IS. You are moving in a direction. You are always moving Forward. You are always Evolving and Changing. It's neither good or bad, right or wrong, up or down, left or right. It just IS. It's Just Going and so at this present time, what is occurring, is that universally, in Your universe—Not in other realms at the time—because it's not necessary—but there are waves or bands of energy that are focused in on what you would call your universe-where Earth resides and it's inhabitants. Because you are in a, an existence, a realm that has a-is the focal point of or is an experiential experience. Experiential is sort of a redundancy but you are an experiment. Earth is an experiment in the way it was set up. And all of it's inhabitants-it's an experiment. So, you, there is more Attention paid to what occurs here by other Beings from other realms because of where this could possibly lead. So what is going on at this time, is there is this Push to Align everything that is alive on your planet with the energies moving through—that are moving through but are also Pulling you and your planet, everything that is alive on your planet, pulling it towards this Higher Vibration is the best way, it will Be another realm. You will call it the 5th Dimensional realm. That is what is going on right now and in order to do that, certain energies that come from the God force or from Oneness, as it resides, it has everything in it, will see the necessity of a certain support in the Type of energy that it moves or directs to this universe that Earth resides in because of where the Evolution and the direction everything is going. So, it will cause the inhabitants of Earth to experience different things in different ways. So, right now, what is going on, is that there has been, of recent times, there has been a rewiring basically. Your DNA in your physical form, is being-the DNA-is being rewired in a way so that it is a better match to the non-physical part of existence. OK? Meaning that the Soul and the Spirit that come into existence-the physical form has been far too dense and therefore-the physical form became-has become-cumbersome for the Soul and the Spirit that it's vibration is becoming lighter so to speak, or higher, right? So what is going on right now, is that the energies are Realigning and Rewiring the Information that is in your DNA so that the human beings that are being Born are coming in lighter but differently. And it always goes on this way but it's-greater leaps have been occurring within-in shorter spans of time-so prior to this, there would have been 20, 30 years span of time, maybe even longer, where you wouldn't really see the changes in the human structure and the way humans acted as in your own lifetime but NOW because you are moving much more rapidly, time is changing, space is changing, the human form is changing, much more-at a rapid, more rapid pace. You have change occurring in the human form to match the non-physical-the Soul and the Spirit-you will see change in 2,3 months period of time. So those entering the human form, within a years period of time, you may have 3 different phases of the type of human in that period of time. Does that make sense? It's very abstract or scientific thinking, I guess. Does that make sense to you?"

Elizabeth: Yeah, that makes sense to me.

Jesus: "Good. Because I did not want to lose you with all of this because it's very important to understand that that is what is going on right now. So, what is your physical form-so-you see these children coming in and they are different. And they are always seen as being different. So, that is a manifestation of this change. But it's necessary. It's absolutely necessary that the physical form change. Otherwise it will no longer be a welcome receptacle or vessel for the Soul to inhabit-the Soul and the Spirit to inhabit because it would be far too dense. It would not be able to-the Soul and the Spirit—would not be able to enter the physical form at all and maintain any sort of long term existence. So, that's why this is all necessary and one of the non-physical features of all this is your emotional body and your emotional body is the focus for those inhabiting the Earth-as human beings-the emotional body is you have your own personal emotional body and then you have the emotional body of the collective consciousness is the best way of saying that. So, those of you coming, each of you coming in, is working on your own personal emotional body and then you're also working and being influenced by the collective consciousness and It's emotional body is the best way of describing it and in order to be Comfortable in 5th Dimensional reality, which is where you are wanting to go, you must be—we have spoken of this—you must be the Master of your emotions rather than the emotions being Master of you. So, right now, this period of time here, is a very intense cleaning house. It's a very intense-taking a look-really at-what have you got on your check list here that you have been carrying with you—maybe for thousands and thousands and thousands of lifetimes that you just refuse to let go of or understand or look at. Some sort of Misunderstanding about what it means to be an Eternal Being. OK? And so, if you are struggling with something-you're seeing it come back again and again and again, it is because it is a belief pattern that is not just part of your physical Human experience but it has become part of your belief structure as a Soul AND an Eternal Being. So there's a difference there you see. And that is why it is much more, I guess you would say Intense, in it's feeling and much—and very important to understand it so that it is no longer controlling and directing where you are when you are in your non-physical state. You see. Does that make sense?"

Elizabeth: Yeah. I think that makes sense. So, what does a person do to control that then?

Jesus: "Well, so, it's a bit like the birthing process-once you begin, and so everybody who's on Planet Earth right now is in their own little mini birthing process here. Because once you've begun this process, there's no going back saying, "I don't like it, it hurts too much.""

Elizabeth: Starts laughing

Jesus: "You know? Right?"

Elizabeth: That makes sense.

Jesus: "Exactly. You have to in some way-Allow it to happen. Whether it be an intervention by the doctor to bring forth the final result Or just nature itself-your own physical form. So you Must keep moving forward because again, everyone must understand that you've all chosen to be here-you were not given this opportunity like, "Oh, OK, sure, why not go down there?" It was not a Casual choice. It was very much you've grown and you've earned the Honor of being On Earth right now and as we have told you, there are a many standing in line waiting to take this same role that You have. So, this is not something to be taken lightly. And you are also contributing to the masses here and moving everyone forward and not just yourself but moving everyone forward because you are all part of that Oneness-can't get away from that-you are not solitary-you are all part of that Oneness."

Elizabeth: K

Jesus: "So, that is what's going on and that's why many of you are seeing things and maybe feeling like you've been beating your heads against the wall-Because these are-when you have an understanding of an Emotion-as it pertains to you-in this lifetime-and you gain understanding and you resolve it, it's a very quick experience and does not usually require a lot of digging-a lot of perseverance, a lot of repetition, but when you have something that is embedded into your Soul memory and has become part of who you are as a Soul, basically, and you've carried it for thousands of lifetimes, well, you're going to find that Understanding comes with greater effort but you Cannot Move Forward without that at this time-this is the whole purpose of Earth is-you are laying also the foundation for future localities—like Earths—to be created. If this works here, let's see if we can do this somewhere else. Set up a similar type of thing. You know it will not be identical—it will be similar."

Elizabeth: OK . . .

Jesus: "Alright?"

Elizabeth: So some people go to therapy to right these-to let go of these patterns that they have-so the process seems to be more than just going to therapy, it seems to be Really questioning yourself as to how to get through this.

Jesus: "Exactly. So, it is-everything that you have that presents itself-as you said, patterns, that presents itself as a pattern in this way, is doing it because it's embedded there for a very long time. Many many lifetimes and it's not going to be taken care of easily because the amount of time that has transpired, the amount of energy that is Stored in those memories-remember that—because it's energy. So the Process needs to be respected in the fact that it will take more time because the Outcome will be an incredible amount of expansion so that's an Incredible amount of energy that will be-will Move the Soul to higher and higher vibrations. So, the best thing for someone to do is-or the purpose of all of this is-when they are feeling that sense of loss or frustration at things recurring and recurring-the pattern-is to Remind themselves that this is all occurring-The Ultimate Point Being-that it is to bring them Back to Reconnecting with Oneness and Understanding that they are Unlimited Beings living only in a limited state of mind but that they are Unlimited Beings with Every Capability of living Unlimited Existence. That is really what it is. And if they can remind themselves of that, then they will move forward and with greater ease reconnecting with Oneness."

Elizabeth: OK. So I'm just going to give a personal experience to see if somebody can relate to it. So, the other day, somebody had said something that one of their friends-they think one of their friends has seriously gone off the deep end and I took that personally and then one of of my other friends said yeah, I've got one of those too so I took that as they were talking about Me. So, I was having a lot of frustration and I was hurt by it and I was sad all day about it but then I realized that if they think I'm crazy NOW just wait until they see what I can do! They ain't seen nothing yet!

Jesus: "Exactly."

Elizabeth: So, is that an example of doing that?

Jesus: "Yes. Absolutely. Because it caused you to reflect on your own being. Did it not?"

Elizabeth: Yes!

Jesus: "You stopped and at first you felt the emotion that you felt and then it caused you to go a little bit deeper, to dig around—because you have experience with this—you dug around-you Found what for you now is The Key and then you brought Understanding. So, remember another thing-very important to remember about patterns—is that they are Necessary because they are Your Tool Box. So, they aren't always meant to be eradicated but they may be the way in which You Use that particular pattern To Expand. So to be Grateful for it because it is your own personal tool."

Elizabeth: That's a great way of looking at it! That's great!

Jesus: "Yes."

Elizabeth: That's great because I did! I felt-at first I felt real beaten down and like crap and then I felt Huge Empowerment-I felt so powerful after that. So it wasn't a bad thing it was a good thing. OK.

Jesus: "Exactly. So when you have something like this-and you probably looked at it and said, "This has happened to me before. This has made me feel this way before." But you got to where you needed to go. If you had a dissimilar experience, you would not have been able to get there as easily Because you would not have had that pattern to Remind You of certain Emotions that are Connected with those experiences for you. So, it's not that your looking all the time to get rid of all of that, it Really Is Understanding. And if you can be gentler with yourselves and know that you have these patterns and that they are tools for you to Use TO Gain Enlightenment. TO Gain that Higher Vibration. TO Move Forward—the problem here is that too many people on your planet take things too seriously. It has become where they believe that they must not Have negative feelings. They must not FEEL certain feelings because they don't FEEL good, they're uncomfortable feelings so they-there's an industry-as you said, therapy-designed to help you get rid of them. Well, many people will continue to have them. Now that is not to say that therapy is not a beneficial experience-that is not what I am saying here because it IS very beneficial but what I'm saying is the approach to looking at things in that way and saying, "Oooh, this is what I do when this is happening so it's a sign for me to open up my eyes and pay attention cause I got information coming to me and I'm not gonna take things too seriously cause I Know that this is all just a huge, huge game or a play and I'm just an actor here and I'm not going to be here for very long and my Truth and my True Life is what exists when I am NOT in this physical form." Ultimately. Correct?"

Elizabeth: Yes.

Jesus: "And that is what we are Hoping we will attain with the work that we are doing here with these sessions and communicating this to people so that we can then have another Surge Forward here on your planet."

Elizabeth: So, I wanna go back to the children that are being born now. So, we won't notice any physical, Physical things about them, it will be more their hearing will be stronger, you know, stuff like that?

Jesus: "Yes. Yes."

Elizabeth: Intuition. Higher intuition, stuff like that.

Jesus: "Yes. Exactly. Higher intuition, certain characteristics about their personality traits and characteristics that will be different than those born a year or two prior to the them-or generations—not to even speak about generations prior. You won't see the Physical changes because the physical form still needs to be—generally speaking-not for everyone-but 2 eyes, 2 ears, 2 legs-but again, it's not for everyone-it depends on what they're doing-but that is where you start from and then move—depending on what you wanna do into other areas-but that you won't see like, going from the norm being 2 eyes to 1 eye."

Elizabeth: Right. OK.

Jesus: "That's not necessary at this point. It would not be for most, a beneficial experience. Now there are those without eyesight-well they are here learning specific-having specific experiences that will bring them to specific Understanding for themselves. So, again, it is all very very relative."

Elizabeth: OK. Um, and then the rewiring that is going on with us. Would that be like the buzzing in the ears.

Jesus: "Yes."

Elizabeth: And pressure changes you feel like that in your head, stuff like that?

Jesus: "Yes. Yes. Absolutely. So, some will be experiencing it and then their physical form will produce headaches or these kind of discomfort. A pressure in some way in their body. And again, it depends on who they are, how their body is made up, where they are living on the planet, how much the energy flows or doesn't flow where they're at so there are many factors that will determine that."

Elizabeth: Is that like when you were talking about-the last time we talked—when you feel a different feeling and it may be the presence of something to just feel that, let that energy go through you?

Jesus: "Yes."

Elizabeth: OK.

Jesus: "Yes. And some Can't because who knows what they are doing-only they know and they may not even know at that time. So they have to also, "K, this is what is occurring at the moment and I have to just accept it."

Elizabeth: OK.

Jesus: "It's not easy! (chuckle) None of this is easy! It is all-it's all in a sense-we make it sound when we speak to you-we make it sound like, "Oh, OK, this is what you have to do and that's all you have to do and be done with it." But that's really not how we see it either but it's meant to give you Understanding so that at least you have a Focus and does not leave you in a place of victimizm or being a victim to life's experiences."

Elizabeth: Right. Because it IS very hard to go through those things. It's when you get through it, it's like, "Waaaah! That was great!!" But it wasn't when you were in the thick of it! (laughing)

Jesus: "Exactly. Exactly. And again, the birthing analogy is the perfect one. When you're in the midst of giving birth there are times when you feel like, "I just don't want to do this anymore." but you know you can't stop, you have to keep going, and then the end result is you have a wonderful experience from that."

Elizabeth: Yep.

Jesus: "Yes. So what else do you want to talk about?"

Elizabeth: Um, let's talk about the hawk that came in the tree when I was talking about Judas the other day at the dinner table. I wanted to talk about Friendship I think and a little about Judas and you and um, just speak about your relationship I guess.

Jesus: "He was a. OK. First let me explain that-you know we talk about life here on Earth and you can have-you reincarnate. And there are many souls that have come through to be Judas. OK? Many souls who have come through and have been The Buddha or have been Joe Smith down the street, OK? Because you have-even though you move forward you have repetition. Remember that. Remember there are many souls waiting to come here to experience life on Earth so one thing that we've noticed is that with your talk of reincarnation and such, many will say, "Well, I am the embodiment—I was at one time Judas or I was at one time John the Baptist." or some other famous figure in history. And another will say, "Well, I was too. I feel that way." We want you to understand that you have all been that. You are characters in a play when you come down here. And each time it might be slightly different for you, but you have taken on that role. OK. That being said, does that make sense to you?"

Elizabeth: Yeah it makes sense to me. I guess. You're not speaking (flip tape) (he was saying that someone who has played the role of Judas could be the person sitting next to me-which was Denise.)

Jesus: "The reason I'm bringing that up is because many of you have Chosen that Role to understand betrayal and to understand many many things. So, what—there was only one Me, however. There were not others coming in embodied as Jesus, OK? But. Judas was—IS cause it is also a present day experience in many ways, the embodiment of the-not embodiment-my relationship with him is what you asked about-it was one of Total Trust and Understanding and Faith In Each Other. He Knew what I was going to have to experience. He was-came to the Understanding through his Own Work for Himself. Those that come in as Judas have come in to—because they have that knowledge of—that I came here to teach, OK? So, the relationship is one-it is a very symbiotic relationship that we had or Have with each other. It's Beyond being my right hand man or my best friend. It's really way beyond that. Beyond brotherhood and all of that. It is All Of That and More. So, that being said, what Judas is-or Portrays-is the Assistance to my experience here in bringing forth that Understanding of the gamut of emotion that goes from betrayal to pure joy to bringing forth understanding of Life Eternal. Judas was the one who understood everything exactly how it needed to go and was the one that was the most in the flow and he was ultimately the one who was betrayed more so than being the one that betrayed."

Elizabeth: Because everyone thinks this way about him.

Jesus: "Yes."

Elizabeth: That we have been taught that he was someone that we should not be liking.

Jesus: "Exactly."

Elizabeth: So let's-we're bringing Judas some-I'm blanking on what the word is I'm looking for-but he's a good guy! Not in the form of good vs bad but you know what I mean.

Jesus: "Yes. I understand what you're saying. He is a very-only those souls who have great understanding, who are very enlightened, are able to take on the embodiment of Judas."

Elizabeth: OK. So he knew that by—That Was part of the plan. He knew that and was that an act of Love then you would call it?

Jesus: "Yes. Absolutely."

Elizabeth: Alright. So when it says in the Bible that you had said that it would have been better for him not to have been born, that doesn't-that doesn't sound like it would be an accurate statement then.

Jesus: "No. And it's not. And remember that the Bible is-are Half Truths in many ways. Because things have been interpreted and misunderstood and twisted around to serve a human desire for power and control. And that is not to say that everything in the Bible is not-it is false— but there are many things that are . . . they cannot be understood any longer by your current mindset and where you are at and how it's been misinterpreted basically."

Elizabeth: K. That was some of my frustration Saturday night. Although the drinking did not help. (Laughing)

Jesus: "No. And a few mind altering experiences and no doubt, things become more exasperated of course."

Elizabeth: Yep. Let's see. What else do we wanna talk about here? (Laughing)

Jesus: (Laughing) It is unfortunate however-just to make a comment about the understanding of the Bible cause there are many Truths in the Bible but much of it was written as parable. Was written as um metaphor but there are many Truths to what was said. It's just that there were Many Things that were either left out or Put In that were not part of that basis of Truth in what had actually occurred."

Elizabeth: Well, it's kinda what I am hoping to do with this.

Jesus: "Yes."

Elizabeth: So, I wanna ask about your Mother, Mary. Did people come to her? Cause we kinda just see her as your mother. What did she do? Was she into herbs? Was she a Medium or Psychic or anything like that?

Jesus: "Well let's say that she was a Very Advanced soul as well with great understanding of this whole process and the purpose of that period of time and what it meant for Humanity so yes, she was like many other women typical of that day because she was living in that environment

210

but she was, as you said, very intuitive. Had great understanding but what was most prominent about her was her Innocence but her Wisdom as well. Those were 2 things. She was a very Wise Being but very Innocent in her Approach to life."

Elizabeth: OK. Um, my daughter wants to know, "Why did God make the trees be the ones to give us air to breathe?"

Jesus: "Well, how can I put this so that she will be satisfied with the answer. Let's say that there was-it was necessary for the planet. There are so many different elements of the planet that need to come together to have balance, correct? So without these things you cannot have-1 thing can't be without the other-etc etc. So those Energies that are embodied in the trees came forth with the purpose of saying that they would be the ones to sustain-be part of the group that would sustain life here in a more passive-well passive isn't the word-but in a more discreet way-the energy of it. So, they manifested as trees and giving forth the what you call it, the necessary-what is the word-what was her question-"

Elizabeth: The oxygen?

Jesus: "The oxygen. Thank you. Because it's symbolic of life force and the trees are an embodiment also of life force here so they hold that energy. They are an energy that holds the energy of life force, itself."

Elizabeth: I wanna go back to talking about God from our last time. So, would God be-it's said that God gives us breath so are we part of the whole body of God?

Jesus: "Yes! Yes. That's the best way of understanding it, yes."

Elizabeth: OK. Alright.

Jesus: "Because if you try to understand it too much with your head, it will only-and that is what happens-it's what happened with you and your drinking bout with your comrades the other evening."

Elizabeth: (hehehehe)

Jesus: "You were trying to-All, yourself included, understand and explain everything with your heads as opposed to understanding and thinking with your hearts and that may seem some what corny but that's not really that way. When we say, "Think with your heart." It means to think in a more expansive way. So if you think about God with your mind, it will try to compartmentalize everything and make it-make associations with what you already know. "Well, the body of God must be like this cause this is what our bodies are like or this is what I imagine the body of God would look like." Right? So you're trying to put it into a framework that makes sense to you. When you think with your heart, you are open to letting the images come to you in forms-the images coming—or the Feeling that will come to you-and that Feeling will carry with it Understanding. So when you do that, you are much Quieter so you are not needing to verify things with words but you do it with a feeling. So, when it comes to understanding say, the body of God or the Bible and what it's teachings Really Are For, it is best to think with your Heart and not with your mind."

Elizabeth: K. Pause. Were you laughing at us when we were doing all that? (laughing)

Jesus: "No, but it's always interesting to observe."

Elizabeth: Yeah, I bet. I don't smoke marijuana but I know a lot of people do and they want it legalized. Is that something that-what are Your thoughts on that?

Jesus: "I don't care. Honestly."

Elizabeth: It doesn't seem like you don't care about much, right?

Jesus: "Exactly. These are human-it's a plant. It is something that has multi purposes, and again, you have the manifestation of there being something there that has medicinal purposes and also practical purposes but because its medicinal purposes bring on Fear in those who want to Control the object that comes to control those who want to use it for medicinal reasons-for healing and such. Again, it's a human condition. We don't see it as being either good or bad or right or wrong. It's just there. We do not even play with or understand-that's not-to say that we don't understand is incorrect cause we DO understand but to use Your terminology we do not understand your Insistence on judgment all the time. We do understand it but we don't because there's no need to judge. And that is what it is with so many things, so, so, so many things and marijuana being one of those things that brings on judgment. Remember, all of these things are there for you to use in whatever way that you feel would work for you. Remember Free Will."

Elizabeth: Yep. How does Free Will work when there's such a plan as the blueprint-how does Free Will come into play when you're in A but you wanna get to C so B you have somewhere to play with. I don't know.

Jesus: "I'm sorry, you'll have to explain your question a little bit more. I'm lost a little bit."

Elizabeth: (laughing) So we come down here with a plan so we'll say my plan, ugh, I know, it's hard for me to explain to.

Jesus: "We can do it."

Elizabeth: So, Free Will would be someone going and shooting someone else. That's their Free Will. But was that in the original plan?

Jesus: "Probably. Don't know. Nobody would really know that. Maybe not even the person doing it. Not until they left their physical form and were able to review their life. So Free Will really is knowing that you have a Choice and again, remember, it's You Humans that put the value on Choice. You put the value of it being good or bad or right or wrong. YOU are the ones that say it is wrong to kill. Now you'll say, "We know that there were the Commandments that were given down." Yes, it is wrong to take a nother's life in regards to those Commandments but really what does It Mean? What. Does. It. Mean? When you stand in judgment of another and their actions, you then put yourself into that cycle of dying and re-birthing continually. So judgment keeps you in continual reincarnation."

Elizabeth: So if you can remove all judgment then you don't have to keep doing it? Reincarnating?

Jesus: "Essentially. I mean there are-might be things that you are here to do. It's not-it's a very complex and intricate experience and Unique To Each Soul and it's Journey here. And you set it up. I mean, you're constantly setting it up the way that you think would be the most beneficial to you. The most fun, what could you learn the most, and so on."

Elizabeth: OK. I'm on board with that. I understand.

Jesus: "OK."

Elizabeth: Last time when we were talking and you were talking about Miriam, the part of the organization, the name of it, I don't know what that is. Can you spell it for me?

Jesus: "I'm sorry, Miriam?"

Elizabeth: Yeah.

Jesus: "It is Mir-"

Elizabeth: No, not her name, the name of the organization that she was part of.

Jesus: "I'm sorry, I don't remember what it was that I told you."

Elizabeth: You said that she was a Grandmother like figure to you and that she was part of an organization and you said the name of it twice but I don't know what the name of it was."

Jesus: "The Essenes?"

Elizabeth: YES! What's that?

Jesus: "It is, I guess the the best would be ESSENES I believe, Essenes and a religious organization I guess would be the best way to describe them. They were the ones who-the Gnostics."

Elizabeth: OH the Gnostic! OK!

Jesus: "Yes."

Elizabeth: I'm a little bit familiar with that. OK, alright.

Jesus: "Yes. And they were a Sect, basically. And I spent much time with them."

Elizabeth: OK. A Sect you said?

Jesus: "Essentially, yes. So a Sect coming from the idea being an offshoot of the-of Gnosticism were the Essenes."

Elizabeth: OK. Alright. We got about 15 minutes. I wanna ask if my doing this book and sharing these messages with hopefully the world, is paving the way for my son, Arron, and what he's going to do.

Jesus: "Absolutely. Absolutely. Again, Free Will. Will he pick up the reins and go in the direction that he planned or will he go in another? But yes, that will give him the opportunity to do it as opposed to having to have to wait for someone else essentially. So that's where Free Will comes in. Your Free Will is presented to you and your Free Will gave you the opportunity to choose to do it or not to do it. And you chose to do it through Free Will which then the affect of that was that your son will then be able to do more of the things that He came here to do."

Elizabeth: OK. That makes sense! Um, John the Baptist. It's said that his parents were very old. Was he orphaned at any point?

Jesus: "Well, essentially, yes, but he was orphaned at an age that he was old enough to-to not-not to necessarily take care of himself but in a sense yes, but he was taken in by a group of individuals. So yes, he was orphaned but when you would say 12, 13, 14 years old."

Elizabeth: OK. Cause I had someone asking about that and then why was he in the desert?

Jesus: "Why he was in the desert? Well. Well why not? Would be really. Why not be in the desert?

Elizabeth: OK.

Jesus: "So I wonder why they questioned why he was in the desert. The desert is an environment-first of all-that is very Prominent in where so much occurred at the time that John the Baptist walked the Earth such as myself and others like that-like us. So the desert provides certain environmental Elements that Promote that Connection to connecting to Oneness. So, being in the desert is a—an experience that is very-removes all distractions-well, even though there Is much activity in the desert but there is just the right elements put together for many. Plus it is what was prominent and still is today for the area in which we lived and at the time that we lived."

Elizabeth: I wanna ask about Baptism. Is Baptism more of a personal choice? A lot of people do it when babies are newly born but I see it as a personal choice.

Jesus: "Yes. And you are right. It is a personal choice. Yet, you must understand that those that do it for another, there was some choice on the part of that Soul that gave permission."

Elizabeth: OK!

Jesus: "Otherwise it would not have occurred. So for an infant, they gave permission."

Elizabeth: OK, alright. My husband wants to know, "Why were we created with such large brains when we only use a small portion of it?"

Jesus: "Because you are evolving and you will be-you HAVE used other parts of your brain that you let—through different cycles, go into-not that you don't use them-but again, you are Evolving so you will be using those parts of your brain that you feel that have been neglected and also, it's all—it's a circuit board basically so yes, you can survive with certain things missing from you, but you-having everything in place puts you in full operating order. So remember that, evolution, your brain is evolving-or is there-and you are evolving in a sense Into that brain and it gives you the Opportunity to use things that you-you know when you come here and you learn things you are using parts of your brain that maybe the generation before you did not use."

Elizabeth: OK. What about Autism? There's a lot of children with Autism. Is that something that I will be able to be healing or is that again, their purpose. Part of their purpose.

Jesus: "It does serve a purpose. There has been-it is a very interesting choice and direction that has kind of been born of your-of Humanity. Those-it's a-I wanna use the word trend but not in the way that is normally understood but it is a trend and there to bring awareness to individuals about Many things but one is about this Need for connectedness. The Need to Be Part Of The Oneness. Those Souls who are embodied in the-who have taken on Autism-are Souls Seeking To Understand the opposite, right? So they are disconnected and very isolated within themselves here because they are seeking to understand the Opposite of that and that is that Connection to Oneness. So, again, you go to the opposite extremes. That is one of the primary reasons for this trend of Autism and that is why it is manifesting in the way that it is."

Elizabeth: So they want to know the opposite of Oneness. So they're not connected to the Oneness through-during their Autism?

Jesus: "Well they ARE but there is the Appearance that they are not and they Feel that they are not."

Elizabeth: So, are they much More, actually?

Jesus: "Well, Ultimately they Will Be. Yes."

Elizabeth: OK. Cause I would think that if they'd be so alone, right, that they would be turning to the Oneness even stronger.

Jesus: "Exactly! That is the Purpose of it. These are souls that have had lifetimes where they were not able to connect to Oneness. They spent their lives here feeling-maybe some of them were what you call Atheists or some of them lost Faith in there being anything—a myriad of reasons. But they were disconnected from Oneness and saw this Autism as a means of connecting to Oneness. Being Forced to connect to Oneness."

Elizabeth: Oooooh

Jesus: "You see? You understood it though in your words that you used made absolute sense."

Elizabeth: OK. Yeah. That's a Great way for parents to see it that way now. That's really good.

Jesus: "Yes. Again, that's-when somebody comes in, there's a reason for it-and such an influx of those with Autism is because in order to-what you are doing here-is you are learning to Master-as I've said this many times, the Emotional body and those with Autism are lacking an emotion. Are they not? That is one of the-they do not have the spectrum of emotion that most humans have. Correct?"

Elizabeth: Right.

Jesus: "So is that what you are going to be like? Yes and no. You will not be Moved by your emotions. So it's really not about HEALING it's about understanding that this is kind of the trend and these are those that are the avaunt-guard. Those who are the first ones who are attempting to be in 5th Dimensional reality. They've Mastered the human-the emotional body—but not to the degree that they can-they're out of balance with it. OK? So they've Mastered the emotional body but to the degree that they've disconnected with Oneness. OK? So, really it's those that with Autism are using the lack of emotion and the disconnecting with others around them in order to force them to connect with Oneness."

Elizabeth: OK. I'm not gonna even try to heal anybody-they're doing themselves a great credit for doing that so I'm not even going to try to touch that.

Jesus: "Thank you. That's exactly what it is. And this may go against what many people would believe and will not agree with this and that is OK also."

Elizabeth: OK. Right. OK. I think that will be it for today.

Jesus: "Very good. I feel that we are complete. So is there anything that I can help you with before I go? Is there anything that you need answered for you for today, on a personal level?"

Elizabeth: On a personal level? No, I feel good that I got over the frustration and now I feel empowered because it was really bothering me but now I feel good about it. And you answered about Arron because he's-I feel like there's just something so very special about him-all my children are special-I just feel like something bigger for him so.

Jesus: "Yes. Yes. So good."

Elizabeth: Do you think there's anything that I need to know? Do you need to tell me something Jesus?

Jesus: "No, I was just asking. That's all."

Elizabeth: (laughing) You don't have any other surprises or anything like that for me?

Jesus: "Well you'll see in the coming days now won't you?"

Elizabeth: I know right?! (laughing)

Jesus: "Exactly. Exactly. Very good. I will then give the microphone back to your friend and we will talk very soon. I love you very much and you have a wonderful wonderful evening."

Elizabeth: "Thank you Jesus. I love you too. You're a great guy. Thank you.

Jesus: "Goodbye."

August 30, 2013

And The Oscar Goes To . . . .

My Saturday started out just like any other Saturday. Our baby was happy and chirping little noises in his crib waiting for my husband, Kevin, and I to come get him. Our other two kids ran upstairs to give us Good Morning hugs when they heard the toilet flush, we all had breakfast together and the cats and dogs had food and water :) The night before, Kevin had made a fire and we all had sat on the swing in the fairy garden overlooking the valley. I had gotten a request for money from someone. At first it was polite and then it got rude. So Saturday morning this was on my mind as I pushed Arron, our 1 year old, in the swing outside by the bird feeders. I kept thinking about how rude this person had been about it and had tried to lay a guilt trip on me. I didn't like that. Then I turned it from him to me because I remembered what Jesus has been teaching me. I began to ask myself, "Why did I ask this person to play that role for me??"

The winds of change, I called them, had blown in that day. They really felt like that!! They were strong and warm and I spent time with Arron up in the pasture walking around just to feel them on me. I posted my Facebook status to "The Winds of Change are Here!!" They brought with them Hope and Energy and Excitement for things to come and Relief because things would now move along more rapidly and a publisher for the book with Jesus would soon be on it's way.

That afternoon, as Arron napped, I decided to catch up on my meditations from the Deepak Chopra/Oprah—21 Day Meditation Challenge. I was more than a few days behind. The one for Saturday was Miraculous Forgiveness but the one that felt and sounded good for me to do was, Miraculous Honor. It had a quote at the top of the page by Marianne Williamson that said, "The world changes when we change. The world softens when we soften. The world loves us when we choose to love the world." and the thought for the day was, "I release and my heart is at peace." During my meditation I saw a patch of 4 leaf clovers, my flame (which was white and very long) and a beach that looked to be in Hawaii that had writing in the sand. I was looking at it from the top of a cliff. I could not quite see what the words said but it looked to be a large Heart shape. After my meditation, I got out my Doreen Virtue deck of Angel Tarot oracle cards. I shuffled all 78 cards and wouldn't you know, here was the Six of Air—"the winds of change are blowing-and it's a favorable wind." !!! :)

I then went outside and walked through the gate in the pasture and thought to myself, "I am not going to be guilt tripped into giving this person money. It's not going to happen because I've learned from the best how to say no to that." And DING! There was my answer! I had asked him to play that role for me so that I would find another lesson that my mom taught me! YES!!!

Gratitude is a wonderful thing!!! I ran down to the barn to tell my husband how it all fit together :)

That evening, at sunset, the sun was a strikingly bright, beautiful orange. I thought about the time that my mom stayed here for a night and how she and the kids and I stood at the cornfield and watched it go down behind the hill. We had bets on how long it would take. I won. I think it was 15 seconds :)

As I saw the sun, I knew. Now was the time to release her ashes! I have had my mom's ashes for many months now and I wanted to do something special with them but I didn't know what. A balloon release didn't sound right and I didn't know exactly WHERE to sprinkle them. Nothing felt right so I had been keeping them in my purse. They were in a little film case. When they came in the mail, I took them up to my bedroom and held them in my hands and wept. I was and AM so very grateful to her sisters and brother for thinking to give me some. My 2 older children took their turns with them too. My son, Adam, is 8. He sobbed and sobbed and then told me, "It's her hand. I know it's her hand."

I ran to the house and retrieved her ashes from my purse and a bed sheet to take up to the pasture. Lexie followed me and sat with me. She asked if she could open the lid and look at the ashes. I said that was fine-just to shield them from the wind. She found a little tiny piece of paper in there that said, "SIT" on it. She asked me, "Are they REALLY Grandma's ashes??" I assured her that they were. I made a mental note of "SIT". I told her, "Go get Dad and Adam from the barn-they won't want to miss this."

All of us stood in the pasture, on the hill overlooking our home, minus Arron, who was in bed already. I then gave my speech that went something like this, "Since I ASKED Grandma to play this role for me, that she did SO WELL, I would give her an Oscar, you know, the golden statues, because she gave an outstanding performance and I thank her SO MUCH for the lessons that she was able to teach me." Lexie then asked me why I would ask her to be like that (meaning so hurtful) and not in a loving way? I was able to say, "Who better to learn from than someone that should BE that close to you but is not? I felt that I could learn the Most having it that way. That was the way that I set that up and she did EXACTLY what I asked her to do so that I would Learn and Grow from it." Then I waited for one of the big wind gusts and began to shake out the ashes. We each took turns with it, ending back at me to shake out the final ones. They were all taken with the wind and it felt good. It felt RIGHT.

Afterward, Kevin and Adam went back down to the barn to continue with their project together of fixing up the scooter and Lexie stayed with me for just a little bit and then went off to play. I was by myself. I welcomed that. I sat with my back against the tree. "SIT" the paper had said. I closed my eyes and felt the base of the tree moving with the wind. I hadn't ever felt that before. The "winds" can move me all they want to but I stand tall and strong and proud for all to see. I talked to my mom and I cried and I admired the beauty of all that was around me and I gave thanks for all of it and especially for my sweet little children and wonderful husband, a list that went on and on.

Ready to go inside, since it was getting dark out, I went to stand up and here A CRICKET came across the sheet and jumped onto my leg! I greeted him and thanked him too because that is very good luck when you see a cricket! In fact, the last time a cricket got my attention in this way was the day before I found our home and then the long, almost 3 year wait and a lesson in Patience finally paid off and we were able to move to Minnesota to be with Kevin :) Yes, crickets are good signs of things to come!

My explanation of WHY I chose my mom to play that role for me made sense to Lexie and that is why I am sharing it here. Because of the example for others that are NOT close with their parents or other people in their lives. To learn how to begin to do this in their own lives.

Today is Friday. The following week. I just found a picture of my mom and Lexie and I on the floor that had fallen out from my bible. I picked it up and stared at it. For the first time I am able to see my mom as this VERY IMPORTANT person in my life-in my JOURNEY here on Earth. I do not see her as I used to. Meaning: Bitter, Manipulating, Selfish, etc, etc. I see her as the Soul that she truly is. Perfect. Because Jesus is right, I do not know what she came here to accomplish. I can only Understand that which was OUR OWN relationship. And I am so Very Thankful for that role that she played. Maybe she might say, "It was an Honor." It does not take away how HARD it was and how PAINFUL and HURTFUL it was when she was alive but it has TRANSFORMED all of that into my "ticket to FREEDOM" as Jesus puts it. Yes, I DID Release and my heart is at Peace. :) It feels good and now I am ready to find the perfect frame for that picture and put it up because I can look at my mom again and it doesn't hurt anymore.

I'm OK With My Crazy! :)

As it turns out, I learned many things from thinking that my friend was talking about me behind my back. I kept asking myself, "Why did I choose her to play that role for me??" I realized that yes, it WAS a pattern! I have been called crazy my whole life-even since I was a little girl.

It was the night that I saw what my friends had said, earlier that morning, was when I became Empowered. My husband had brought home the new GI Joe movie and that inspired me to the "You ain't seen nothing yet!" attitude. The next day I was doing a Deepak Chopra meditation. He spoke of Presence. I realized that she was teaching me this also. I not only needed to stop checking Facebook so much and put my phone down more and be present with my family but I was able to see that by being present-in the moment-it didn't matter what Anyone said about me. In this moment, they are not in my presence and nowhere even close to me. In this moment I appreciate what is going on with me and around me. This moment, NOW, is all that matters. I choose Presence.

After this realization, I felt good but knew that there was something else in it for me. Beyond the empowerment and presence. I felt that it still was not complete. I continued to ask myself what that was. What was I missing?? Well, a few days prior to all this happening, one of my Wonder Woman sisters, (Compassion) had suggested reading "Tapping the Power Within" by Iyanla Vanzant. I told her I would join her because I hadn't read any of her books yet and knew hardly anything about this amazing woman that I respect very much. I checked the library and they did not have a copy of it so I told my daughter, Alexis, that we would go to Barnes & Noble on our shopping day together. That morning I had a vision of another one of Iyanla's books. This one was "PEACE from Broken Pieces". I didn't see the name of it but it was the color of the cover-bright yellow-that I saw. I thought, "Watch, Barnes&Noble won't have Tapping but they will have this because THIS is the one I am supposed to be reading." And sure enough! When Alexis and I got to Barnes&Noble, here was the discount table right when you walk in the door. I found Dr. Wayne Dyer's books, "Excuses Begone!" and "The Shift" for $5.95 and picked up copies of those in case someone I knew could use them. Then I saw Iyanla's book on the bottom shelf for $5.95 also!! YES!!!! I couldn't believe these great finds On Sale!!

Before Alexis and I left, we moved all of Iyanla's books to the top of the table so that people would see them better :) Hehe.

A couple nights later I was able to start to read it. On page 24 is where I found my answer. Iyanla talked about the Pathology of family. "It's why no one talks to so and so or talks about them as soon as they leave the room." It sparked something in my heart. A truth. I immediately thought about my friend and her parents. They talk about people all the time! And I'm not saying that in a mean way, I'm just saying that is what they do. She only talks about me because she learned it from them! This made my heart realize the Truth and I began to cry. NOW I understand!! :)

CHAPTER 10

Emotions Are Your Tools

In the 2 weeks following the last session with Jesus, I was busily going through all of the tapes and reading along with what I had transcribed so that I had it all Just as He said things. As accurate as possible. I had a feeling that things were wrapping up and it needed to be ready to go.

September 4, 2013

Jesus: "Hello my friend."

Elizabeth: Hey, Jesus! How are you?

Jesus: "I am doing well, of course. And how are you?"

Elizabeth: Feeling anxious, um, the Holy Spirit dove fell off my necklace this morning so I'm curious as to I think that we might be wrapping this up. Is-would I be correct in thinking that?

Jesus: "Yes. So why would that make you feel anxious? Have you asked yourself for wrapping this up, why do you feel anxious about that?"

Elizabeth: About wrapping the book up?

Jesus: "Yes."

Elizabeth: Uh, I feel anxious because I think it will be new things that I'll be having to do, out of my comfort zone so I might be a little nervous or apprehensive about that but I REALLY want these messages to get out to people so I'm just like, I want it to happen so that people can start doing these things in their own lives when they read this stuff so.

Jesus: "Absolutely. So, again, the feeling of anxiousness is, you've identified it. That's the important thing. And this goes for Anyone who is dealing with something—the Awareness of what you are experiencing in that moment-it does not mean that it will go away or that it shouldn't

226

be there or it's good or it's bad, it Just Is, you are experiencing that at the moment and being in a certain emotional state is a way of receiving information from your Own Bodily System telling you certain things and it's Not Always Bad. It's not always something that you want to get rid of and That is Key Here. One of the messages we're hoping that WILL come across is WHEN you feel anxiety WHEN you feel anger when you feel these what you call Negative emotions, they're Not Always something that you want to-in fact they AREN'T things that you want to take and say, "Let me get rid of this!" without Understanding and I think that has come through here. Understanding. And you may continue to have these experiences-emotional experiences-because they are your Tools. They are Your Tools. What you Use to Gain information about your experience, your environment, your own awareness, your Own Path. So, when you run from them or shy from them or fear them, then you add another element of experience there that you have to first have to deal with-the running from, the fear, the resistance as you call it, and then get down to what the Information that is contained in the emotion. If this is the message that comes out to the world through these teachings here, our discussions here, that there is Valuable, Valuable Insight, Information in regards to that. You have an emotional body for a reason. And the reason being is that it's like a radar. If you think of radar-how radar is used for a vehicle. A vehicle will use radar to know or a compass would be a better example. You have a compass that tells you what direction you are going. Radar tells you what obstacles are in the way or what might-there's something there-you don't know what it is-but there is an object in front of you. Look at your emotions as being that as opposed to, "-Gasp-Oh, I'm feeling this and I must get rid of it or I'm feeling that and I must get rid of it." Or, "This must not be a very good experience for me because I'm feeling negative." Well Maybe Not. Really Be Patient. Be Slow in Reacting and take things with a Little Bit Less Seriousness. These are the messages we are hoping to bring forth. Now, yes, we are winding up This Phase of this experience but you will continue going on with this because it's never ending. There will be-we want that you maybe complete this section and then look for ways to bring it to the public. We will do our part. You do your part. And all of us working together, we will bring information to the world that is necessary for individuals to Find that sense of Peace. Especially right now that things are Soo much in-up in the air-so to speak or taking on such a tone of strangeness for so many people. So it's important that they have tools necessary and this is what-this is a handbook in a lot of ways. So it may not be extensive. So yes, I would say, we will continue to have our conversations but you will take this, what you have now, and begin to think about offering it to the public."

Elizabeth: OK, I figured that's what was going to happen. So that's good to hear from you!

Jesus: "Yes. Yes. We could go on. But we will probably move in other directions, do other things, it's to be seen. Build on this. Let's begin with this. Let's test the waters with this. Let's put it in a way-let's see what the reaction-what we can create from what we already have right now. I think we have enough to begin with. Let's put it that way."

Elizabeth: Alright. So we're starting out with little ripples and see where they go.

Jesus: "Yes. Yes. Absolutely."

Elizabeth: OK. So when I'm trying to get people's attention, like, to you know, say, "Oh, I wanna pick this up and I wanna read this!" What do I tell them to get their attention?

Jesus: "Well, what sort of ideas-cause you have ideas. How has it impacted you is really-that is why you were the recipient, in a way, and the Medium was the vessel. Because you will be-it's not that the Medium will not be involved in the promotion of this-of course she will be. But you have a very important role here because you have the responsibility that you have of being out there in a certain way that is Your Responsibility that is a different responsibility than the Medium's. Of course, this is like everything in life-but when you are-THAT aspect of it-the Excitement is what YOU bring-the element that YOU bring to this because the Medium cannot sense it in the same way as you but You bring the Excitement!"

Elizabeth: Giggle

Jesus: "Because you've experienced it-First Hand."

Elizabeth: Yes! That's why I think why I get so excited cause I KNOW it works! Cause I've been using it! So.

Jesus: "Yes. So, that's where you'll begin because it's-you'll speak to others about how this came to you. Your initial attempt at reaching people was the indicator of your ability to involve people in-at that level-By personal experience and telling others what you have done and how it's very simple if you allow yourself to observe it In That Way."

Elizabeth: Right.

Jesus: "Does that make sense?"

Elizabeth: Yes.

Jesus: "OK. So you see how you are-being the recipient in this way, your Excitement, and you Applied this-what you have learned-you're more clear headed about it in the sense that as it's coming to you directly as opposed to the Medium who is only filtering it, absorbing it internally, may listen to it and read it later and see it a little bit differently later-her experiential feedback is different than yours."

Elizabeth: Right.

Jesus: "So, so much of that IS from you explaining to others how you heard these messages, you felt compelled to bring this forth, and you'll see that that's the beginning point. Remember, everything has that kind of beginning and just be gently guided as to where you need to go from there."

Elizabeth: OK. So, I think I would probably do better talking to people, like publishers and stuff, probably in person cause they can SEE my Excitement! SEE how much Passion I have for it. So. Do I need to take a class where a publisher will be so I can speak to him? Or?

Jesus: "These are all possibilities. If you Can, then do that. You know by getting out there and your Enthusiasm is Infectious and that's what you carry. And that deep Faith that you have and your Enthusiasm. THAT is what is going to be reaching these people. Remember that. Remember the Energy of it."

Elizabeth: OK. OK. I'll do that. So I could possibly just bring that energy with whatever words that I use because it's the energy that I'm putting into it. They'll feel it when they read it?

Jesus: "Yes."

Elizabeth: OK. Alright.

Jesus: "OK. So. What questions have you for me as we conclude this first section of our experience together?"

Elizabeth: Um. Well, I wanted to ask you if "Sins" is a Man-made word.

Jesus: "Well. OK. Depends on how you are asking-what you are wanting to know from that. Sin is an expression of a-of an energy. OK? So nothing is right or wrong, good or bad. Sin indicates that something is wrong. That there is a punishment to it. REALLY what it is, it's a type of-A Sin-the energy Behind that word-where it has it's origins-is in that Sin is a blindness to experience. OK? So when you sin is when you judge something-you are sinning in a sense because you are not in a place of being as receptive as possible. OK? But it does not carry with it punishment. Only-the only punishment-is that it becomes a hindrance for you. But again, when we view all of what we understand as our teachings here, if there is no right or wrong or good or bad, everything is Just Is-than how can Sin even exist? So where did that come from? And the way you understand Sin-in your world-it is Man-made. But there IS an energy that could be-it has it's origins in that—and all it is is when someone-a Soul-continually experiences the same pattern when they are in human form and does not Allow themselves Enlightenment through experience. Is the best way of putting it. Where the origins of it-Then the rest became Man-made."

Elizabeth: OK. Alright. That's a good explanation cause that's what I was kinda thinking so I just wanted you to clear that up cause . . .

Jesus: "Cause it's out there."

Elizabeth: Yeah. From when we were talking about the second coming and stuff um, there doesn't seem that there is a sense of urgency for people to turn directly To You, right? Because you were saying that people are of a higher vibration that Don't necessarily believe in you and that's OK too. So, is-just Finalize-is there a sense of urgency for people to turn to you?

Jesus: "No there is not. But turning to me is-when you say that, really what I AM, what is meant by that is the Christ Consciousness Energy. Turning to the Christ Consciousness Energy rather than turning to me. So when one says, "Turning to Jesus." Really what they want to understand from that is Allowing Christ Consciousness Energy to thrive Within Them."

Elizabeth: OK.

Jesus: "Allowing what is External Christ Consciousness Energy to touch and aflame within the Human Soul of Christ Consciousness Energy so that it is Alive within you."

Elizabeth: Beautiful!

Jesus: "Sometimes I'm eloquent. Sometimes. Not all."

Elizabeth: Um, let's see. Um, I know. My brother, when he was little, he had a premonition. He had a dream that he caught a goose on the ice. So then he told my mom that he did that and then when we went up to our cottage that weekend, he DID find-he caught a goose on the ice! So my question is, why do some people deny themselves those abilities instead of going further into that?

Jesus: "Well, it's because of many factors and it really depends on an individual. What they are here to experience. What-how much they have become Human in a sense with not-in disconnecting with their more spiritual or metaphysical side or aspect. So it really depends on the individual. The reasons for not allowing that to flow through them-there has been great resistance to it-set forth by your traditional religions. They've been acting as the Resistance that is Necessary for the then expansion forward. Right? Whenever there is something-that pendulum that swings to one side, it will then cause, it reaches it's culmination point and then there is an Explosion of some sort and then everything goes to the other extreme. You see that ALL the time. In nature, and you see that all the time in your Human experience. So too with things like this. There's been such denial from the masses that these things can't exist. That you-but it's necessary for then it to come out in full force because it is a necessary state for existing within this 5th Dimensional Realm that you are all moving into."

Elizabeth: OK

Jesus: "So it's a way of learning and it's a way of teaching How To exist in that realm.

Elizabeth: So when people have things like that that happen like that to them, it's kinda just like a little planted seed and whether it's gonna grow or not. Right?

Jesus: "Yes. Yes. Exactly. But it's an indication of what is to come."

Elizabeth: OH OK!

Jesus: "For everyone. They will all be. That's what's available for everyone when you reside more in this 5th Dimensional Realm, yes."

Elizabeth: OK. The 5th Dimensional Realm-do we know a time frame of when that might happen or is that all depend on where we're going err.

Jesus: "Well you are already sometimes in-like on the edges of that 5th Dimensional Realm. That's why things are so Intense right now. Why you've been having these different eclipses and solar flares and all the different planetary upheaval. It is because of the changes that are occurring for the planet itself and how she is adjusting her vibration and then the humans on the planet, you are, your physical forms are adjusting-that's why many have been going through different physical experiences that have been intensified. Or emotional experiences as well because you are-you know like the snake shedding it's skin-it's a process. The butterfly that starts off in his cocoon, then becoming a butterfly-it's that moment before becoming a butterfly there is-it's very painful and such. So, that's-you are at times-like on the edge of the 5th Dimensional Realm but right now you are still traversing Between the worlds so to speak. So the time frame is hard to say because it's already there-it's just some are there more depending on where they have brought their vibration to."

Elizabeth: OK. And when you speak of the different realms-those are-is it like a curtain?

Jesus: "Yeah."

Elizabeth: So if I was to look just past my feet it might be just beyond my feet.

Jesus: "Yes."

Elizabeth: (chuckle) that's so neat. I wanna see stuff. Am I gonna start seeing stuff? Cause I've been asking. This is a personal question.

Jesus: "Yes. What kind of stuff have you been asking to see?"

Elizabeth: I wanna be able to see Spirits.

Jesus: "OK. You are wanting to see them in a way in which they cannot always present themselves. And you do not have that as your-it's not a necessary thing for you to see them in the physical the way that you've been wanting to see them. Because of who you are and how you will be experiencing 5th Dimensional Reality. You won't want to see them with your physical eyes. We want that you understand that you can see them with your energetic body. That's why. They are there. It's just a different type of seeing that you have. You want to be able to Let Go of that desire to see them with your eyes that way. THEN when you begin to sense them and experiencing them with energetically, once you get comfortable with that, then to potential for seeing them with your eyes will increase."

Elizabeth: OK. Alright. I was kinda thinking that maybe I should just let that go.

Jesus: "Yes. And just say, "OK. Let me just experience it at an energetic vibrational level."

Elizabeth: OK. Cause I was outside walking around this morning with Arron and I was thinking, well, if I did see you, if You or Mother Mary appeared in front of me, I'd wanna run to you and give you a hug. And then I thought, well, maybe I wouldn't be able to do that. But. If I have the feeling of giving you a hug, right then and there, then you'd be able to feel that anyways. Right?

Jesus: "OK. I will tell you something. When you-I reside in all of you. And you know that. When you hug another-you are hugging me."

Elizabeth: OK.

Jesus: "So, I know you want to see me as you remember me but I no longer have-that was a very short period of time-I no longer have that as my way of Being. It was very temporary so if you were to see me in that way, it's really not what is Truth. But if you were to sit and open up to the Energy of me-what-who I am-Then you would feel the embrace and it will be much more profound but you can begin when you embrace another. Ask to feel the Christ Consciousness or the Jesus within them-however you want to do it because That's Really what it's about."

Elizabeth: (sniffles) That makes me cry! Cause it's True.

Jesus: "Yes. And then when you do that for another-it Ignites it Within Them-as I've said before-grows-makes it stronger within you and within yourself and the other as well."

Elizabeth: That's really good. OK. I have to compose myself now.

Jesus: "Yes. Because so many-and the same-it's because it is one of-that is what I did here-the bringing forth the Christ Consciousness and opening the pathways for that. And each soul that incarnates has now the makeup-the DNA-the Gene-whatever-of the Christ Consciousness within them. So there is Always. No one comes without that now. That is what **I** brought. Opening up that pathway. Earth did not have Christ Consciousness prior to my experience here."

Elizabeth: OK. Thank you for putting it that way because I wasn't looking at it that way before so.

Jesus: "Exactly. Exactly. So Now you will see and your experience with others will increase quite a bit. It's going to change the way you relate."

Elizabeth: OK.

Jesus: "Because you will be looking to FEEL that within another and then you feel it within yourself and that's-and not feel who they are as a Human Being but Who They Are as an Eternal Being, essentially and that's what you will be connecting with and that is what everyone can do! That's just not for you. This is what EVERYONE can do! Cause if you think about it, you are an energy Being and if you embrace another, say you embrace another out of the joy of seeing them and having them close to you, that is an energy exchange that's closer to Christ Consciousness than hugging another because they are sad and you feel sorry for them and need to comfort them because you feel sorry for them. But when you embrace them, when you have that, and you embrace them knowing that they are ALSO part of this Oneness that we say—the Christ Consciousness-they have the opportunity of then having that ignited within them."

Elizabeth: So they may be able to feel that then.

Jesus: "Yes."

Elizabeth: OK. I'm gonna go start huggin people! (laughing)

Jesus: "Yes. It teaches-Yes! You asked and you received. It's just-and this is what we are hoping that will come forth for those who open themselves to this information. Is that they will stop the interpreting their experience in the ways that they have been and start to see-they say, "I ask and it's not coming" and all of this and it's there! It's there! It's just not in the form the way you have perceived it or have your expectations of it. That's what's important. How you are expecting it to come and how it really is. So stay open to that."

Elizabeth: Oh, that's what I was thinking this morning, actually. (Laugh)

Jesus: "OK. Good."

Elizabeth: I was thinking, yeah, expectations, remaining open, how they yes. OK. Good.

Jesus: "Yes."

Elizabeth: Expectations aren't-can they work negatively against a person?

Jesus: "Absolutely. Because it can keep your attention focused in a direction and not—that is not necessarily the way that you Really Want to be going or how—You Miss Out on things if you look at it or experience it with that-with expectation. Missing out on that potential of being surprised or of learning something new."

Elizabeth: Right. So, the expectations that I hold for this book, I should just not worry about it. My husband keeps saying, "Don't worry. God's got it all OK." but I feel-but I have this certain role here so where-am I doing OK with like with my role of what I need to do for it?

Jesus: "Yes, absolutely! That's why there's been a flow."

Elizabeth: OK. Cause I don't wanna screw it up. (Laughing)

Jesus: "No. Neither one of you are screwing it up, by any means. So remember, it is something that there's something for both of you to learn in this and others and we're making an attempt to reach a larger audience here with this information. So you will be patient and see what ends up happening."

Elizabeth: OK. I'm gonna go on to a question. My daughter wanted to know if there was a reason for war. There are things going on in Syria right now and I'm concerned. Sigh. When people take action. It should be for the good of all and I don't know. Do you have any thoughts of that?

Jesus: "Well. So the purpose of war?"

Elizabeth: Yeah.

Jesus: "Would be, the purpose of war really is, again, from chaos—from chaos comes Order. Chaos comes Order. And It's The Way Things Are On Earth. And in many parts of the Universe. There's chaos and in the chaos 1. And if you think about, you have little wars going on all the time. People who don't get along and bicker with each other and call each other names. That's a war, is it not? It's the same Energy. It's Absolutely the same energy when someone has a negative feeling towards another individual and feels that a sense of retaliation or vindictiveness that's the same energy of War. So, it's going on all over the place. And if you ALL through this Here, understand that Everything Is Energy and Understanding it and it's Messages that it's carrying and the Vibration of it, it will Certainly help you in Understanding and being more Accepting of conditions that are part of just the way things are. To keep balance you have to-at this time-have to have Chaos. And then there's Order. Chaos and then there's Order. At this time. Your ultimate goal is to NOT have to have chaos to the degree that you have it, in order to have Order. OK? That's part of this Heaven on Earth where you are able to Raise the Vibration of the Planet and those on the Planet to a level where chaos and resistance No Longer have the same service as they do right now."

Elizabeth: Will this book be able to help people go beyond that then? I mean, it's helping me, so.

Jesus: "Yes. So there you are. You're the example. It's helping you and you're someone who has already a lot of enlightened ideas and understands a lot so think about the every day individual and what that will mean for them."

Elizabeth: OK. Maybe touch on, going back to the importance of respecting your body.

Jesus: "Yes."

Elizabeth: I don't know. Obesity is a very big thing but is that-I'm assuming I'm judging then so maybe obesity would just be another certain path that somebody has? (Note: I now smell strong cigarette smoke as I type this question up and we are not smokers so I'd like to include smoking also to this).

Jesus: "Yes. That they're choosing. Yes."

Elizabeth: But ultimately, should we be taking care of our bodies?

Jesus: "Yes. It's the vehicle that you are using to inhabit Earth. It's how you-how-otherwise, why bother with the physical form?"

Elizabeth: Right.

Jesus: "Just say, you know, come down here and be Energy Beings and nothing more. Without the physical form . . . . you know, it becomes very difficult for certain experiences to occur but with the physical form-it's the vehicle-it's just the way it is. So when you disrespect the physical form, there's consequences because of the way it's made up and it's OK, it's neither good nor bad but is it hindering you? Is it serving you? All of these questions you must ask yourself. Is it serving me to Be obese? And maybe it is. Because there's something that you're learning there. So, in order to learn it, you chose obesity. But does that mean that you are stuck as an obese person forever? No."

Elizabeth: OK. Maybe just because I like to exercise and it makes me feel good that I'd like other people to be feeling good too, so.

Jesus: "Right."

Elizabeth: I don't wanna force my views on people but.

Jesus: "True. True. But it IS important how you use your form. Yes."

Elizabeth: Alright. Oh, when you were telling about animal reincarnation you were saying that animals are less defined, more united, they are more like one. They are half individual and then my tape got flipped and I didn't get the rest of what you were saying so can you kinda finish on what you were saying? You were saying they were in their own evolution also.

Jesus: "Yes. So animals, essentially what they are is they have-everything has consciousness. Everything. And animals have consciousness that is more of a mass rather than an individual consciousness. Like Humans are more individualized in their consciousness and you can tell. So, whenever you have that for an animal, they are more connected, let's say, and United in with the Oneness and with each other than Human Beings are because their path is different as well. Does that answer your question?"

Elizabeth: Yeah, that helps. Yeah. So I suppose that's how an animal can tell if a person is a threat or not because they must be reading their energy. They must-can they read energy better than we can? For now?

Jesus: "Yes. Absolutely. Absolutely."

Elizabeth: OK. Alright. Just another plug for people to be nicer to animals! (laughing)

Jesus: "Yes. Yes. Treat them with kindness. They Are there In Service but that doesn't mean abuse is OK either."

Elizabeth: Right. Is there anything else you wanna tell us when we don't know much about you in the Bible? Is there anything else we should know that we might be interested in?

Jesus: "Hmm, let me see. What else. Well, that I was fluent in languages of other lands. I just knew them so I was sometimes considered a-I was a bit of a spectacle in a sense because I could walk into a foreign land and speak their language."

Elizabeth: Wow!

Jesus: "Yes."

Elizabeth: OK. What else? (laughing)

Jesus: (A little laugh) "Yes. Well, that—some things have to stay Hidden for the moment. For the very fact that your planet isn't ready for it. And it is part of what will be coming out. So. That-when we talk about-when you ask about my life when it was on Earth-some things, if they were to be revealed Now, would have an adverse affect or not be accepted. It just wouldn't be-it's not the right time for that information to come out. But let's just say that I had lived a very Long and Healthy life, as you know, and things even after my quote un quote "death" there was still an existence that I had created."

Elizabeth: OK. We'll leave it at that then.

Jesus: "Yes."

Elizabeth: I was going to ask you about Alzheimer's and when I was thinking about it, I saw the face of a baby. So, are people with Alzheimer's kind of assisting humanity in the same way of when people are dying of disease or whatever, going in between the worlds and getting rid of that cellular memory-like detaching the clingingness to life? To the Human form?

Jesus: "Yes."

Elizabeth: OK.

Jesus: "So, you're seeing an infant. What does that mean for you?

Elizabeth: Um, it means that infants, they come in with open possibilities. They don't have any set guidelines. They don't know any of that yet. So.

Jesus: "Yes. So, someone with Alzheimer's is going back to that state of pureness."

Elizabeth: Yes. Yes. OK.

Jesus: "Yes."

Elizabeth: Um, people would like to have a cure for that. Is there any kind of cure for that? Or?

Jesus: "There is a cure for everything."

Elizabeth: OK.

Jesus: "But will there BE in your lifetime? Possibly. There will Definitely be changes in the way it affects people. They're already beginning to do that. And that, see, they serve a purpose too-it's that constant pendulum swinging back and forth between what is easier to deal with than what is more difficult to deal with and swinging back and forth, back and forth."

Elizabeth: It seems like we're all taking our turns just doing our own part in helping all of us together as One.

Jesus: "Yes. Absolutely. Because that is what you are doing."

Elizabeth: Yeah. Um . . . Oh, I know what I wanted to ask. So, disease such as cancer can be manifested because of things like Unforgiveness and other emotions. Are there other physical things-I'm just gonna use deodorant as an example because it's got Aluminum in it. So they think that maybe the aluminum could cause the cancer sooo but I don't believe that I could get cancer cause like you said, disease can't exist in a body-in someone that doesn't believe in the disease to begin with. So

Jesus: "Right."

Elizabeth: Are there outside influences creating the disease besides us just us in our heads and our emotions?

Jesus: "Well, to a certain degree but then it would hold true for all. So everyone who used deodorant would all get cancer. Would that not be a more accurate statement if you were going to say that? What Human Beings need to Focus on is Why One and Not the Other?"

Elizabeth: OK.

Jesus: "You definitely live with much-with a greater number of toxic-you live in a more toxic environment, absolutely. You don't have the pureness of air and cleanliness of the water that was at one time. But there were-you are also not living with diseases that were-would cut a life short during My time. The thing is, is finding a Balance here. And finding what-why did this occur? What is-something like cancer is a very hard thing to find one definite and specific cause because there are so many and things will-you weaken your system by using certain things and certain behaviors that will weaken the system. That's all it is."

Elizabeth: So it's really-it goes back to listening to your own intuition of how you feel something's good for you or it's not.

Jesus: "Yes. Absolutely. Because that's what your body's communicating to you."

Elizabeth: OK. Alright. Good.

Jesus: "OK. Good."

Elizabeth: Um, I wrote a wonderful story about my healing with my mom this weekend. I'm just so proud of it.

Jesus: "Oh Good."

Elizabeth: I'm not just so proud of the story but oh, it's so nice to be at peace about my mom and being able to look at her picture and not-just like only seeing her as you know, a teacher of mine. So and to be Grateful. I wrote about it so other people can use what I learned.

Jesus: "Yes! And that's very important that these things are kept in mind and that you continue to utilize them in this process that we've begun here."

Elizabeth: OK. So I was thinking about adding it to there. So I think I will add it to the book then too.

Jesus: "Yes."

Elizabeth: Just as an example so. There was a couple things I was gonna add actually. My personal experiences. I didn't think that would be too big of a deal for you would mind that so.

Jesus: "No. No. Because remember that this isn't something that I've decided to do, it's something that We have decided to do and whichever direction it goes it's because it is seen as being important for the experience at hand."

Elizabeth: OK. Um, I'm gonna ask a personal question. I, sometimes I'm not so affectionate to my husband and he kinda takes it personal but I kinda feel like I'm independent in that kind of way so I don't want him to feel bad when I'm not giving him hugs and kisses but he kinda makes me feel like I'm damaged somehow. Am I really-do I need to work on something with that?

Jesus: "From what I can see, for you, it is as (flip tape) (He was saying that this can be true for others also-not just for me) but you are also dealing with, as was spoken of before, with the Medium, with-OK-you are a type of-you have your personality and ways in which you regenerate and recharge require periods of solitude and if you are not getting them then you will tend to kind of pull all your energy in within you so that you Can recharge and conserve what you DO have so that it will grow as opposed to doing it out of a sense of some sort of problem within you."

Elizabeth: OK. That makes sense. I'm gonna let him hear that (laughing)

Jesus: "Yes. And for him it is a-because he feels when there is a-an exchange of affection by physical contact, that is how he is expressing and feels that expression of love. Maybe after you've heard today about how you can connect with his-by being affectionate with him-that you will ignite within him even more of his Christ Consciousness and his in you-you might be more willing to-to experience it because you're Not damaged goods, it's just the way you are and the way he is and how what he needs so trying to find balance and still respecting each others individual needs is WHY the two of you are together."

Elizabeth: To teach each other that.

Jesus: "Yes."

Elizabeth: To help me. Yes. And for me

Jesus: "For Both of you."

Elizabeth: Yes, for both of us. Thank you.

Jesus: "Because of who he is and what his needs are but you two chose this lifetime to find balance with this so it will be a constant back and forth and what's important here is to continue to love and respect each other throughout these experiences. I can guarantee you that when once you are out of this child bearing stage, you will be more affectionate than what you are right now because you know-you'll be approaching life a little bit differently. Right now your energy is being in a sense sucked by 3 little ones."

Elizabeth: Yeah. Good. That gives me something to look forward to! (Laughing)

Jesus: "Yes. Yes, and you'll see. You'll see. Especially you have one that is very young and that-especially within their first year of birth-for as life they will—Are independent but they are So dependent on the mother for survival that that does-I mean on an energetic level-it keeps the energy out. The energy is focused in on this Soul and it's survival. That goes back to when man first appeared on Earth how many billions of years ago-whenever that was-how they-it's a means of survival. So, you are also dealing with something that is a genetic memory-so to speak-going back to-well this is instinctual. It is something that was necessary as being parents. If the mother did not focus all of her energy on the infant, the infant was at greater risk of not surviving as opposed to-now it's Different! So, but there's still that cellular memory there and that's why your energy goes into Mostly your youngest. That energy for others-there is not a lot left over. At the moment. But that will change."

Elizabeth: OK. I kinda feel like my other two are now old enough where they, you know, I feel like-we're still teaching them, you know, to be respectful and all that but I just feel like there's not as much as the need to-as much as the little one-that goes without saying but I don't know.

Jesus: "You are—this is just what it is and many many females have the same situation as you and feel the same way but they might force themselves to be more affectionate with their spouses or their spouses don't have the same needs but-you aren't dealing with something that is so unusual or strange, that's for sure."

Elizabeth: Right, right. I knew that. Yes. Well I'm glad that we're talking about it now so that they can read that so.

Jesus: "Yes."

Elizabeth: Um. Then there's something else I'll talk about too. So, I'm SO happy that my kids are going back to school today (laughing)

Jesus: (He's laughing too!)

Elizabeth: SOME mothers-they get really sad about it but I'm just really happy so it shows how much of a difference there is from one person to the next but yeah, I'm just-I'm really happy. (Laughing)

Jesus: "Yes, so see, you, and this is common with those on the path such as yours-and who have had experiences such as yours-that it is-you are very much In Need of Your Own Personal Space. Every Day. Different times of the day. When that is not given to you, it tends to Drain you. And then of course you have your past life experiences that are related to this, but it will tend to drain you. And that—taking the time that you need to experience your own inner quiet is very important, for you, for rejuvenating."

Elizabeth: OK. So, for us people that need to do that, we should not feel guilty about that.

Jesus: "No. Absolutely. You are following a need with your own special, unique combination of physical and non-physical expressions that you have right now and that you call, "Beth".

Elizabeth: OK. Well, what's my original name?

Jesus: "You do not have an original name."

Elizabeth: So Nobody does??

Jesus: "No. You were just a blob of energy."

Elizabeth: HA!!

Jesus: "I don't mean to be so light about it. You didn't really have a name."

Elizabeth: OK

Jesus: "Because you are energy. That's something that's more reserved for Humanity and Earth's individuals. We do not call each other by names when we are not in the physical. We are more recognized by our energies."

Elizabeth: Oh that makes sense.

Jesus: "Yes."

Elizabeth: So, OK. Um, anything else we wanna talk about before we wrap up for today?

Jesus: "I want that this not end here. That you do not see this as an ending because it is not an ending. It is an installment. OK? This is something that is-IF all goes as we are planning, would be ongoing for a very very long time and will open up doorways to other experiences for you and the Medium that are very important. Those experiences of working together. You are not Free Yet to explore all possibilities that are awaiting you. You will need some more time to finish child rearing and I don't mean that you need to be finished but where you have more independence from your children. And that's around the corner. That's not far off. But you still need a year or two in terms of Earth time. Correct?"

Elizabeth: Yep. Yep.

Jesus: "So, things will start to lighten up for you, you will see in this year. This may still be a testing year in regards to that, but this is a preparatory year for you and the Medium and this is something that-if you continue on-you are creating a foundation for things and you will see that doorways will open up into other things that you can possibly do here. One thing leads to another. And this is true with anything in life. So, I would really encourage you to just look at this as we are ready to put This Section out there but that you and I will continue to speak. Whether we make this second part into this same type of book or it becomes something that is done in a different way. Really is to be seen. But let's get out what we can right now. You're-there's Much to be explored in regards to this. So having the Patience and the Openness and realizing that everything takes-some things can happen overnight and other things will take more time for them to grow and you understand this. So just being where you are at right now is very very important."

Elizabeth: OK. The Medium would like to know, where she should direct her energy.

Jesus: "Alright. I am just taking a pause here to not be influenced by the Medium who becomes both excited and cautious at what comes through because she feels she can-she's so powerful in that she can affect the message that comes through so that she doesn't believe it. But that is her problem, is it not?"

Elizabeth: Yeah.

Jesus: "Yes. As she is learning. So, what direction. There is no direction that is incorrect. There is a purpose to all of this that is still unfolding. If she is to come through this with the outcome that she is desiring here because she has created all of this-to be again, Patient. Day by Day. But if she is observant, she will see that it's not the physical response. She is being more patient then and more hopeful and not falling into the usual despair that she normally would-that-it is SO like the butterfly in the cocoon. It really really is. And if she can hold on to that image, that will help her. The direction. No direction is incorrect here. But that she will have more insight within the next 15 days of your Earthly time-she will get some more insight and that will help her. And I know she will not believe this but I will tell her that this Phase of where she has been at for a very very long time is ready to conclude. She is ready to let it go as well and let it be what it was and stop carrying it around. That is important for her to understand that she is ready to just let it go-she does not need to understand. She understands but she does not need to understand it all but that she can just let it go and that we will take care of that which she has been protecting for a very very long time."

Elizabeth: OK. Thank you.

Jesus: "You are welcome."

Elizabeth: OK.

Jesus: "So, anything else that we need to talk about?"

Elizabeth: No I don't think so. I think the messages that we're bringin are good for people.

Jesus: "Yes. This is a very good-because what I will tell you is you do not want to inundate them with too much."

Elizabeth: OK.

Jesus: "They will want more. But you—not—because there have been many who have done this and many who have already brought forth many of these messages so they have done it in their own ways so the public has gotten both more sophisticated And more cynical in regards to this so that's why, rather than give them a lot about a lot-we are giving them a little about a lot."

Elizabeth: OK

Jesus: "And then it is telling them that is Up to Them to take this and do what they can but this is a Manual. This is a Textbook in short form of "How To" in this case and this is-we are going to grow from here. You and I are not done talking to each other so don't think this is the end of things."

Elizabeth: I don't.

Jesus: "Good. Good. It's very important because the Medium knows that and you should as well. So you will continue on. Whether-and you will see-whether it's just to have a discussion-the three of us-the Medium being the 3rd. That's what it will be maybe and from there we will come up with other things for us to do."

Elizabeth: OK! Alright! Cool!

Jesus: "Because there is also-there is-the next phase will involve more of the what you call, The Mother Mary and we want to understand The Holy Spirit and The Mother Mary more."

Elizabeth: GREAT! Is that why The Holy Spirit dove fell off my necklace today?

Jesus: "Yes. So you see-we're dealing with something here that you had an idea on-this initial talking with the energy of who I am. And that's one. Now we will be going into the more abstract and less delved into arena of The Virgin Mary and The Holy Spirit-what does that mean. Because The Holy Spirit is something that is not talked about OR understood by many and that is where we will be going into next."

Elizabeth: AWESOME!!! YAY!!!!

Jesus: "Yes. Yes."

Elizabeth: I was Hoping that would happen-so-Holy Spirit and Mother Mary, yes! Yes. :)

Jesus: "Yes. Yes. So that's why I said this is just the first of many different encounters that we will be providing."

Elizabeth: OK. Can I say Hi to everybody that's there again? (laughing)

Jesus: (He's Laughing!) "Don't you everyday?!" (Through my laughing I think I hear Him say, "All day long.")

Elizabeth: Yeah I do!

Jesus: "Yes. You miss everyone so much but you are doing well. You are connected very much. This has helped you very much to connect more with life as opposed to longing to be back over here. What we have done over the past few months has given you the opportunity to connect with us-as you said, to say hello to everyone over here-so you have grounded yourself more into life more willingly than you were a few months ago."

Elizabeth: OK. Good! Good!

Jesus: "Yes. Yes."

Elizabeth: Sigh

Jesus: "So we I think are done for today!"

Elizabeth: We are! Thank you!

Jesus: "The next time when we meet we will talk about what we will be doing with more detail in regards to all of this in what we want to bring forth in regards to The Holy Spirit and Mother Mary and where we will begin with that. So that will be-our next one will be our introductory to the second one of our books. But now you must work on this, I know, and bring it all together so it makes something cohesive and readable for all who are waiting for it to come."

Elizabeth: OK. Good! Alright! High Five!

Jesus: "High Five and I of course love you very much and we talk all the time so I will say hello to everyone even though-and they all say hello back to you—and everyone is smiling here with great love for you and the Medium and all who are open to us. Even those who are not. Yes."

Elizabeth: Awesome! Thank you! Love you too guys! Bye everybody!

Jesus: "OK! (Laughing) Goodbye."

Elizabeth: OK Bye!

Laurie: Oh Beth you're so funny! You're like, "Bye you guys!" I'm laughing cause I can see them all, right? And they're like this-this huge-you know just a vast group of individuals just smiling and they're all popping up as your saying that. I'm like, "Oh my God!"

Elizabeth: REALLY?

Laurie: Yeah, yeah.

:)

September 8, 2013

AMEN!!

"An infinity of forests lies dormant within the dreams of one acorn."—Dr. Wayne Dyer

"The greatest achievement was at first and for a time a dream. The oak sleeps in the acorn; the bird sleeps in the egg; and in the highest vision of the soul, a waking angel stirs. Dreams are the seedlings of realities . . ."—James Allen

These quotes that Dr. Wayne Dyer posted today on Facebook spoke directly to me. I shared it on my wall. Then the kids and I went outside to play catch. Adam was pulling Arron around in the little red wagon and they were so cute so I went to get my phone to take pictures. I then tucked the phone on the side of my hip, just inside my shorts. Arron was playing with a ball so I went to go be with him. We were under an Oak tree and I chose one of the leaves off the ground to carry with me-remembering what Dr. Wayne had posted. All of a sudden, I heard music! It was coming from my phone. At first I thought someone was calling me but the song was not familiar to me at all so I wondered what was going on. I pulled my phone out of my shorts and looked at the screen. It was the song titled, "Amen" by Kid Rock off of the Rock N Roll Jesus album (great album by they way)!!! What?! I didn't even know this song was ON my phone!! My husband must have put it on there last month. The whole album was set to play and the thing is, is that Kid Rock is down on the list of albums #1. #2. Amen is the second song on the album-not the first and #3. I don't listen to albums. I just have a set playlist titled, "Beautiful Mother's" or "Patti's Fun Music" that I listen to. NEVER albums. So just now when I looked at all the albums Kevin had put on there, I was really surprised! I am just so excited so I am blabbing :) When I saw the name of the song, "Amen"

I KNEW this was NO accident. You bet I sang along with the chorus of "Amen's"!! This was a present in a way. To let me know that Divine Timing is at hand.

Last night I stayed up till 11:30p.m. working on transcribing Jesus and I's last conversation for this book. I became tired and went to bed before flipping the tape to side B. Many, many nights I have stayed up late getting this book ready for all of you. This has been a labor of Love and it brings me incredible joy to know that so many will benefit from this! If you allow these teachings into your heart, you will never be the same. I keep saying it, but this book is a journey. A journey that continues to bloom. Over and Over and Over again.

"You're the example. It's helping you and you're someone who has already a lot of enlightened ideas and understands a lot so think about the every day individual and what that will mean for them."—Jesus

When I went to bed last night, I was worried about how I was going to get the attention of a publisher. When I woke up, Doreen Virtue had posted 2 things about Divine Timing and I went, "OK. I know this is a sign for me to RELAX." So that is what I set my intention to for today. Even before getting out of bed. Then I used the Angel Tarot app on my phone and chose one. The card was Renewal. Part of the meaning is, "near the end of a project" and "Rest easy, knowing that you've prepared well." Perfect!! :) Thank you, Angels! NOW, after the song and the Oak tree, I FEEL that everything is going to plan. Everything came together. Just like the book getting into your hands will. I am letting my expectations go and I'm riding the wave and just TRUSTING. Having an experience seals everything together. I will carry this around with me and go back to the feeling of it, if and when, I ever have worry creep back in. I will think about seeing "Amen" on my phone screen and put myself back into the Gratitude and Surprise that I felt.

A few nights ago I had a dream. My friend Barbara and I were in a classroom full of people. She was wanting me to hand out business cards for my 1st book, "Love, God" and I said I didn't have any so she pushed me to get up in front of everyone and start teaching what Jesus has been teaching me. I was a little apprehensive about it but at the front of the room, with everyone looking at me with their attention, it all flowed wonderfully. It filled me with such confidence! So much so that when I woke up, I carried it into now. Thank you, Barbara!!! Then the Next night I had a dream that I was in an American Gladiator like type of obstacle course. I ran super fast, jumped over things and pulled myself up all effortlessly and won!! I feel I am preparing for the next part of this plan. Oh boy!! Yes! I'm going to be speaking to people! Let me at it because then people will feel my Enthusiasm and Faith first-hand!! That is what Jesus says I bring to this. He says, "You know by getting out there and your Enthusiasm is Infectious and that's what you carry. And that deep Faith that you have and your Enthusiasm. THAT is what is going to be reaching these people. Remember that. Remember the Energy of it."

Energy. It's all Energy. Can you feel my Energy through these words that I type? Jesus says you will be able to! As I write these words, I am SUPER EXCITED!! "You bring the excitement!"-Jesus :) That's so awesome to hear!! :)

AMEN!! AMEN!!! AMEN!! YES!! Things are happening!! Things are moving!! And "forests" will grow!!!!! AMEN!!

About the Author

For more information on Laurie Stimpson or if you would like a reading from her, please visit her website at www.lauriestimpson.weebly.com

Get to know Elizabeth Riebe at www.elizabeth-ohmygod.blogspot.com and www.elizabethcookfaith.com